Exploring Christian Ethics

Exploring Christian Ethics
Biblical Foundations for Morality

Kyle D. Fedler

WESTMINSTER
JOHN KNOX PRESS
LOUISVILLE · KENTUCKY

Scripture quotations, unless otherwise indicated, are from the New Revised Standard Version of the Bible, copyright © 1989 by the Division of Christian Education of the National Council of the Churches of Christ in the U.S.A., and used by permission.

Scripture quotations identified as NIV are from *The Holy Bible, New International Version,* copyright © 1973, 1978, 1984 International Bible Society. Used by permission of Zondervan Bible Publishers.

Book design by Sharon Adams
Cover design by Pam Poll Graphic Design

First edition
Published by Westminster John Knox Press
Louisville, Kentucky

This book is printed on acid-free paper that meets the American National Standards Institute Z39.48 standard. ♾

PRINTED IN THE UNITED STATES OF AMERICA

06 07 08 09 10 11 12 13 14 15 — 10 9 8 7 6 5 4 3 2 1

Library of Congress Cataloging-in-Publication Data
Fedler, Kyle D., 1965–
    Exploring Christian ethics : biblical foundations for morality / Kyle D. Fedler.—1st ed.
      p. cm.
    Includes bibliographical references and index.
    ISBN-13: 978-0-664-22898-9 (alk. paper)
    ISBN-10: 0-664-22898-4
    1. Christian ethics.   2. Ethics in the Bible I. Title.

BJ1251.F43 2006
241—dc22   2005042423

To Shirley Guthrie,
who taught me the importance,
beauty, and joy of Christian theology

CONTENTS

Preface

*P*lanes, barber chairs, and dentist offices are the worst, but it occurs in many other situations where I am thrown together with strangers. They ask me what I do for a living, and for a split second I am tempted not to speak the truth, because when I reveal that I teach Christian ethics I often get drawn into a conversation about ethical issues. Don't get me wrong; I love to talk ethics. It is what I do for a living. The reluctance comes from the fact that so many people that I meet lack the concepts, vocabulary, and framework that would give our conversation some common ground.

In such situations, people will often ask my view on an issue, and I quickly become frustrated over my inability to communicate it because we do not share a common ethical vocabulary or a common biblical worldview. For example, in conversations about capital punishment, I usually divide my objections into deontological and utilitarian considerations. But most people are unfamiliar with these basic ethical categories. More importantly, it is quite difficult to explain to someone who is not familiar with Scripture why I oppose capital punishment. This is not simply because they may not know *the particular passages* that mention capital punishment, but because they may not be familiar with the larger biblical context into which I want to place my views.

This unfamiliarity with both secular and biblical ethics is not restricted to people I meet in public places. I find the same to be true of many of the young Christians I teach in my ethics courses and even of the older Christians I teach in adult church school. Many of them lack the conceptual and biblical tools to articulate clearly their ethical views. All Christians know that the Bible is an essential resource, but when it comes to formulating a coherent ethical framework they are often confused about how to use the Bible responsibly. They are often at a loss as to the overall theological and moral narrative that holds the Bible together, so they resort to pulling verses out of the Bible and trying to apply them to their lives.

This book is designed to provide a basic overview of ethical theory and biblical ethics. The goal of this book is not to provide answers to modern ethical dilemmas faced by Christians. (For those persons already conversant in ethical theory and biblical studies, there are other fine works available.) The reason I do not take this approach is twofold. First, it is usually the case that applicable portions of Scripture need to be read within the larger scope of the Bible, and many Christians are unfamiliar with that larger narrative. Second, the Christian life is greater than the sum total of answers to moral quandaries. Being a Christian involves the development of a particular kind of character. And the shape of that character is determined by the story that we tell about God's ongoing journey with human beings from the beginning of time until the end of time. To live the Christian life, we must learn to see the world through the lens of the Bible, the book that tells that story.

For these reasons, I have not divided the book into particular issues in ethics such as human sexuality, war, medical ethics, and the like. I do discuss such issues as violence, sexuality, family, and wealth, but always and only within the larger biblical story. To do otherwise runs the risk of leaving the reader with only fragments of a larger picture. For example, readers will have a very truncated view of Jesus' attitude toward wealth unless they understand his pronouncements within the context of such broader biblical themes as sin, covenant, the image of God in humanity, idolatry, and the kingdom of God. Failing to understand the larger theological context is like building the upper floors without a strong foundation.

Exploring Christian Ethics: Biblical Foundations for Morality is written for those Christians who want the foundations necessary to begin formulating a biblical worldview. I have written it for people with little or no background in theology or ethics. I try to keep the technical jargon to a minimum and to avoid entering into long discussions with other thinkers. This book seeks to guide those who wish to develop a strong biblical foundation for doing ethics and living the moral life.

Part 1 begins with an introduction to basic ethical theory, because Christian ethicists share certain concepts, vocabulary, and approaches with other ethicists. But even when dealing with commonly shared concepts such as egoism, deontology, utilitarianism, and virtue, I seek to present them from a Christian perspective.

Part 2 of the book is devoted to an exploration of the biblical resources for creating a Christian moral framework. After an entire chapter examining the various ways in which Scripture can be used in Christian ethics, we will explore those sections of the Bible that have been most influential in shaping the Christian worldview in relation to morality and ethics: creation and fall, the Mosaic covenant, the prophets, the teachings of Jesus, the life of Jesus, and the letters of Paul.

Each of us is a small but important part of the great pilgrimage of God with human beings that began at the creation of the universe. My hope is that this book will help you understand the larger journey that constitutes God's past and present covenant relationship with human beings. If we can understand the broad outline of God's journey with us, we are in a better position to do the kinds of things and develop the kind of character that God expects of traveling companions.

Acknowledgments

Ethics, by its very nature, involves dialogue. I cannot possibly thank all of the dialogue partners who have influenced and shaped this book. I would like to thank certain individuals, however, who gave me particular assistance: Professor Walter Schuman of Ashland University for sparking the project, Professors Wyndy Corbin and Scott Seay of Ashland University for their comments and encouragement, and Professor James Childress of the University of Virginia for reading and commenting on an early draft. Special thanks go to Professor David Aune, my colleague at Ashland University. Not only did he provide ongoing and extensive comments on early drafts, but he was invaluable in the development of chapter 10.

I wish to thank all of my ethics students at Ashland University who gave me useful feedback on the manuscript when it was used as a textbook.

A major portion of the book was written with the help of a summer writing grant from Ashland University for which I am grateful.

Learning the Christian language is vital to living as a Christian. Until we can learn to speak the Christian language we will not be able to see the world through the lens of the Christian faith. This language will contain familiar terms such as "virtue," "compassion," and "justice." Yet these terms might be understood differently within a Christian context. And then there will be new and unfamiliar vocabulary: image of God, covenant, kingdom of God, Decalogue, purity, and the like. By learning this language we will begin to enter into the thought-world of the biblical writers.

To summarize, one goal of this book is to help you examine your own use of moral language and concepts so as to become more aware of how you make ethical decisions. The second goal is to become familiar with the main tenets of Christian ethics. For those of you who are actively involved in a Christian church, these two might be closely connected.

Types of Ethics

As we begin our journey, it is helpful to be familiar with some common ethical distinctions that will clarify our thinking. Ethicists divide the field of ethics into three branches: descriptive, prescriptive or normative, and metaethical.

1. *Descriptive ethics* is not geared toward asking what people *ought* to do or how they *should* feel. Rather, it is concerned primarily with discovering how people actually behave, think, and feel in relation to morality. "Public support for capital punishment in America is declining." This is an example of descriptive ethics because it is a purely descriptive statement. "The decline in support for capital punishment is unfortunate given that capital punishment is right and necessary." This second statement moves us out of the realm of mere description because it is judging the morality of such a state of affairs. It moves us into normative ethics because we are making moral judgments about what is right and wrong.

As beginning ethicists, you should be on guard against falling into two very common traps whereby you make *normative* claims from *factual* evidence. For example: "Most Americans support capital punishment for murder, therefore capital punishment for murder is morally right or defensible." This is a very common mistake. Unless one is a complete relativist, the popularity of a position does not *determine* its moral rightness. You may have a greater burden of proof if you stand in stark opposition to commonly held morality, but the fact that something is widely held as moral or immoral does not make it so.

A second trap usually takes some form of the following: "It may be right for people to do X, but nobody ever does, so we should not say that X is a duty." For example, "There is nobody who wouldn't defend himself or herself against attack, so pacifism is wrong." Once again, we find a confusion of normative and descriptive ethics. If one is engaged in trying to establish goals or rules to live by, it is not enough simply to say that people do not generally act this way. The purpose of normative ethics is to set standards, even if those standards appear stringent or even unattainable by most people.

2. *Prescriptive or normative ethics* is the type of ethical inquiry that "prescribes" certain actions, behaviors, or modes of feeling and thinking. It seeks to establish "norms" for acting, thinking, and feeling. A norm is a rule. It is not simply what is "normal," but what "ought" to be. When we engage in normative ethics we are seeking to establish the right or good ways of acting, thinking, or feeling. Most of what we will do in this book is normative ethics. We will be asking not simply how people do, in fact, make moral decisions and shape their moral identities, but rather how they *ought* to do so. I will be proposing certain rules, ideas, and virtues that *should* shape the Christian life. For example, we will be examining what Jesus said and did and how his teachings and ministry ought to shape our lives as contemporary disciples.

3. *Metaethics* involves the investigation into how people use moral language and the ways in which they go about making ethical decisions. Metaethicists ask such questions as "What is the meaning of the word *ought* or *must* or *good* or *wrong?*" How do people use such terms? How do people go about deciding what makes an action right? In this way, metaethics is somewhat abstract. Philosophers who engage in metaethics are like grammarians; they are primarily concerned with how moral terms are used and how they fit together to make moral sentences. This field also includes questions of moral epistemology (how we *know* right from wrong). The discussion of deontology and utilitarianism in chapter 2 is a metaethical one.

Levels of Normative Ethical Inquiry

Much of this book deals with normative ethics because it focuses on the question "How ought Christians to act, feel, or think?" Throughout the book we will try to maintain a balance between two closely related aspects of normative ethics: *decisionist* and *virtue.*

Decisionist Ethics

Decisionist ethics focuses on the question "What ought I to *do?*" It often deals with situations of moral perplexity. Moral perplexity emerges when we are confronted by two or more courses of action and we are unable to decide which is the right one. This is often called "quandary ethics" because it deals with moral quandaries or moral dilemmas.

Virtue Ethics

Virtue ethics is a type of normative ethics that downplays the importance of particular tough decisions in favor of an examination of the characteristics or virtues that a good person develops and displays. This approach to ethics deals not simply with moral quandaries or instances of moral perplexity, but with the question "How ought I to *be* or *live?*"

Virtue ethics seeks to establish a model of the "good life." The "good life" does not mean what it means in modern America, namely, a life of financial and physical well-being. The good life, as the focus of so much ancient Greek and Roman moral philosophy, is that for which human beings are designed, the manner of living that most fully fulfills our function as human beings. For example, is it better to live a life of study and contemplation, or a life of activity? Is wealth or poverty incompatible with a properly lived human life? Is it better to raise a family, or serve humanity by remaining single? Should one even worry about other human beings? Should one try to live in a simple manner?

Virtue ethics also seeks to answer the question "What kind of person should I be?" What kinds of characteristics or virtues make a good person? Humility? Generosity? Mercy? Joyfulness? A sense of humor? The moral life is about developing a certain kind of character that is certainly reflected in actions but is not reducible to a set of actions or positions on tough issues.

Finally, virtue ethics also addresses the question "How does the good person *respond?*" Throughout this book, I contend that a major part of becoming a moral human being is learning to respond to things in the right way. So much that happens in our lives is beyond our control. A loved one hurts us. Do we respond with anger or forgiveness? Someone else gets the job we thought we deserved. Do we respond with resentment or humility? We see someone else in pain. Do we feel pleasure or compassion? Emotional responses, far from being outside of our control and thus beyond the pale of morality, are a central feature of the moral life. How we respond to both the blessings and the "slings and arrows of outrageous fortune" is arguably a better barometer of our moral character than where we come down on abstract issues or hypothetical dilemmas.

Virtue ethicists remind us that moral inquiry should not focus merely on how we act in situations of great moral difficulty or what we think about tough moral quandaries such as abortion or capital punishment. Ethics involves the kinds of persons we are and how we respond emotionally to the daily events of our lives. What is the good life? What is a good person like? How does a moral person respond? These are central questions. How you deal with particular moral quandaries will depend a great deal on the kind of person you already are. Therefore decisions, character, and visions of the "good moral life" are closely intertwined.

Throughout this book I will seek to strike a balance between decisionist ethics and virtue ethics, between an emphasis on decisions and a focus on broader questions about the virtues and the good life.

Christian Ethics

Although the category of "Christian ethics" did not emerge until about three hundred years after the death of Jesus Christ, the earliest Christians were deeply concerned about ethics and morality.[1] One reason that so many early Christian writers focused their writings on ethics was the need to refute false accusations against Christians raised by their non-Christian neighbors. Many of these early defenders of the faith (called "apologists") were less concerned with showing that Christian doctrine was logical and believable than with demonstrating the *moral* superiority of Christianity over paganism. Non-Christians accused early followers of the Christian Way of being irreligious because they did not sacrifice to the pagan gods.[2] Other accusations against Christians ranged from incest (a misunderstanding of calling one another "brother" and "sister") to cannibalism (a misunderstanding of the celebration of the Lord's Supper). But more importantly, they accused Christians of being immoral:

> Is it not then deplorable that a gang . . . of discredited and proscribed desperados band themselves against the gods? Fellows who gather together illiterates from the dregs of the populace and credulous women . . . and so organize a rabble of profane conspirators, leagued together by meeting at night and ritual fasts and unnatural repasts . . . they despise temples as if they were tombs; they spit upon our gods; they jeer at our sacred rites; pitiable themselves, they pity (save the mark) our priests; they despise titles and robes of honour, going themselves half-naked![3]

Modern Christians may find it ironic that a society that engaged in infanticide and gladiatorial games viewed Christians as morally suspect. But it is clear that one reason early Christians were so concerned with ethics was in response to such attacks.

The concern with living the proper life was not merely a reaction to outside criticism, however. Morality is central to the very core of the Jewish and Christian belief systems. Let us turn for a moment to those Judeo-Christian faith commitments that led Jews and Christians to place such a great emphasis on living a life not just of right belief but of right action, disposition, and attitude—a life where both the "hands" and the "heart" are carefully regulated and cultivated. I will expand on these faith claims later in the book. For now I will simply highlight them.

At the risk of oversimplification, the Christian universe consists of three components: God, the created world, and human beings. Faith claims about each of these contribute to the overall Christian emphasis on morality and ethics. Put differently, it is what Christians profess to believe about God, human beings, and the created world that makes ethics so central to Christianity.

God: God Acts in History, and God Is Just

Let us begin with two claims that Christians make about God that make morality so vitally important: (1) Yahweh is a God who acts in history, and (2) Yahweh is moral.[4] The God revealed in Scripture is a God who acts. For those of us raised in the Christian tradition, this seems self-evident. But it was not always so. Many people in the ancient world believed that God created the world and then simply set it on its course, much as a watchmaker builds a watch and then lets it run, without interfering with its workings. But Deism (as this view is called) is contrary to what Christians believe. It contradicts the witness in the Old Testament of events such as the exodus, where God intervened to save the Israelites from their Egyptian captives. More importantly, it is contrary to the very foundation of Christianity, namely, the incarnation (or becoming "flesh") of God in Jesus Christ, who was a particular human being *in history*.

The Christian confession that God acts in human affairs is a warrant for Christians to take seriously what happens in this world. In other words, we have a God who is concerned not simply with "heavenly" or "spiritual" things, but with the daily events of this earth. Therefore, we are also called to be concerned with things of this earth: with whether people have food and clothing, with what we do with our bodies, with whether outsiders are treated with dignity and respect, and so forth.

But it is not enough simply to say that God acts in history. Ancient Romans also held that their gods (Jupiter, Apollo, etc.) acted in history. But in contrast to these gods, Christians worship a God who is absolutely just and unimaginably compassionate—in a word, *moral*. Yahweh is a God who intimately cares for real people in real situations. The God of the Bible is no theoretical God of the philosophers who sits alone thinking God's own inner thoughts. No, the God revealed in Scripture enters into the messy world of human life and wills and demands justice:

> For I the LORD love justice,
>   I hate robbery and wrongdoing.
>   (Isa. 61:8)

> Who is the King of glory?
>   The LORD, strong and mighty,
>   the LORD, mighty in battle.
>   (Ps. 24:8)

> The LORD, the LORD,
> a God merciful and gracious,
> slow to anger,
> and abounding in steadfast love and faithfulness,
> keeping steadfast love for the thousandth generation,
> forgiving iniquity and transgression and sin.
>   (Exod. 34:6–7)

Note how many moral characteristics are attributed to God: just, loving, compassionate, gracious, steadfast, powerful, and glorious. This is a far cry from the immoral and petty gods we find in many ancient religions.

Because our God is a just, loving, and compassionate God, *we* are called to be just, loving, and compassionate. In other words, for Christians, there is a profound connection between our worship of God and our treatment of our neighbor. As our exploration of biblical ethics will make clear, how we treat our neighbor is not a distinct or different arena from how we relate to God. Love of neighbor and love of God go hand in hand. In other words, morality and religion are two sides of the same coin. The manner in which we conduct ourselves toward the world and toward our neighbors is part of our worship of God.

World: The World Is Good but Is Not God

While we will examine this at greater length in chapter 5, for now it is enough to observe that for Christians, the world is considered a *good* place. Despite the sin, injustice, and misery that are so prevalent, the created world is not evil. God loves and cares about the world, and therefore what happens in this world is a concern of God's. God does not care merely about our "spirits";

what happens to our created, material bodies here on earth is also important to God. Therefore, it should be important to us also. It is not enough for Christians to focus on the spiritual well-being of themselves and others; they must tend to the physical care of God's children also. The idea that the world is good is at the very heart of Christian ethics. It is a foundational idea that acts as a warrant or justification for Christians to concern themselves with issues of poverty, hunger, justice, sexuality, warfare, and the like, because all of these involve the real, everyday treatment of the physical.

Humans: Made in the Image of God but Sinful; Redeemed by Christ

The most foundational claims that Christians make about human beings are: (1) They are created to be in harmonious relationship with God and one another; (2) they have disrupted both of these sets of relationships; and (3) the results of our sin are overcome in the life, death, and resurrection of Jesus Christ. In coming chapters we will see that the first two claims are characterized under the theological headings of "image of God" and "sin." We will also explore the Christian confession that Jesus Christ has come to restore these broken relationships. For now, it is important simply to recognize that the first two claims make morality an important aspect of Christian life. Human beings are created *in order to be* in a reciprocal relationship with God. Their creation was neither accidental nor arbitrary. God has a purpose for creating you and me and everyone who has come before and will come after. That purpose is so that we can gratefully enter into a mutually loving relationship with God that brings glory to God and joy to human lives. As the opening lines of a famous catechism say: "Man's chief and highest end is to glorify God, and fully to enjoy him forever."[5] Human beings are not created as slaves or mere robots. God desires to be in intimate communion with human beings while we live on earth and not simply when we go to heaven. A central part of Christian ethics is learning how we are to relate to God.

But we are also created to be in relationship with other human beings. And because we are created for community with others and not simply for lives of isolated autonomy (self-rule), we must discover how it is that we are to properly relate to our fellow creatures with whom we share the earth. Love, capital punishment, wealth, poverty, government, warfare, marriage, friendship—all these ethical issues are central to the Christian life because they touch upon the foundational Christian claim that humans are created to be in relationships of mutual love, concern, and respect with one another.

On the other hand, we have distorted both sets of relationships: our relationship with God and with one another. Our relationship with God is not what it was designed to be. We rebel against God, make other things into gods, pretend to be gods ourselves, or simply ignore God altogether. Our relationship with our creator is fractured and disrupted.

The same is true of our relationship with our fellow creatures. Whether it be with our parents, our brothers and sisters, our next-door neighbors, our bosses, or our "enemies" in other nations, we have chosen to shatter the harmony and mutuality that God intended. Christian ethics is founded on the belief that while God created us to be in proper relationship with God and neighbor, we have disrupted those primary relationships. Much of Christian normative ethics is a searching effort to discover how to mend our relationships with our neighbors and to live in harmony with them.

Faith Claims and Ethics

We have spent the last few pages in an initial exploration of some of the most basic Christian faith claims. The rest of this book will expand on these. What is absolutely essential to recognize at this point is the intimate connection between faith claims and ethics. If Christians really do act and feel differently than the rest of the world, if we are at all distinguishable from nonbelievers in terms of morality, it is because of *what we believe* about the universe. Our faith in who God is and what God has done in Jesus Christ transforms us. As Paul writes, "Do not be conformed to this world, but be transformed by the renewing of your minds, so that you may discern what is the will of God—what is good and acceptable and perfect" (Rom. 12:2). Because Christians see the world differently, they act differently. If Christian morality has been overrun by secular morality, that is only a symptom. The underlying cause is that many Christians no longer view the world from a Christ-centered and biblical perspective.

We live in a world that downplays the reality of ideas and beliefs, as if only the material, the scientific, and the quantifiable were real. As Donald Luck observes, we need to discover that "as remote and comical as fussing with ideas may seem, ideas are real and very important. They change the world."[6] The ideas that we maintain about God, the world, and our neighbors largely determine who we are and how we act. If I envision everyone outside my small circle as hostile competitors in a dog-eat-dog world, then I will form my behavior, virtues, and emotions around that belief. If I believe that all poor people are lazy, then that perception determines my behavior and response to poor persons. But if I believe that all persons are made in the image of God, then that faith commitment will shape my actions, feelings, and virtues. If I believe that God is ultimately in control of history and will one day bring justice and peace on earth, then that faith commitment will shape my actions and attitudes.

As we begin our journey, it is vital that we dig below the surface of what Christians *do* in order to discover the vision of reality that shapes their very being. In your own exploration, continually ask yourself, "How does what I believe affect how I behave, think, and feel?"

Itinerary for the Coming Journey

Exploring Christian Ethics is divided into two major sections. Part 1 will introduce you to some basic concepts and ideas in the field of ethics. These ideas and concepts are common to both Christian and secular ethics. However, we will approach them from a biblical perspective. Chapters 2 and 3 introduce the three main approaches to ethics: deontology, utilitarianism, and virtue theory. We begin with some basic ethical theory that is common to Christians and non-Christians because God also works through human reason to guide us. Part 2 moves us to more specifically biblical material. It is my contention that we cannot understand Christian morality or learn the language of Christian ethics without immersing ourselves in Scripture. I therefore begin part 2 with a discussion of the various ways that Scripture might be used in Christian ethics. In chapter 4 we will also briefly examine other sources of Christian guidance such as tradition, reason, and experience. Chapters 5–10 constitute the heart of our exploration, the highlight of our journey, in which we will create a strong foundation for Christian ethics by examining the key source of guidance for the Christian life: Scripture.

Chapter 2

What Should We *Do?*

Approaches to Ethical Decision Making:
Egoism, Deontology, and Utilitarianism

CASE STUDY

John and Bill had been close friends for many years. They were next-door neighbors in the same small Ohio town and attended the same Christian church. Both were good students during high school.

They were therefore pleased when both were admitted to the same college. As part of their orientation, John and Bill signed a pledge not to cheat and to report anyone who did. The semester started well, with both young men taking premed courses with the hope of becoming doctors and starting a practice together. Their goal was to start a free clinic to serve the working poor. But Bill ran into difficulty after several weeks. First, his father suffered a severe heart attack, and then his girlfriend indicated that she no longer wanted to continue their long-distance relationship.

John and Bill were in organic chemistry together, a course that was critical for getting into medical school. Bill was not well prepared for the midterm, which counted for half their grade and was graded on a curve, based on the outcomes of all the students in the class. As the exam ended and they walked out of the classroom, Bill breathed a sigh of relief. "Well," he said, "I think I did OK." "Great," replied John. "I think I did pretty well, too." Later that night, after a few beers, Bill said to John, "Can I tell you something in confidence?" "Sure," said John. Bill proceeded to tell his good friend that he had taken notes to the exam and had used them for his answers. John was shocked because he had always known Bill to be honest and trustworthy. He told Bill that he should go to Professor Williams and admit what he did. Bill replied that he would never cheat again, but that he wouldn't turn himself in because he "knew" that other students were cheating, too.

The next day, John was called into Professor Williams's office. The professor said, "I know that you are good friends with Bill. I suspect him of cheating on the midterm. He has denied it. Do you know anything about it?"

John is faced with a tough decision. He must decide upon a single course of action, but he is unsure of the right course. How does he decide? It would help to know what makes an act "right." What characterizes those actions that are "right," "good," or "righteous" from those that are "wrong," "bad," or "sinful"? If we can isolate what makes something good or right, then this might help us to make the proper moral decision.

Ethical Egoism

One way to decide which action to perform is simply to ask the question "What is best for me?" This mode of reasoning is called *ethical egoism*. Ethical egoism says that decisions should be based on the following principle: *Everyone should act so as to maximize his or her own benefit*. This is the mode of ethical reasoning behind the oft-repeated phrase "Look out for number one."

In the case study above, if John were an ethical egoist, then he would argue that the right thing to do is whatever is best for himself. On the one hand, John might believe that telling the truth is the right thing to do, not because truth telling is inherently right or because more people would be harmed by lying than by telling the truth. Rather, from an ethical egoist perspective, telling the truth is the right thing to do in this case because when everything is said and done, honesty will work toward John's own benefit (however he calculates that). On the other hand, if he felt that lying to Professor Williams would save his relationship with Bill and he values that relationship, then he might argue that lying is the right thing to do.

Almost all Christians recognize that ethical egoism is a poor way to live life and that a life lived merely in pursuit of self-gratification is an impoverished one. At the very heart of Christianity is the claim that loving and serving other human beings is part of the good life. Jesus explicitly rejects ethical egoism by calling on his followers to place the needs of others above their own: "Whoever wants to be first must be last of all and servant of all" (Mark 9:35).

Yet we must be careful about assuming that the moral life is always one of complete self-sacrifice. There is a place for consideration of oneself in the Christian life. Jesus was not an ascetic, that is, someone who promotes self-denial and seeks to avoid all pleasures in life. Jesus is depicted as drinking wine and feasting and going to parties. According to Christians, life is a precious gift of God, a gift that is not to be treated with contempt. Concern for one's own physical, emotional, and spiritual well-being is part of caring for God's gift. However, as we shall see when we turn to Scripture in part 2, ethical egoism is the antithesis of a biblically formed moral life.

Psychological Egoism

In contrast to ethical egoism, *psychological egoism* says that people always act out of some degree of self-interest. Psychological egoism is a descriptive view, not a normative one. It simply *describes* the way people act; it does not say that people *ought* to act in their own self-interest. A psychological egoist would say that in making his decision John will inevitably act in his own self-interest.

Two things should be observed about psychological egoism. First, it is a difficult theory to refute, because it is notoriously difficult to discern or isolate someone's motives. Think about our example above. John might not lie because of the commandment "You shall not bear false witness against your neighbor" (Exod. 20:16). But he also might not want Bill to get into more trouble. Or he might hold some deep, almost unconscious, anger toward Bill. All of these motives might be mixed together. How do we decide which is the real motive?

Moreover, psychological egoists can always find self-interest, even in seemingly altruistic (i.e., self-giving) actions. For example, take the famous story about the young Abraham Lincoln's explanation of his saving little piglets from drowning in their trough. Lincoln, who had just been arguing that even seemingly good acts are motivated by self-interest, was confronted by someone who asked, "'Now Abe, where does selfishness come in on that little episode?' 'Why, bless your soul, Ed, that was the very essence of selfishness. I should have had no peace of mind all day had I gone on and left that suffering old sow worrying over those pigs. I did it to get peace of mind, don't you see?'"[1] Lincoln argued that he really performed the action out of selfishness, to make himself feel better. Is that what is meant by a "self-interested" motive? Does feeling good about doing good make someone selfish?

Although I have raised some questions about psychological egoism, we should recognize the partial truth behind psychological egoism as seen from a Christian perspective. Many Christian thinkers have agreed with Paul that "there is no one who is righteous, not even one. . . . All have sinned and fall short of the glory of God" (Rom. 3:10, 23). Protestant Christians, in particular, have always held that, other than Jesus Christ, human beings are incapable of acting in a totally pure and good manner; all human acts are tinged with sin. When we turn to the chapters on biblical ethics, we shall see that the Bible does not view human nature through rose-colored glasses. Human beings, even the founding fathers and mothers of the faith, are portrayed as weak, sinful, disobedient, lustful, and greedy. And despite how they are often portrayed in stained-glass windows and children's books, the apostles of Jesus were as weak, unfaithful, and disobedient as you and I. The Bible is starkly consistent in its portrayal of human sin. From the sin of Adam and

Eve in Genesis 3 to the idolatry and violence of the book of Revelation, humans are depicted as creatures that continuously violate the image of God by their sinful disobedience.

But psychological egoism and the Christian doctrine of sin are not equivalent. First, psychological egoism generally argues that all actions are equally selfish. The Christian doctrine of sin says that all actions are tainted by sin, not that all actions are equally sinful. All human beings are sinful in God's eyes, but not all are equally guilty of the same sins. As the great American ethicist Reinhold Niebuhr puts it, "Men who are equally sinners in the sight of God need not be equally guilty of a specific act of wrongdoing in which they are involved. It is important to recognize that Biblical religion has emphasized the inequality of guilt just as much as the equality of sin."[2] Second, psychological egoism as a philosophical perspective fails to capture the Christian claim that human beings, while sinful, are also transformed by their faith in Jesus Christ. Psychological egoism leaves no room for spiritual development and transformation. But many are the Christians who can witness to their own moral and spiritual transformation upon confession of faith in Christ. Hearts, minds, motivations, and desires are all changed. The apostle Paul says it is like becoming an entirely new creation: "So if anyone is in Christ, there is a new creation: everything old has passed away; see, everything has become new!" (2 Cor. 5:17).

Yes, we might be driven by sin. But contrary to psychological egoism, sin is not our nature; it is the violation of our nature. In Christ we see the true form of humanity, and Christ lived without sin. One day we will regain our created nature when we are raised fully with Christ. And that transformation into our true selves is already being initiated right here on earth when we, through faith, become united with Christ: "We know that our old self was crucified with him so that the body of sin might be destroyed, and we might no longer be enslaved to sin. For whoever has died is freed from sin" (Rom. 6:6–7). In Christ we have been set free from the destructive cycle of sinful self-centeredness. We no longer must prove ourselves worthy by the acquisition of fame, power, or money. We know that we have been made right with God and are thus set free to live lives of mutual self-giving love.

Deontology

If ethical and psychological egoism are unsatisfactory approaches to deciding what makes an action "right," how should we decide? Two modes of deciding whether an action is right have prevailed over the past two hundred years, each of which focuses on one particular aspect of a human action. Human actions can be broken down into three parts: the agent, the action itself, and the consequences of the action.

Consequentialism argues that the consequences of an action should determine its morality. *Virtue theory* claims that we should focus on the agent performing the action, as we shall see in chapter 3.

In contrast to these two theories stands *deontology*. This moral method focuses on the nature of the action itself. For deontologists, the moral life is seen primarily as adherence to a set of rules or principles. Does the action adhere to a rule that we find morally obligatory? Is the action a duty that is required of the person? Deontologists contend that there is something inherent in the very nature of certain human actions that makes them right or wrong. It is not simply a matter of the consequences of the action being good (consequentialism) or that the action reveals something about the nature of the person (virtue theory). Rather, certain acts have qualities that (at least initially) make them right or wrong. Key themes in a deontological system include obligation, fairness, rules, justice, and, especially, duty. In fact, the term "deontology" is derived from the Greek *deontos*, meaning duty. *A deontological method of doing ethics stresses the notion that certain actions are inherently right or wrong.* Therefore it is important to discern those rules or laws that dictate which actions are right and which are wrong. Once we discover them, we must adhere to them. As we return to our opening example, if John were a deontologist, he would decide which rules apply in this case and then choose a course of action based on those rules, rather than merely on the consequences of his actions.

Christianity and Deontology

From its very beginning, Christianity has struggled with the place and function of rules or laws. There is a long history, from Paul (first century) to Augustine (fourth century) to Martin Luther (sixteenth century) that has warned against "legalism," the almost slavish adherence to rules. Protestant Christians, in particular, place great emphasis on what is called "justification by grace." This idea, drawn from the writings of Paul, contends that human beings are saved by a free gift of God, not by anything that they can do for themselves. In fact, many Christians believe that attempts to make oneself appear righteous in God's sight by good deeds and following rules (or the Jewish law) are actually a reflection of human sinfulness. It is a sign that humans are too proud to accept God's free gift of forgiveness in Jesus Christ (see chapter 10).

As evidence that we should be wary of an overemphasis on rules and laws, some Christians point to Jesus' criticism of a group of Jewish leaders called the Pharisees. This group of first-century Jews developed traditions to promote strict adherence to the 613 commandments in the Torah (the first five books of the Old Testament). In addition to addressing acts such as killing, stealing, kidnapping, and lying, these laws dictated all aspects of life: what kind of clothing one could wear, whom one could eat with, how to wash one's hands in preparation for meals, and the like. In addition, one large set of rules had to do with what counted as "work" on the Sabbath, as any kind of work on the Jewish Sabbath (Saturday) was forbidden.

Strict adherence to these Sabbath rules brought many of the Pharisees into conflict with Jesus. Jesus often criticized them for following the letter of the law but abandoning the spirit or principle behind the law: "Woe to you, scribes and Pharisees, hypocrites! For you tithe mint, dill, and cummin, and have neglected the weightier matters of the law: justice and mercy and faith. . . . Woe to you, scribes and Pharisees, hypocrites! For you clean the outside of the cup and of the plate, but inside they are full of greed and self-indulgence" (Matt. 23:23, 25). Here Jesus seems to be saying that strict adherence to the law is less important than the virtues of mercy and justice, that one must first change one's heart and then the actions of the hands will follow. As in Jesus' day, we find many legalists among us, men and women who are so focused on adhering to preestablished rules that they find little room for compassion or forgiveness.

In our zeal to avoid falling into legalism, we must take care lest we fall into a position of *antinomianism*, the stance of being against (*anti*) all laws (*nomoi*). Antinomianism fails to appreciate the place and importance of rules in the Christian life. First, much of the Old Testament is structured around the gift of the law. Second, as we shall see in our exploration of Jesus' teachings, Jesus himself often appealed to Old Testament laws. Finally, rules or laws set limits on the way we might try to achieve certain goals in life. There are limitations to what we as finite, sinful human creatures can and ought to do, even in the pursuit of some good goal.

Deontologists focus on the action itself because that is the one thing that is within our control. We often cannot control the consequences of our actions, but we can control our own behaviors. Many Christian deontologists contend that it is not our duty to make the world come out right; that is God's work. There are limits to what we can do, even with good intentions and even in the hope of making a situation better. The phrase often used by deontologists is "The end does *not* always justify the means." In other words, the goals that humans strive for (the "ends") do not justify or make right any means to achieve them.

Put differently, deontologists contend that certain actions are inherently right or wrong, regardless of the consequences. We cannot do anything and everything to achieve a desired state of affairs. For example, Bill has the worthy goal of becoming a small-town doctor, believing that he could do much good by healing people and seeing them through difficult times. Ultimately, even if more good may come from his cheating on this one single exam, that does not make it right, according to any deontologist who holds a strong rule against cheating. The end or goal of serving others, no matter how worthy, may not necessarily justify his cheating on the exam or lying to his professor.

Christian deontologists argue that our duty as human beings is to follow the rules that God has provided, even if following such rules might sometimes lead to greater suffering. Two examples might help clarify this line of thinking:

Example 1. John Howard Yoder, an influential American pacifist, holds that it is our duty to be peacemakers. We cannot wage war because this is both the example of Jesus and a command of Jesus (Matt. 5:38–48). To the criticism that this seems to shirk the responsibility of making the world safe and just, Yoder contends that it is not part of our responsibility to ensure that the world turns out for the best; that is God's responsibility. Stanley Hauerwas summarizes Yoder's position when he says that "the task for the Christian is to obey and it is ultimately God's business to bring the kingdom of this world into his realm."[3] Indeed, even if the good consequences of going to war might outweigh the bad, that does not make the deed right. Taking human life is inherently immoral, and no good benefits will make it moral, according to the deontological thinking of Yoder.

Example 2. A second example comes from the field of bioethics. In some cases, terminally ill patients are in severe physical and emotional pain. Their deaths are mere weeks or days away, but that time seems unbearable. The idea of relieving them of their pain by hastening their death is called euthanasia. Many men and women have proposed that the benefits of hastening the inevitable outweigh the dangers; therefore euthanasia is morally acceptable.

However, deontologists such as Gilbert Meilander criticize such reasoning. Meilander is sympathetic to the belief that it would be better if the person were not in such pain. We may even wish and pray that the person would soon die. However, Meilander argues, just because we might want something to be the case does not mean that we can do anything in our power to achieve that goal. "Those who know themselves as creatures—not Creator—will recognize limits even upon their obligation to do good. As creatures we are called to do all the good we can, but this means all the good we 'morally can'—all the good we can within certain limits. It may be that the Creator *ought to do* whatever is necessary to bring about states of affairs which *ought to be*, but we stand under no such godlike imperative."[4] Ultimately we are not responsible for the person's sufferings, if the only way to ease them is to kill the person. Allowing suffering in such a tragic situation is not the same as causing it or being responsible for it. However, we *are* responsible for our own actions. And one thing that we are forbidden to do, in Meilander's view, is to act in such a way that we intentionally cause someone's death in order to relieve suffering.

What we observe in these cases is what ethicists call *limited negative responsibility*. Negative responsibility is responsibility not just for what we *do* but for what we *allow to happen*. Deontologists claim that we have a very *limited* negative responsibility; they focus on what we do rather than on what we allow to happen. If certain groups of people in Iraq are tortured or killed by the Saddam Hussein regime while the citizens of the United States do nothing, that is the responsibility of the Iraqis if the only way to stop such violence is to go to war. Those who refuse to confront violence with violence are not to be blamed, even if they could have prevented suffering by using force, according to pacifists. Our duty is to do what God commands, and that includes not killing our brothers and sisters. Likewise, if the sick person suffers, we are not responsible for that. However, if we were to hasten the sick person's death, we would be responsible for that action.

Almost all deontologists hold that we *are* responsible for seeking justice, alleviating pain, and saving lives. In fact, most would say that we have a duty to do so. However, we cannot do anything and everything in pursuit of these goods. We can only pursue these goods by doing actions that are not inherently immoral. In other words, we cannot do evil in pursuit of good.

Issues Involved in Deontology

With this overview of deontology, let us turn to some of the issues involved in deontological thinking. Deontologists contend that certain acts are inherently moral or immoral. Therefore, there is a great emphasis on rules in deontology, since rules dictate which actions are obligatory and which are prohibited.

First Major Issue: Which Rules?

Which rules or acts are inherently right or wrong? What rules should we live by? Many answers to these questions have been proposed. The most famous deontologist, the German philosopher Immanuel Kant, proposed a number of what he called "categorical imperatives." They are imperatives (commands) that are not dependent upon any condition or situation. They are therefore categorical, as when someone says, "I categorically deny that." Two of these categorical imperatives are:

1. Never act except in such a way that you can also will that your maxim should become a universal law.
2. Always treat other persons as ends in themselves and never as means only.

The first of these rules is a variation of the rule of universalizability, that we should act as we would expect anyone else to act in the same situation. It is a more abstract form of the wisdom of our mothers who said, "What if everyone did what you did?" Kant's second formula says that because human beings are of the highest value, we should always treat other people with the greatest of respect and never use them simply as a means to a greater good. Any action where I treat someone else merely as an object is forbidden. Such a rule would be an important limitation if followed because it would mean that we could not sacrifice one person's well-being for the greater good of many others.

Some Christian Rules or Principles   It would be premature at this point to discuss Christian rules and principles at length since we have not yet examined the main source of rules in Christian ethics—the Bible. At this point let us simply look at several other rules or sets of rules that have been foundations for Christian morality.

1. *The Decalogue.* Also known as the Ten Commandments, the Decalogue is one candidate for a set of rules that should stand as a foundation of Christian ethics. We shall examine it in more detail in chapter 6.

2. *Love.* Jesus said, "'You shall love the Lord your God with all your heart, and with all your soul, and with all your mind.' This is the greatest and first commandment. And a second is like it: 'You shall love your neighbor as yourself'" (Matt. 22:37–39). This is the rule of *agape*—Christian love—which we will explore in chapter 9.

3. *The Golden Rule.* "Do to others as you would have them do to you" (Luke 6:31). Some variation of this rule has been found in a wide variety of philosophical and religious systems, from Confucius to the Stoics. As we saw above, it has much in common with Kant's categorical imperative. For Christians, the Golden Rule is closely connected to the command to love our neighbors as ourselves; both share the common idea that we are to view the needs and desires of others as equal to our own. As Harvey McArthur puts it, "It is intended to shatter the radical self-centeredness that obscures our awareness of the rights and needs of others."[5]

Which rules or principles we choose to live by are central to a deontological system. It is important to remember, however, that deontology is more of a method for doing ethics than a substantive theory of morality. This is to say that deontologists, including Christian deontologists, generally agree on how we should do ethics and how we should build a system of morality. But they often disagree on what that system will look like because they might disagree on which rules or principles should guide our decision making.

Second Major Issue: Applicability of Rules

The first question that you should ask of any deontologist is "What rules or principles are you working with?" The next major question about deontological systems is *how to apply* these rules. The question of applicability can be broken down into two parts: meaning and weight.

Meaning: What Is the Meaning of the Rule?   We have seen that Jesus tells us to "love our neighbors." But how? What counts as loving our neighbor? Does loving my neighbor mean that I must like my neighbor? Does it mean that I must sacrifice for the good of my neighbor? And if so, how much? Is it loving to provide welfare for neighbors I don't know? Can I kill certain neighbors to protect other neighbors? Can I hurt my neighbor to protect my family or myself? All of these questions involve the meaning of neighbor love (*agape*), which we shall discuss at length later. What I want to highlight here is simply that citing a rule is only the first step. We must ask what the rule actually means.

Let us return to the case of John and Bill. As a deontologist, John has already determined that one rule is "Do not lie." But now he must determine the meaning of that rule. Would it be a lie to say, "I did not see him cheat" or "I have no conclusive evidence that he cheated"? Both of these statements are literally true but seem intended to deceive Professor Williams. John may also believe that Professor Williams has no right to the information and therefore that he is free to say, "I have no knowledge about this," without it being a lie.

It is often the case that disagreement increases as the specificity of rules increases. Whereas we might all find common ground by agreeing to the principle "Love your neighbor as yourself," we will soon find ourselves disagreeing over what this actually means when we begin applying it to complex situations such as nuclear power, gay marriage, freedom of speech, or warfare.

Weight: What Is the Weight of the Rule?   In deciding how to apply a rule we must first ask about its meaning. But even if we agree on the meaning of the rule and that the rule applies in this situation, we might still disagree as to the weight of the rule. When ethicists talk about moral weight they are referring to the stringency of the rule. Rules can be understood to have different weights or stringencies.

Rule of thumb. A rule might simply be a "rule of thumb." As such it carries no moral weight, and breaking it is not seen as a moral infraction. "Never bunt with two strikes" is a rule of thumb in baseball. But no coach will be said to be immoral if he does not follow it (stupid, maybe, but not immoral). Moreover, the rule does not need to be followed in all cases; it really just helps the person gain a sense of direction, a helping hand based upon past experiences. "Honesty is the best policy" is seen as a rule of thumb for many people. This "rule" says that, in most cases, it is best to be honest. But that may not always be the case, and this rule acts simply as a helpful guide. "In interior design, objects on a table should be grouped in threes." While this is a good rule of thumb, it is not always true. (Utilitarians, as we shall soon see, hold almost all rules as rules of thumb.)

Absolute. On the other extreme, a rule might be absolute. This means that in all cases where the rule applies, it must be followed. Several of the examples of deontological reasoning given above assume that at least some rules are absolute. For the Roman Catholic Church, the prohibitions against abortion and contraception are absolute rules. This means that no matter how beneficial the possible outcome, they are prohibited. The rule is absolutely binding.

Prima facie. One reason that many people shy away from thinking about rules as absolutes is that there are many cases where more than one rule or principle might apply. In fact, it is usually the case that a moral question arises because of a *conflict* of rules or obligations.[6]

In the case of John and Bill, various moral obligations or rules seem to apply. There is the principle of loyalty to friends and the keeping of confidentiality. But there is also the principle of honesty, as well as the issue of justice or fairness to their classmates. Be loyal to friends. Do not divulge information given in confidence. Be honest. Be fair to all people. If all of these rules are absolute, then John is in a complete bind. There is no possible way of doing all of the "right" things.

One way of beginning to make sense of this complexity is to say that rules have *prima facie* weight, or more accurately, that they are *prima facie* binding.[7] This means that they carry some moral obligation but are not binding in all cases. *Prima facie* means "at first view." At first view, such rules *are* binding; if no other rule or principle conflicts with the *prima facie* rule, it must be followed. They are more than rules of thumb because they are binding in most cases, but they are not absolute in that they can be overridden temporarily if they come into conflict with a weightier obligation. Such an understanding of the weight of rules helps make sense of the fact that we normally understand ourselves to be under a number of rules that often conflict with one another.

Many if not most moral dilemmas, like the one facing John, arise as the result of a conflict between competing principles. Take another example:

It is generally recognized that a physician has an obligation to be honest to her patients. But Dr. Johnson has just unsuccessfully tried to save the life of seventeen-year-old Chris, who was injured in an automobile accident. Chris's brother, Jonah, was also severely injured in the accident. While Jonah is being worked on in the emergency room, he asks Dr. Johnson if his brother is OK.

Here we see two competing principles. Dr. Johnson feels strongly that it is not right to lie to patients. But she also feels that giving Jonah a completely honest answer at this point will be harmful. Consequently, the *prima facie* principle of truth telling is in conflict with another *prima facie* principle, that of not harming others (nonmaleficence). All things considered, she decides not to tell him. Her actual obligation entails overriding one *prima facie* obligation for another. The principle of veracity (truth telling) has been overridden in this case. This does not mean that the principle of truth telling played no role or had no weight. Nor does it mean that nonmaleficence always outweighs veracity. Certain conditions must be met for one *prima facie* principle to override another, and even then the overridden rule continues to play a role in a number of ways. What follows are some of the rules that govern the process of judging between competing *prima facie* rules or principles, lest we use the notion of *prima facie* rules as a smokescreen for simply picking and choosing which rules we wish to adhere to in any situation.

1. One *prima facie* rule overrides another when "better reasons can be offered to act on the overriding norm than on the infringed norm."[8] We must be willing and able to provide good, publicly justifiable reasons for overriding a *prima facie* obligation. This obligation to provide good public reasons for overriding one principle for another keeps us from using the conflict of principles as an excuse for doing whatever we feel like. It makes us accountable.

2. Overriding a *prima facie* rule should be a last resort. If there is any way of respecting both rules, then that way should be considered. So in the case of Dr. Johnson, lying should be the last resort. If it is possible not to lie and not to harm Jonah, she should do so. Again, this distinguishes *prima facie* rules from mere rules of thumb.

3. We should seek the action that least violates the principle being overridden. In our case, the action that least violates the overridden principle of veracity (truth telling) should be followed. Therefore, it is better for Dr. Johnson to say something like "I don't know" than "He seems to be doing super! He should be in to visit you as soon as you are better." As one set of ethicists put

it, "The agent seeks to minimize the negative effects of the infringement."[9] This criterion represents an acknowledgment that overriding a *prima facie* obligation does not mean dispensing entirely with that obligation.

4. Finally, the principle that is overridden leaves what philosopher Robert Nozick calls "moral traces."[10] In our case, the moral trace is the felt need to apologize at a latter point for lying. So Dr. Johnson might come to Chris at a later date to apologize and explain her reasons for lying. She might also feel some guilt or regret. If the principle of veracity were just a rule of thumb, it would be difficult to account for this need to apologize and the feelings of guilt.

Prima facie rules create a presumption or burden of proof. Most people contend that there is a strong *prima facie* obligation to tell the truth. Anyone who lies must overcome that burden of proof and justify the lie. So in the case of John and Bill, John may hold that telling the truth is a *prima facie* obligation. Yet he may feel that in this case the initial presumption against lying can be overridden based on other moral obligations such as keeping confidences among friends or not doing things to harm other people.

We shall see that in Christian ethics, many of the faith claims made by Christians create strong moral presumptions against certain kinds of behavior. For example, the fact that human beings are created in the image of God creates a strong *prima facie* obligation to protect human life. Some ethicists would consider the protection of human life an absolute principle, but most Christians see it as a strong *prima facie* obligation, an obligation that can be overridden in particular cases when the principle of protection of life comes into conflict with another very important principle or rule.

Some deontologists and deontological systems mix absolute and *prima facie* rules. For example, for Roman Catholics the rule against lying carries significant moral weight but is not absolute. However, rules such as those against abortion, contraception, or homosexuality are absolute, so they always outweigh any *prima facie* rules.

Understanding rules as *prima facie* binding is certainly less clear-cut and more complex, requiring greater sensitivity to the intricacies of a situation than a system of absolute rules. But for many people, this way of understanding the weight of rules seems to capture the complexity of the moral life better than an absolute or rule of thumb understanding of rules.

Whether we hold rules to be rules of thumb, absolute, or *prima facie*, in order for rules to function properly as guides to the Christian life it is absolutely essential that we understand the rules within our shared theological vision of what God has done and is doing in the world. In other words, the rules that Christians live by must be seen in the context of the story revealed in the Bible about who God is, who human beings are, and the purposes for which God has created us. We should be very wary of simply ripping rules out of the Bible without regard for their context and then applying them to our current situation, since the meaning of the rule might have been quite different in its original setting.

Rules have always played an important part in Christian morality because we believe that God has set certain limits on human action and certain boundaries for human behavior. Scripture provides us with many such rules. Moreover, rules function as guides for the proper way to live out God's intentions for our lives by showing us how to love God and neighbor.

As important as rules are, however, we do not worship rules. There is a danger of following rules so slavishly that we lose sight of the relationships that the rules are designed to foster. This is what Jesus means when he says, "The sabbath was made for humankind, and not humankind for the sabbath" (Mark 2:27). The keeping of Sabbath was a very important law. But when it got in the way of love, compassion, and healing, Jesus felt free to break it.

Finally, there is a danger of self-righteousness. Many of us can point to individuals who believe that they are worthy of God's love and grace because they follow all the laws of Scripture (as they interpret them). Jesus is constantly scandalizing those people who are strict followers of Hebrew law (such as the priests and scribes) by arguing that the "sinners" and the unrighteous are beloved by God and are able to hear the invitation by God to enter into God's kingdom (Matt. 21:31; Luke 14:7–23).

Consequentialist Ethics

Deontologists tend to focus on the nature of the act, claiming that certain acts, because of their inherent quality, are moral or immoral (or at least carry some moral weight). They therefore stress the importance of rules, because rules capture the ethical qualities of certain actions.

But actions are not isolated events. Actions are performed with particular goals in mind, and actions have consequences. *Consequentialists* contend that actions are to be judged not by some inherent quality but by the consequences that they produce. The main type of consequentialism is called *utilitarianism*. The most important early proponents of utilitarianism were Jeremy Bentham (1748–1832) and John Stuart Mill (1806–1873). Mill and Bentham argued that actions do not have some inherent quality that makes them moral or immoral. What makes an action right or wrong are the consequences of the action. Those actions that result in good consequences are good, and those that result in bad consequences are bad.

Of course, this does not get us very far until we know what counts as "good" and "bad" consequences. Both Bentham and Mill argued that the ultimate good is pleasure or happiness and the ultimate bad is pain or unhappiness.[11] So when deciding between two courses of action, one must perform the action that will result in the greatest amount of good for the greatest number of people. One must calculate the benefits to all people that will result from an action and then subtract the harms that will accrue to others and oneself. The action that has the greatest overall "utility" (proportion of good consequences to bad) is the right action. Bentham argues that this is the only principle of morality: "By utility is meant that property in any object, whereby it tends to produce benefit, advantage, pleasure, good, or happiness . . . or . . . to prevent the happening of pain, evil, or unhappiness to the party whose interest is considered."[12]

Utilitarians hold that there are no intrinsically good or bad acts, and that intentions and character are only important when it comes to judging *persons*. But when determining the right action, there is only one rule: *Do the greatest good for the greatest number.* This is a simplified version of the principle of utility described by Bentham. Utilitarians are generally suspicious of the language of intrinsic value or inherent rightness. To argue, as deontologists often do, about inherent rightness is to ground morality on something that can be neither demonstrated nor measured. Utility, on the other hand, is both measurable and demonstrable, they argue. If you want to know if an act is right, examine its consequences.

In the case study that opened this chapter, John must weigh all of the consequences of lying, not lying, or evading the question. The moral action will be the one where the good consequences of his action outweigh the bad consequences. So, among other things, John might consider the following:

- the effect of his action on Bill's future
- the effect on the class of allowing Bill to cheat on the exam
- the consequences for their friendship
- the possible consequences of getting caught lying

Once John has taken into account all of the possible consequences of different courses of action, he must act on the principle of utility. He must act in whatever manner will create the greatest amount of good for all persons involved.

As a mode of moral reasoning, utilitarianism has a number of attractive elements. First, there is something intuitively very appealing about utilitarian thinking. In our own lives we will often forgo a lesser good for a greater. We often try to achieve an overall maximum of good in our lives, even when the benefits are remote. For example, you might forgo the current pleasure of eating a piece of cheesecake because you suspect that a week or year from now you might be overweight. A second intuitively appealing aspect of utilitarianism is that it seems natural that we should seek the very best outcome for the most people if we want the world to be a better place. Third, utilitarianism is markedly egalitarian. Each person counts as one and only one. The benefits and harms to others receive the same weight or consideration as benefits and harms to oneself. Fourth, utilitarians argue that we have extensive negative responsibility, thus reminding us that *not* acting is a kind of action that requires moral justification since both acting and *not* acting result in consequences.

Difficulties of Following a Utilitarian Approach

Despite its appeal, there are many difficulties or questions that a utilitarian mode of ethical reasoning poses. Let me simply raise a few of these.

Difficulty of Judging Future Events

One problem is the difficulty of judging future events. How do we know what consequences will occur as a result of our actions? Utilitarian thinking, argue its critics, requires a great deal of guesswork. For example, John is unsure of what might happen if he lies. He must do quite a lot of moral guesswork in making his decision. Is it possible to imagine all of the future effects of one's actions?

Personal Difficulty of Living by Utilitarian Standard

To live by a utilitarian mode requires a great deal of work. Instead of living by certain standards and rules, utilitarians must calculate benefits and liabilities to all persons resulting from each and every action they perform.[13]

Determining What Counts as a "Good"

Utilitarianism has not gotten us very far unless we can more precisely define what counts as a good or bad consequence. We must still determine which values go into the utilitarian calculation of liabilities and benefits. Are pleasure and pain the only values that need calculation, or are there other values that must be considered? What about some of the following values: freedom, beauty, equality, land, economic well-being, education, scientific knowledge, pleasure, and health?

Issue of Incommensurable Values

"Incommensurable values" are of different types; they cannot be compared. They are like apples and oranges. Are consequences really as quantifiable and comparable as utilitarians imply? How do we weigh or balance some of the values identified above? A prime example of this is the issue of economic benefits versus ecological preservation. How are we to measure ecological damage against economic growth and health? This is the debate that is currently taking place over whether or not to open areas of the Alaskan wilderness to oil exploration. It can be quite difficult to balance harm to the environment with the economic benefits of obtaining more oil and natural gas. Another example might be the balancing of human freedom and human life in cases where nations go to war to protect people's freedom and self-determination.

Do the Ends Justify the Means?

Finally, a fundamental question for this approach to ethics is whether desirable ends always justify any effective means. Can some means (actions performed to achieve a goal) be ruled out because of some intrinsic, inherent feature, even if they would be very effective? Are there not some actions, no matter how beneficial, that are simply wrong? This is the reasoning behind the opponents of embryonic stem cell research. Stem cell therapy has the potential to cure many devastating diseases such as Parkinson's, diabetes, and Alzheimer's, as well as to help paralytics. However, to do so, embryos must be destroyed. Opponents contend that no matter how good the consequences or ends, the means to those ends cannot be justified. Utilitarians argue that such moral squeamishness leads to greater suffering and harm for many desperately ill people. Therefore, the benefits of stem cell research outweigh any negative consequences.

Christianity and Utilitarianism

Strengths of Utilitarianism from a Christian Perspective

Is utilitarianism consistent with a biblically grounded Christian ethic? From a Christian perspective, utilitarianism has several strengths. First, utilitarianism presupposes a world that is somewhat predictable in terms of cause and effect. Christians claim that God, as the loving and powerful architect of creation, has designed a world that is good and predictable so that human creatures will have a place to grow in love for God and neighbor (see chapter 5 on creation). Utilitarianism presupposes a world that is predictable and orderly.

The second strength of utilitarianism from a Christian perspective is its emphasis on human well-being. Utilitarians stress the real, measurable effects of our actions upon people's lives. They remind us that we do not live and act in a vacuum; our actions (or failures to act) have real and often life-changing consequences for many other people. This accords nicely with a central tenet of Christian ethics. As we shall see when we turn to the law and the prophets, a recurrent biblical theme is caring for people's physical well-being. Concrete concerns about the daily conditions of life pervade the laws given by God. For example, coats taken as collateral must be returned before nightfall so that the borrower has something to sleep in (Exod. 22:26–27). Likewise, the prophets rail against such mundane matters as using unfair scales in the selling of wheat or taking bribes in court cases. And Jesus tells us that we must feed the hungry and clothe the naked (Matt. 25:31–46).

In their suspicion of rules, utilitarians rightly warn us against placing rules above human beings, against hiding behind obligations so that we can avoid the real work of loving our neighbor. Joseph Fletcher, in a model of Christian utilitarian reasoning, argues that love, which he defines as maximizing the good consequences, is the only law: "Love, unlike law, sets no carefully calculated limits on obligation; it seeks the most good possible in every situation."[14] Christian utilitarians can point to Jesus' own attitude toward the law in support of their position. For the sake of helping actual human beings in pain, Jesus himself was willing to break many of the laws Jews held sacred.

A third strength of utilitarianism from a Christian perspective is that it is markedly egalitarian. Everyone counts—and everyone counts equally. Historically, Christians and Jews may not always have lived up to the biblical claim that all persons are created in the image of God. Nevertheless, this is central to the biblical vision of humanity. Old Testament law, the prophets, Jesus, Paul, and James all warn against showing favoritism to the rich and powerful. All stress the importance of treating the poor and powerless as equal to the rich and influential. Utilitarianism says that we do not place our own well-being above that of our neighbor or even our enemy. Moreover, we do not favor our friends and relatives over strangers.

Weaknesses of Utilitarianism from a Christian Perspective

In the end, however, utilitarianism's major strength is also the reason that Christians might reject it as a mode of ethical reasoning. It is too one-sidedly humanistic on a number of fronts, according to many Christian critics.

First, Christians recognize values other than human well-being. Especially to be rejected is hedonistic utilitarianism, which argues that pleasure is the only value that must be calculated and human pain the only disvalue. Loyalty, honesty, devotion to God, concern for the created order, self-control, and justice are just a few of the things that Christians value in addition to human pleasure and avoidance of pain.

Second, the focus on human well-being and flourishing recognizes no limits upon human action. It is so entirely focused on reducing human suffering and increasing human well-being that it refuses to recognize divinely imposed limits upon human action. There is a kind of *hubris,* or pride, that goes with utilitarianism, say its Christian critics. Utilitarians assume that we can do anything and everything to increase human well-being and decrease human suffering. Recall Gilbert Meilander's observation: "Those who know themselves as creatures—not Creator—will recognize limits even upon their obligation to do good. As creatures we are called to do all the good we can, but this means all the good we 'morally can'—all the good we can within certain limits. It may be that the Creator *ought to do* whatever is necessary to bring about states of affairs which *ought to be,* but we stand under no such godlike imperative."[15] Another way of saying this is that utilitarians fail to recognize that we have obligations to God as well as to our fellow human creatures. God is the ultimate value, not humans.

Third, many Christian ethicists claim that utilitarianism is too one-sided as a moral theory because it places entirely too much emphasis on human *action.* The Christian life is much more than a series of discrete actions. It involves the development of a set of virtues or character traits that reflect our basic assumptions about who God is and what God is doing in the world. I will say more about this theory of virtue in chapter 3.

In conclusion, the utilitarian stresses the human obligation to act in such a way that we create a better world for all human beings. As Christians who are created for fellowship with others and commanded to love our neighbors as ourselves, we recognize the same obligation. However, we also recognize that we are placed under other obligations.

Therefore, in my opinion, the best approach is to say that the principle of utility is a *prima facie* obligation. Christians have a *prima facie* obligation to help others and to avoid harming them. But Christians have other obligations imposed by God, and there might be times when these obligations must override the principle of utility. We may have to choose a course of action that will *not* result in the greatest good for the greatest number. We will recognize that God has placed limitations upon our pursuit of the normally admirable ends of relieving suffering or benefiting others.

Chapter 3

How Should We *Be?*

Virtue, Character, and Responsibility

*I*f someone were to ask you whether a person that you know is a good person, you would probably not say, "Let me tell you what choice she would make when faced with a moral dilemma." Rather, you would probably say something like, "Yes, Shannon is a good person. She is warm and honest and caring and humble." Or you may say, "Frank is kind of stingy and jealous and is always getting angry." Whether you know it or not, you are engaged in what ethicists call *virtue ethics.* In the previous chapter, we explored several answers to one of the key moral questions: "What should I *do?*" Certainly, how one behaves is a central concern not only for professional ethicists but also for anyone trying to live a good moral life. But to restrict morality only to actions is to have an impoverished view of what makes up a good person. This is especially the case in Christian ethics. Since Christian ethical thinking began, Christians have argued that it is not enough simply to follow a prescribed set of rules or even to do the right thing. One must also develop a certain set of character traits. To be a truly good person, it is not enough that one simply do the right things; one must also feel the right way and do the right things with the right motives and intentions. In other words, one must possess a certain kind of character.

This way of thinking about morality is called virtue ethics or character ethics and focuses less on the question "What should I *do?*" and more on the question "What kind of person should I *be?*" Without a doubt, the two questions are related, but recently, virtue ethicists have criticized the overemphasis on deciding what to do in morally tough situations. Virtue ethicists such as Stanley Hauerwas have criticized the preoccupation with what they call "quandary ethics" or "decisionist ethics." "Morality is not primarily concerned with quandaries or hard decisions; nor is the moral self simply the collection of such decisions."[1] While recognizing the importance of decisions, virtue ethicists observe how seldom we encounter situations of real moral perplexity such as that faced by John in Professor Williams's office or Doctor Johnson in the emergency room (see chapter 2).

Yet every day we are in the midst of developing our character. Whether we are compassionate, humble, and joyful, or envious, angry, and cowardly, these are elements of our moral being that are relevant each and every day. They may often get expressed in actions that fall below the ethical radar screen of people who are looking for momentous events of great moral decision making.

What kind of person are you going to be? In many ways this question is both prior to and more important than individual decisions. It is prior to individual decisions because it will determine how we see a moral situation and how we respond. This is what Jesus means when he says, "Either make the tree good, and its fruit good; or make the tree bad, and its fruit bad; for the tree is known by its fruit. . . . The good person brings good things out of a good treasure, and the evil person brings evil things out of an evil treasure" (Matt. 12:33, 35). Jesus contends that, like good fruit that comes naturally and inevitably from a good tree, so too do righteous *actions* come forth from a righteous *person*.

This priority of character and virtues over actions is manifested in Jesus' own teaching ministry, for he often reinterprets commandments such as "Do not kill" or "Do not commit adultery" to mean "Do not be angry" and "Do not lust" (Matt. 5–7). Jesus is calling his followers to a higher righteousness that involves a transformation of the entire person, not just their actions. As John Calvin remarks about the relationship between actions (duties) and virtues, "It would not be enough duly to discharge such duties unless the mind itself and the heart first put on the inclination to righteousness, judgment, and mercy."[2]

Let us take a closer look at a virtue approach to ethics. Since virtue theory has a long non-Christian history going back to Plato, Aristotle, and the Stoics, we will begin with a general discussion of this approach. We will then move to a more specifically Christian treatment of virtue or character.

What Is Virtue?

A virtue is a type of habit. "Habit" is a technical term that has been used for over two thousand years to describe an inclination or disposition to act, think, or feel in a certain way. Habits are tendencies or patterns of behavior or thought.

Virtue is a type of habit—but a habit to do or feel or think what? It helps to understand the origin of the word. "Virtue" is the English translation of the Greek *arete*, which means "excellence." Originally the term was not restricted to human skills. The *arete* of a knife is its sharpness, and the *arete* of a blanket is its warmth. Everything has an end (*telos*) or goal or purpose for which it is designed. The knife is designed to cut; thus, its *arete* is its sharpness. The same is true for human beings according to most virtue ethicists, such as Aristotle: "Just as we can see that eye and hand and foot and every one of our members has some function, should we not assume that in like manner a human being has a function over and above these particular functions?"[3] Human beings are designed a certain way with a particular end or purpose. Therefore, the virtues are those characteristics that, when practiced, make us better people. As sharpness makes good knives, human virtues make good people.

A virtue is a habit to act, think, or feel in a way that disposes a person to its proper end. The Latin term *virtu*, from which we draw the English "virtue," reflects this meaning. Its origin is *vir*, which is the root for "man" (as in the word "virile"). Virtues are those habits that make us truly human, that help us live our lives in the properly human way. Christian virtues are those habits of thinking, feeling, and acting, that make us truly Christian persons.

Let's flesh out this rather bare description by highlighting some of the key elements that most virtue approaches share.

Elements of Virtue Theory

Virtue Ethics Focuses on the Whole Person, Not Just Particular Actions

Virtue ethics shifts the focus from particular, discrete actions to the person who is performing the action. This is why you will find very little discussion of the morality of particular types of actions in the writings of classical virtue theorists such as Plato and Aristotle. Instead of deciding what makes an act right or wrong, these ancient Greek thinkers (and their modern-day counterparts) discuss at length what makes a person virtuous. In place of discussing good and bad *acts*, virtue theorists discuss what makes a good or bad *person*, a person of virtue or vice.

Morality is less concerned with those rare instances in which we have to make difficult moral decisions, and more with what Birch and Rasmussen elegantly call the "quiet social vocation of soulcraft."[4] For virtue ethicists,

> the work of morality [is] directed less to the resolution of moral quandaries ("what would you do if . . .") than to the deliberation of how we should live, with special concern for the sorts of persons we should be. This side of the moral life brings *moral formation* to the fore and accentuates moral education and training for the good life as key elements of ethics.[5]

Virtue ethics focuses on the formation of a kind of character or identity that makes us most authentically human. To be virtuous is to have and practice those patterns of behavior, thought, disposition, and feeling that make us "good."

With this shift in focus from the act to the person, it is no longer sufficient to decide whether this or that particular act is right or wrong. Now one must propose some vision of what constitutes a person of virtue or vice. This is to say that virtue theory rests on some conception of the ideal human life and that how one defines a "good person" is dependent upon our broader understanding of what the world is like, who God is, and how human beings are related to both the world and God. In other words, what counts as a "good person" will greatly depend upon the story or narrative one tells about the nature of the universe. This is what Hauerwas and Pinches mean when they say that virtue ethics begins from "'somewhere' . . . in contrast to ethics done in the theoretical mode of modernity that tries to begin from nowhere."[6]

This all sounds very abstract, so let's see if we can make our exploration more concrete. I was once helping to record the times at the end of a bicycle race. One of the competitors whom I had known from previous races came across the finish line. He had won the race after being behind two other riders much of the afternoon. I said to him, "Congratulations. Nice riding to catch those two guys in front of you." To this he responded, "Oh, I was just toying with them the whole time." I was immediately put off by this answer because it struck me as displaying a profound lack of humility. I expressed my opinion to someone next to me who said, "Oh, that's just the way it is in mountain bike racing. Cockiness is a virtue; it helps you win."

The conversation did not go any further, but if it had, my fellow judge might have asked me, "Why do you think humility is a virtue?" To this question, my response would begin with an appeal to Scripture's call for humility. But if the person asked why the Bible thinks humility is a virtue, I would have to tell a much larger story about God's greatness and our human sinfulness. The story would be a Christian interpretation of who God is, what God has done, who human beings are, and what our destiny is. In other words, humility is a virtue in Christianity because of the grand narrative we tell about God, Jesus Christ, creation, human sinfulness, and the redemption on the cross, in addition to an explanation of how we are called to be servants because our Lord became a servant. To explain why humility is part of what it means to be a good person would require an explanation of why humility is a constitutive part of what it means to be a good *Christian*, because my understanding of "good person" is defined by my Christian faith.

But in a world like that of mountain bike racing where not everyone is Christian, "good person" might be defined largely in terms of "good mountain bike racer," and therefore humility might not be considered a virtue. More broadly, if someone were to say, "I don't think that God created human beings or saves them, and I also don't think human beings are all that bad," then humility might not be on their list of virtues that define a good person.

How people define a "good person" is part of a much larger set of convictions and beliefs about the way they see the world. As a Christian, it might be very hard for me to defend my understanding of the virtuous life without appealing to the particularities of the Christian story. So if a non-Christian asks me to defend generosity as part of the virtuous life *without* appealing to the Christian story, I will be in foreign territory. I might be able to make some argument about the common humanity of all people, but even this is grounded for me in my Christian worldview.

Virtue Ethics Places Actions within the History of the Person

Virtue ethicists criticize deontology and utilitarianism because they are preoccupied with difficult moral quandaries. But virtue ethicists also criticize deontology and utilitarianism because these modes of moral reasoning approach these quandaries in a way that abstracts them from the person who is making the decision. "Should one go to war? Should one have an abortion? Should one give money to the poor?" Such questions are asked and answered in the abstract, as if the kind of person one is or wishes to be has no bearing on the decision.

We do not come to each act as a blank sheet of paper. We confront moral situations with a history of moral decision making and character development that goes back to our earliest childhood. The very fact that we recognize a situation as moral or immoral is the result of a long history of decision making that reflects and shapes our character. Deontologists and utilitarians often assume that we can simply describe a situation from a neutral perspective, identifying key moral elements. Underlying this assumption is a blindness to the richly textured stories and values that give shape to human life. Let us take several examples. For some people, the decision to use birth control is a serious moral problem; other people do not even see it as a moral issue, but simply a medical and practical one. The very fact that some people, such as Roman Catholics, view birth control as a moral issue is a result of their particular religious character. For most people, the practice of eating dairy products such as cheese and milk never strikes them as a moral decision. For those of us who are vegetarians for religious reasons, eating milk and cheese requires deliberation and justification. If a person is not compassionate and generous, the issue of whether to give to a charity or buy himself a new car presents itself as merely a monetary question and not a moral one. This is to say that all people have characters that they have developed over their lifetimes. Whether or not they view a situation as morally difficult is the product of that character.

Because of this deeply ingrained moral character, virtue ethicists contend that in most cases a virtuous person will not need to think about rules or principles, but will simply act in the virtuous manner because she has developed a certain type of character or set of virtues. Have you ever heard someone say, after doing something that looks heroic, "I am no hero; I couldn't have done anything else," or "It never crossed my mind not to do it"? What this reflects is that most of our moral actions, from minor, everyday honesty and courtesy to the occasional heroic act, are usually not the result of careful moral consideration but rather emerge spontaneously from our character, a character shaped by our values, commitments, worldviews, and previous actions. They are like good fruit that comes forth naturally from the good tree.

This emphasis on the whole person is also reflected in the insistence by virtue ethicists that one cannot judge a person by a single action, nor does one become virtuous by a single act. As Aristotle put it, "One swallow does not mean summer."[7] You would not call a person honest or caring simply because he displayed that character trait once or twice. He must have a pattern of expressing that virtue.

You and I may sometimes act out of character, but if we do this too often, people begin to reevaluate their impression of our moral character. Persons of virtue must ultimately be consistent in their displays of virtue. Persons of virtue have an integrity about them. Not only do they act and feel consistently, but they act and feel consistent with their beliefs and values. They can be trusted to act in conjunction with their beliefs even when the chips are down. In fact, this steadiness of character is one of the overriding characteristics of a person whom we call virtuous.

For Virtue Ethicists, Acts Both Reflect Who We Are and Determine Who We Are

One of the central presumptions of virtue ethicists is the dialectical relationship between character and actions. On the one hand, our *character is reflected in our actions.* If you want to know whether a person has the virtue of humility or wisdom or patience, you observe whether that person behaves in a way that reflects these virtues. What kind of persons we are determines how we are going to act in a given situation. Whether we make a stand when someone tells a racist joke or whether we "let it slide" depends on how courageous we are. The presence or absence of the virtue of forgiveness will determine whether or not we seek revenge against someone we feel has harmed us. Our character determines our actions.

Not only do our actions reflect our character, but *our actions determine our character*. For example, according to Aristotle, Aquinas, and other virtue ethicists, if we want to acquire the virtue of courage, we should act courageously. If we want to develop the virtue of compassion, we should act in ways that resemble compassionate behavior. "We become just by doing just acts, temperate by doing temperate acts."[8] Actions shape our character. If you act in a certain way long enough, you will likely begin to develop certain virtues or character traits that are connected with those ways of acting.

Virtue Ethics Focuses on Motivation and Intention

In virtue ethics, there is a considerable emphasis on intention and motive. It is not enough that a person does what is right; a person must do what is right with the right motive, intention, feeling, or disposition. The truly virtuous person will *desire* to do what is right. The virtuous person does not just perform the right action; she does what is right with the right motive or intention. According to Aristotle, "Anyone who does not delight in fine actions is not even a good man; for nobody would say that a man is just unless he enjoys acting justly, nor liberal unless he enjoys liberal actions, and similarly in all the other cases."[9] For deontologists and utilitarians, the important thing is whether the act gets done or not. For virtue ethicists, there is a much greater concern with the act getting done with the right motive, since what is really being judged is not so much the act, but the agent performing the act. Philip Melanchthon argues that we should not look at the "external masks of men; the Holy Scriptures look at the deepest, incomprehensible affections. Since a man is governed by these, the scriptures judge the acts according to the motivation behind the affections."[10]

This last claim raises some interesting questions that the reader may want to consider. The first has to do with the voluntariness of virtue. Deontologists and utilitarians argue that we should focus on actions because actions are within our control. But whether we have a certain virtue such as courage or humility seems largely outside of our control. We can try to act justly or act compassionately, but can we force ourselves to enjoy acting in such ways? Second, is it necessary that we have the right motive for an act to be moral? Here we might want to invoke the distinction between act and agent, saying that a good act done with a bad motive should lead us to praise the act but not the agent. If I give money to a charity with the goal of being praised or getting a tax break, is the act no longer morally praiseworthy? Third, what if we act out of multiple motives? What if the person gives to the charity because she has compassion for the people it helps *and* hopes to get a tax break and be praised? Despite these questions and issues, there is something intuitively correct about the virtue ethicist's emphasis on motives and intentions. Truly moral people seem to be those who act virtuously, not simply out of some abstract sense of what they *ought* to do but because they *desire* to do so.

Emotions, Dispositions, and Virtue

One significant contribution of virtue theory is that it has reintroduced the importance of emotion in the moral life. Both utilitarianism and deontology are quite suspicious of emotion. Deontologist Immanuel Kant argues that emotions are a hindrance to acting out of duty. One should put aside emotion and act solely from a sense of duty, doing what is right according to universal principles. For utilitarians, emotions can often get in the way of the objective calculation of good or bad consequences.

But virtue ethicists see emotions as central to the moral life. Emotions and virtues are closely connected. Many virtues or vices—such as courage, sympathy, and envy—are so closely connected with emotions as to be almost indistinguishable from them. But some emotions are not identified specifically with a virtue or vice, such as anger, grief, joy, and shame. I contend that part of what it means to be a good person is to learn to *feel* the right way toward the right things.

This may sound very strange. Most of us have grown up hearing that "you can't judge emotions" or that "there is no such thing as good or bad emotions." We are told that we cannot control what we feel, and that all emotions are acceptable as long as we express them appropriately. What lies behind such thinking is the idea that emotions are completely outside of our control, that they are irrational and uncontrollable.[11] People contend that emotions simply "come over us" and that we are moved by them, as a sheet is moved by the wind. Emotions are portrayed as being somehow separate from our rational faculties, beyond our ability to shape or train.

And so we are told not to judge people's emotions but only their actions. I think this is a misunderstanding of both emotions and the moral life. Emotions are not blind forces that simply overcome us; they are closely connected with what we believe and what we value. If I become extremely angry because my son spills apple juice in my car, then you have learned something about what I value, namely, my car. If I feel sad when Sheila dies, it is because I valued Sheila. You may not have particularly liked Sheila, so you do not feel sad.

Because emotions are related to what we value, they can be judged, just as our values are. For example, if Bill gets pleasure out of watching a child torture a dog or cat, that is wrong. It is not enough for Bill to say, "It is a feeling. I can't control my feelings." Likewise, if a person fails to feel anger at the sight of someone unjustly wronged, that is a failure of virtue. And it is not morally neutral if a person fails to feel sadness at the loss of a loved one or joy at the success of a friend.

Part of becoming a virtuous person is learning to feel the right emotions about the right things. Anger, for example, can be moral or immoral depending upon the object. If I become angry that the United States ranks dead last among major industrial countries in the percentage of GNP that it gives to poor nations, that is moral anger.[12] If I feel angry because I cannot find a parking space, that is a morally questionable emotion.

Since emotions are derived from what we value, we can learn to transform our emotions by changing our values. Through prayer, study, imagination, and action, we can transform our emotional responses to the world around us. For example, to transform the emotion of envy, you might concentrate on the many blessings in your own life. To develop greater compassion, you may engage in a practice of praying fervently for other people. To lessen the emotional anguish of grief, you may follow John Calvin's suggestion and meditate upon the resurrection. In the end, Christians are called to a purification of the whole person—behavior, thought, *and* feeling.

Christianity and Virtue/Character

There is little doubt that modern Christian virtue ethicists have helped Christians reclaim a central feature of Christian ethics. While the language of character formation has never completely disappeared from everyday Christian discourse in families, sermons, or Sunday school, the reemergence of the language of virtue among professional Christian ethicists is a welcome sight, because the development of Christian character is absolutely central to the Christian life. To be a Christian is to be shaped by the values, commitments, and worldview of the community of faith to such a degree that one begins to internalize certain virtues and dispositions. To be a Christian is not merely to act in certain ways. Nor is being a Christian merely to believe certain abstract doctrines. While belief and action are vital to being a Christian, one must also allow oneself to be shaped and molded into a particular kind of person, to develop a set of virtues that reflect what we as Christians claim to believe about the world.

Virtue and belief go hand in hand. Recall our earlier discussion about the connection between virtues and the larger view of what it means to be a human being. Christians have a particular understanding of what a human being ought to be like. As we shall see, much of this is shaped by an imitation of Christ. But our understanding of the kinds of persons we should be is integrally connected with our beliefs. For example, Paul claims that forgiveness is a key virtue. Why? Because of what he believes that God has already done for us, specifically, forgiven us our sins. Jesus tells a parable in which a man is forgiven a huge debt by his king. After leaving the presence of the king, the man runs into a servant who owes him a small sum that the servant cannot pay. The man has the servant thrown into jail until he can pay. When the king hears about this he says, "You wicked slave! I forgave you all that debt because you pleaded with me. Should you not have had mercy on your fellow slave, as I had mercy on you?" (Matt. 18:32–33). In this parable, the king represents God, and therefore Jesus is saying that we should show mercy because God is merciful and has forgiven us.

To use the ethical lingo, what we see here is the connection between the *indicative* and *imperative*. An indicative is a sentence or statement that says, "This is the case." It "indicates" something. An imperative is a command: "Do that," or "Be like this." As we shall see in discussing the ethics of Paul, the Christian life moves from the indicative to the imperative. In other words, we are first told what God has done (indicative) and then how we are to act in response (imperative).

Because Christians believe certain things about who God is and what God has done, we should display certain virtues. As Birch and Rasmussen put it:

> To belong to a people of God means *the formation and transformation of personal moral identity in keeping with the faith identity of the community.* This encompasses more than virtue and character formation, but they are indispensable components. Moreover, the *scriptures* of the community are a prime medium for moral formation.[13]

By internalizing certain biblical stories, language, symbols, and ideas, Christians begin to experience the world in a particular manner. The shaping of this way of experiencing the world lies at the heart of the project that we are engaged in—normative Christian ethics.

Virtue and Sanctification

Christians have a particular way of talking about developing the kind of character that reflects God's intention for God's human creatures. We call it *sanc-*

tification (from Latin *sanctus*, meaning "holy")—to be made holy. To be holy is to be set apart. Christians are called to be different kinds of people. As Paul says, "Do not be conformed to this world, but be transformed by the renewing of your minds" (Rom. 12:2). We no longer base our understanding of the good person on what the world tells us, but rather on what we learn about God through Jesus Christ. We become set apart, sanctified. This does not mean that we take a "holier than thou" attitude. We are made holy only insofar as God transforms us. God is the central actor in our transformation; therefore, we have nothing to boast about. It does mean that we are willing to recognize that we may be called to be witnesses to a different vision of the good life, to be ready to actively resist the temptation to simply conform to the world around us. We should develop a kind of Christian character that is shaped by our grand understanding of what God has done in the history of Israel, what God revealed in Jesus of Nazareth, and what God continues to do through the Holy Spirit.

What might such a character look like? We will explore this question further as we discuss the Bible in future chapters. For now let us simply begin with an overview of the Christian character. There are many, many virtues identified throughout Scripture. Some of the prevalent ones found in the New Testament are:

Humility/meekness	Matt. 5:5; Col. 3:12; Rom. 12:16
Forgiveness	John 8:1–11; Col. 3:13
Patience	Col. 3:12; Rom. 12:12
Hope	Rom. 12:12; Heb. 6:19–20
Courage/faith	Luke 8:22–25; 1 Cor. 16:13
Generosity	2 Cor. 8:1–15; 9:6–15
Sympathy/compassion	Col. 3:12; Matt. 14:14
Love	1 Cor. 16:13; Rom. 12:9–10
Truthfulness	Eph. 4:25
Gentleness	Col. 3:8; Phil. 4:5
Kindness	Col. 3:12
Self-control	2 Pet. 1:6
Joy	Gal. 5:12; John 16:12; Phil. 4:4

Paul refers to some of these as "fruits of the Spirit." By this, he means that these virtues will emerge when persons have received the spirit of Christ into their lives. When believers receive the spirit of Christ, they will act like Christ did.

We will examine the ways in which Christians imitate the virtues of Christ in chapter 9. As you read the assigned Bible passages in the coming weeks, ask yourself which virtues seem to be prevalent.

Cardinal Virtues

Ancient Greek and Roman thinkers such as Plato, Aristotle, Seneca, and Marcus Aurelius spent much time discussing the virtues. A general consensus was reached among them on what are called the "cardinal virtues." They are called "cardinal" because they were the "hinge" (Latin, *cardo*) on which all the other virtues hung.

Wisdom / Prudence

This is the crowning virtue of the cardinal virtues. Wisdom, or prudence, is the ability to know how properly to exercise the other virtues. Courage becomes a vice if we simply rush into dangerous situations with little regard for our safety or that of others. For example, a store clerk refuses to hand over cash to three armed gunmen. This may be an act of courage but it is not a virtuous act. Courage can become mere rashness without prudence. The wise man also is able to see the intricacies of a moral situation. He has what James Gustafson calls *discernment*, the ability to identify the relevant factors in any given situation and a sensitivity to moral complexities. Have you ever known someone who was able to see things in a situation that simply did not occur to you? This person has moral wisdom.

Courage

Few us of will ever get to exhibit courage by running into a burning building to save a child, but we often confront more routine situations that require courage. A person tells a racist joke and everyone laughs, but one person confronts the jokester. A student who refuses to abandon his or her moral beliefs in the face of peer pressure displays the virtue of courage. Courage can manifest itself in many different forms. It may involve standing up for one's convictions in the face of ridicule or outright attack. It may involve saying something to a friend or family member that will make one unpopular. It may mean taking a new job or pursuing a new path that is unfamiliar and challenging.

Justice

Justice is the virtue of acting in such a way as to give persons their due. This can take two forms on the social level: retributive and distributive. *Retributive justice* is the institution of punishment for wrongdoing. So when a burglar goes to jail or a corporation is fined for polluting, retributive justice is being served. *Distributive justice* involves the means by which we distribute the goods of society: money, jobs, land, and the like. Justice is a virtue not only on the social but also on the individual level, although it can be exceedingly difficult to practice justice in an inherently unjust society such as a repressive dictatorship. On the individual level, just persons are generally characterized by the ability to see beyond the narrow confines of their own self-interest. They are willing and able to weigh the interests of others in their moral deliberation. Just persons have developed the moral skill of seeing the effects of an action or policy on all persons involved and then acting in a way that is fair. Of course, what counts as fair is a subject for debate. As we shall see when we turn to the Bible, economic justice involves more than simply giving each person what he or she has earned. So whereas egalitarians, Christians, or libertarians may disagree on what counts as fair, just persons are ones who will adhere to their notions of fairness, even when to do so might be detrimental to themselves or their group. Here we see the close connection between justice and courage and why most virtue theorists have argued for the unity of the virtues, such that it is impossible to fully have one without the others.

Temperance or Self-Control

Unfortunately, this term has been almost exclusively identified with abstinence from alcohol. But temperance is much more than abstaining from alcohol or other temptations such as drugs, chocolate, caffeine, and the like. It is to be in control of one's actions in all that one does, not being completely driven by impetuosity. It involves restraint and moderation in all things and living within God-given limits. Part of becoming a mature human being is learning to accept and live within one's limits. We cannot do or have all things. Nor can we simply pursue our own good at the expense of others. "Temperance is a matter of linking what you choose and what you refuse in a whole pattern of life that makes it possible for you to live a good life for yourself and, indeed, to contribute to the good lives of others."[14]

Christian Cardinal Virtues: Faith, Hope, and Love

Most Christian ethicists agree with the Greeks that justice, courage, temperance, and wisdom are important virtues. In fact, these four "cardinal" virtues can all be found in Scripture. However, Scripture cites three other virtues as central: "And now faith, hope, and love abide, these three: and the greatest of these is love" (1 Cor. 13:13).

Faith, as we shall see when we explore the thought of Paul, is not simply an intellectual assent to some church doctrines. Faith is understood as *trust*. It is assurance or trust in the faithfulness and promises of God. For Christians, even if one has justice, wisdom, courage, and temperance, this is not enough to live the truly good life. These are incomplete unless one has faith in Jesus Christ.

The same is true of **hope.** Most people would not normally think of hope as a virtue, but it is central to the Christian life. In fact, it is hard to picture the Christian life without hope. Hope does not mean naive blindness to the cruelties and difficulties of life. Nor is hope simply an optimism about the ability of human beings to improve their lot. Our hope is not in ourselves; our hope is in the promises of God. As we shall see when we discuss the prophets and Jesus' proclamation of the kingdom of God, Christian life is characterized by a hopeful anticipation of God's complete reign on earth. Christians can become as discouraged as anyone else at the state of the world. In fact, their sensitivity to the suffering of others can leave them more vulnerable to despair. But we can never lose all hope, no matter how dark the times, because we wait in longing expectation for the fulfillment of God's promises. Christians are called to live not simply in the shadow of the cross of Christ but in the light of the empty tomb. If the cross of Christ is the symbol of ultimate despair, then the resurrection of Jesus from the dead is the warrant for Christian hope in the midst of despair.

We shall discuss the virtue of **love** at length in a later chapter. But this is the virtue that binds all other virtues together. As Paul says, "As God's chosen ones, holy and beloved, clothe yourselves with compassion, kindness, humility, meekness, and patience. . . . Above all, clothe yourselves with love, which binds everything together in perfect harmony. And let the peace of Christ rule in your hearts" (Col. 3:12, 14–15). In this admonition to the church at Colossae, Paul connects love with peace and harmony. A single Hebrew word encompasses all of these terms: *shalom*. The goal and capstone of the Christian life is shalom—peace, harmony, and love between all human beings and between human creatures and God.

Other Key Christian Virtues

One exercise you might want to try for yourself as we read through Scripture is the identification of three or four important virtues that would most clearly identify the Christian. Certainly, faith, hope, and love are central, but what other virtues most clearly distinguish the Christian life? I propose the following three.

Forgiveness

A spirit of forgiveness characterizes Christians. This virtue is prevalent throughout the New Testament. Jesus calls upon us to forgive others (Matt. 6:12, 14; John 8:1–11; Matt. 18:21–35). Jesus forgave those who accused and mocked him on the cross (Luke 2:34). Ultimately we are called to forgive one another because God has forgiven us our sins through Jesus Christ: "Be kind to one another, tenderhearted, forgiving one another, as God in Christ has forgiven you" (Eph. 4:32). We forgive because we are forgiven. In a world where revenge, lawsuits, and self-seeking are rampant, a spirit of forgiveness is a distinctive mark of being a disciple of Christ.

Humility

Christians are characterized by a profound sense of humility. This humility arises out of several foundational beliefs. First, Christians confess that God is the creator of all things. We do not create ourselves. God created us out of an overflow of divine love; God did not need to create us and does not need us to be God. Our very being, as well as everything that we have are gifts from God. Second, just as Christians proclaim that their existence is a gift from God, so too do we believe that our salvation is a gift from God. As we shall see when we come to Paul's writings, Christians are put back into right relationship by a free gift of God, not by their own efforts or righteousness, for "all have sinned and fall short of the glory of God" (Rom. 3:23). These two beliefs (that God is the source of all things and that no one is saved by his or her own efforts) lead the Christian to a deep sense of humility. There can be no boasting when we recognize that all we have and all we are is a gift from God.

Joy/Thanksgiving

Finally, a central Christian virtue is joy. This may strike many as strange, since Christians are often portrayed as serious and somber. But Christians believe that Christ is the "good news" of God. They have faith in what God has done. They have hope for what God will do in the future. Therefore, they live lives of joy in the present, with thanksgiving for what God has done and will do. As Paul says, "Rejoice always, pray without ceasing, give thanks in all circumstances; for this is the will of God in Christ Jesus for you" (1 Thess. 5:16–18).

Conclusion

For virtue ethicists, the good life is not simply a matter of doing the right things. It involves the ongoing task of shaping one's very self, of developing a certain set of virtues, emotions, and dispositions. This is certainly the case for Christians. The Christian life involves more than believing certain things or doing certain things. The Christian life is a total transformation of one's character in light of our beliefs about what God has done and continues to do in the world.

PART 2 Biblical Foundations
for Morality

Chapter 4

The Use of Scripture and Other Sources of Christian Guidance

*W*e have come to see that the moral life revolves around the answer to two broad sets of questions. The first set is: "What should we *do* if we want to live moral lives? How should we behave? How do we decide what to do in particular situations?" This set of questions focuses on the decisionist aspect of ethics and morality and has elicited two general approaches over the last several hundred years in the realm of secular or philosophical ethics: deontology and consequentialism.

The second set of questions focuses less on particular decisions than on the development of a set of virtues or character traits. The primary question is not "What should I *do?*" but "How should I *be?*" Virtue ethicists pursue the question "What kind of person should I try to become?" Virtue ethics has a long history within the non-Christian realm, going back to Plato, Aristotle, and the Stoics.

Christians have employed all three of these ethical methods (deontology, utilitarianism, virtue). But the Christian approach to ethics differs from the secular philosophical approach in one very important way. Whereas philosophers ground their efforts in their experience of the world and (more importantly) in human reason, Christians contend that there are two more sources of wisdom and guidance. Christians agree that human experience is a source of guidance and that human reason can help us decide what to do and who to be. But Christian ethicists diverge from philosophical ethicists in their appeal (1) to the traditions of the Christian church and, most importantly, (2) to the Bible. These are the four recognized sources of Christian guidance or wisdom in the Christian tradition: *the Bible, tradition, experience, and reason.* Let us now explore these four sources of moral guidance in the Christian life.

Scripture

It is not too much to say that the one thing other than belief in Jesus Christ that unites Christians more than any other is the Bible. It is also one of the greatest sources of division and controversy. Scripture unites Christians in that anyone who calls herself a Christian is not free simply to dismiss the Bible as irrelevant. She may quarrel with it, question it, investigate it, and emphasize some parts over others, but she may never simply say, "I am going to do Christian ethics without the Bible." To be a Christian is to be in conversation with the biblical text. The fact that Christians (as well as Jews and Muslims) are referred to as a "people of the book" reflects the fact that Scripture stands as the bedrock of the Christian life. The Bible can never be simply dismissed as irrelevant or peripheral.

The Bible is the life story of the people of Israel, Jesus Christ, and the early Christian church. But it is not merely the life story of a people; it is the story of their relationship with their God. It is through the stories of God's dealings with the Jews and early Christians that we come to know *who God is* and *what God wills*. This is to say that God reveals God's self in the history of these peoples. The Bible is the witness to that revelation and the vehicle through which God reveals God's self to us. However, the vehicle is not to be worshiped; that is idolatry. On the other hand, anyone who claims to completely dismiss the Bible as irrelevant and immaterial is placing himself outside of the realm of Christianity.

This is especially true for Christian ethicists. Since the very beginning of Christianity, Christian ethicists have argued over the way in which Scripture should be used in ethics, the meaning of particular passages, the importance of various sections of Scripture, and the very nature of the Bible itself. But no ethicist is free to completely ignore the Bible and still claim to be a *Christian* ethicist. What unites all Christian ethicists is their common appeal to the revelation of God as witnessed in Scripture.

Scripture as a Source of Debate

Simply because all Christian ethicists employ the Bible as a source for guidance does not imply that there is a uniform understanding of how one is to use Scripture. How to interpret Scripture often causes divisions among everyday Christians. Christian ethicists are no different in this regard. Such disagreements can take place on two broad levels. Ethicists might disagree on the interpretation of a particular verse, story, or passage of the Bible. This is an *exegetical* disagreement. Exegesis is the process of "drawing out" the meaning of a portion of Scripture (Greek: *ex* [out of] + *agago* [to draw] = to draw out). For example, ethicists might disagree on what Jesus meant by "Blessed are the poor in spirit" (Matt. 5:3). Some might argue that Jesus is praising those who lead lives of spiritual humility and hunger for God. Others might argue that the "poor in spirit" are those who are financially poor as a result of their loyalty to the precepts of God, resulting in their rejection by society. What we have here is an exegetical debate over the exact meaning of this particular passage.

On the broader level, we might find disagreement not simply over how to interpret a particular passage but on how one understands Scripture as a whole. This involves the issue of *hermeneutics*. Hermeneutics is the method of reading texts. The presuppositions one brings to Scripture are incredibly important. As with scientific investigations, the methods that one employs often determine the outcome of the investigation.

Some people claim that they do not come to Scripture with any hermeneutical method, with any presuppositions. They usually do not say it this way; rather, they claim that they are "literalists," that they take the Bible literally. We see this attitude in the bumper sticker that reads, "God said it. I believe it. That's it." The assumption of this slogan and those people who call themselves literalists is that they are not engaged in any kind of interpretation. This is simply wrong. There is no such thing as an uninterpreted reading of Scripture. Everyone engages in interpretation. Reading, by definition, involves interpreting what words mean. The scribbles and lines on a page of the Bible have no meaning in and of themselves. They have meaning only insofar as we understand that they are words. But we have been *taught* what words mean. If nothing else, we come to Scripture with a preconception about what certain words mean. Certainly, some interpreters lean toward a more *plain* reading of Scripture, but this does not mean that they are engaged in a literal, noninterpretive reading. To read Scripture is, by definition, to be engaged in a process of interpretation. Let us look at some reasons why.

First, most of the Bible is made up of stories. In fact, most of Jesus' teaching was done in parables, which are little stories. Stories cannot be read literally, even less so parables. So-called literalists often argue that we are to read Scripture "literally" except for passages that are clearly meant to be "poetic," for example, those that talk about God's "hands." Certainly, we can read some passages in a more plain sense and others with a more poetic touch. But we must decide which are poetic and which are to be read more literally, and this involves us in hermeneutical decisions and thus interpretation.

On the opposite end of the spectrum from literalists are those who claim that any hermeneutic or any exegetical rendering is equally valid. Simply because people disagree with one another does not mean that there is no way of adjudicating various interpretations. Just because people disagree does not mean that everyone is equally correct. This is an improper move from the descriptive to the normative.

In the next few pages I will identify some of the challenges of using Scripture in ethics. This is not for the purpose of questioning the importance of the use of Scripture or its central place in Christian ethics; rather, it is with the purpose of showing that the use of Scripture in ethics is not a simple process, as if one might be able to use the Bible as one uses an owner's manual: Check the index, look up the appropriate passage, and find the one and only answer for a problem on a given page. As Old Testament ethicist Christopher Wright observes, "The great failing of this practice is that it does not take the Bible seriously for what it is—that is, fundamentally a story, with a beginning, an end, and a middle."[1] The use of Scripture in ethics requires struggle, thought, investigation, and discussion with other Christians. Most of all it requires a great deal of time reading the Bible. There is no need to read an entire owner's manual to learn how to change the burned-out headlight in your car. Passages of the Bible are one part of a very large whole and must be read within the context of the entire story and overall movement of the Bible.

Reading Passages in Their Historical, Social, and Literary Context

One of the most difficult challenges for Christians is learning how to read passages of Scripture in their larger historical, social, and literary context. This is also one of the most contentious issues in the church, namely, the degree to which we should take the historical and cultural context of the Bible into account. Some people argue that many of the acceptable customs and binding laws practiced during the biblical period are no longer applicable because we live in a very different time and place. For example, the prohibition against lending money at interest (Deut. 23:19) is grounded in a society in which usually only the very poor borrowed money as a means of survival. Since we now live in a very different type of society, this prohibition may no longer apply. Another example is the biblical position on slavery. Many Christians contend that one cannot simply apply the command for slaves to "obey their masters" from first-century Palestine to modern society.

Many Christians worry that this type of hermeneutic not only challenges the Bible as the inerrant (i.e., without errors) word of God, but opens the gates for simply choosing which passages apply and which do not based upon criteria outside the Bible. This is a legitimate concern that must be taken with the utmost seriousness, lest we simply read into Scripture what we want to hear. We must be wary of substituting *eisegesis* (reading meaning *into* the Bible) for faithful *exegesis*.

Yet failure to understand the historical and social context of a passage can also lead to a misuse of Scripture. By ripping passages out of their literary, social, and historical context, Scripture has been wrongly employed to justify such things as slavery, the burning of witches, the Holocaust, and the taking of land from the American Indians. We must take great care lest Scripture become just another tool by which the powerful oppress the powerless.

A second danger is taking passages out of their larger biblical context and assuming that all passages are equally important, what Edward LeRoy Long calls the principle of "flat equivalency":

> One need only imagine how certain texts could be chosen and strung together under a presumption of flat equivalency to realize how readily the Bible can be used in ways that mock the fundamental premises of a moral perspective: "Cain slew Abel"; "Go Thou and do likewise"; and "What Thou doest, do quickly."[2]

One of the skills that you, as a budding Christian ethicist, should begin developing is the ability to recognize when passages are simply being ripped from their original context to support a given claim (a practice known as "proof-texting"). Yes, there is great diversity within Scripture, but that does not mean that all readings are equally valid or defensible. It is important to discern the larger unity of vision within the Bible and to base one's exegesis upon its dominant lines. For example, one might appeal to the instances of God's commanding the Israelites to kill women and children in warfare as support for total war or even for the use of nuclear weapons in a modern war. However, we must read such passages against the backdrop of the more dominant themes of the compassion, justice, forgiveness, and mercy of God that we are called to imitate.

While recognizing and celebrating the diversity of voices in Scripture, we must also seek to discern the dominant and overarching vision of God and God's will that is revealed in Scripture. So if we wish to discover a biblical view "on any matter, we must surely seek to let the Scriptures speak as a whole . . . [b]ringing the matter into the light of each of the main phases of the Bible's story. . . ."[3]

Ways of Using Scripture in Ethics

Beyond the issues of context and diversity stands the most prevalent issue regarding the use of Scripture in ethics.[4] *How* do we use Scripture in ethics? This hermeneutical question is clearer if we explore the various ways in which we might "apply" Scripture to morality and ethics. James Gustafson has identified the following ways of using Scripture but argues that they are not mutually exclusive. In fact, we probably want to use several of these methods, even if we may end up emphasizing one over the others.

Law: Use the Bible by Finding Specific Laws to Follow

This is one of the most common uses of Scripture in ethics and moral decision making. Obedience to laws is a central theme in Scripture as we saw in our discussion of deontology. However, we shall see that the use of Scripture as a source of rules or laws is not without difficulty. More importantly, using the Bible *only* for laws or rules is to have an extremely narrow understanding of the function of Scripture in the moral life. To live as a Christian means more than simply obeying rules. It involves a transformation of the entire person, coming to see the world through the lens of the Bible as we seek to develop character traits, virtues, and ways of interpreting the world.

Using Scripture primarily as a book of rules raises specific problems. First, most of Scripture is not laws. In fact, laws and commands make up an extremely small portion of Scripture. In the Old Testament, only in the books of Exodus, Leviticus, and Deuteronomy do we find large portions of law. Most of the Old Testament consists of stories, poetry, wisdom, and prophecy. The same is true of the teaching and preaching of Jesus. Except for his Sermon on the Mount (Matt. 5–7), Jesus provided relatively few commandments. Therefore, using the Bible primarily or exclusively as a book of rules is to ignore vast sections of Scripture.

A second difficulty is determining what counts as a rule, law, or commandment. This may seem like a simple question, but it is not. There are clearly sections of the Old Testament that are in the form of laws, such as the Ten Commandments and surrounding sections of Deuteronomy and Exodus. But what about other types of commands? When Jesus tells the rich young man to sell everything he has and give it to the poor, is this a commandment for *all* people, or only for that young man? When Paul tells the Corinthian congregation that they should not begin a meal until all are present, is this a command for us today? When Jesus says that anyone who does not leave his mother and father is unworthy of him, is this a command, or simply a statement?

Third, what do many of these laws mean? For example, what does Scripture mean by "Honor your father and your mother"? Does it mean doing whatever they request? Does it mean caring for them in their old age regardless of the cost? Does it mean never disagreeing with them? Laws require interpretation; the meaning is not always self-evident.

Fourth, how do we apply the laws for today? This is the broader question that we have been pursuing throughout this entire section. But more narrowly, we observe that there are many modern situations that are completely alien to the Bible: cloning, nuclear war, acid rain, school vouchers, and so forth. There are no laws dealing directly with these and similar modern issues.

Fifth, what if there is a conflict between commands? What happens when there is a conflict between, for example, the command not to lie and the command to protect the powerless? In other words, are Old Testament laws understood as rules of thumb, *prima facie* binding, or absolute? Of course, we might want to say that some laws are only *prima facie* binding and others are absolute. Of all the 613 commandments in the Hebrew Scriptures, most Jewish legal scholars believe, all are *prima facie* binding except three. As Harold Schulweis notes, "Jewish ethics allows itself few immutable absolutes. The notable exceptions are the three absolutes which prohibit murder, incest, and idolatry."[5] So, for example, when it comes to protecting human life, all 613 commandments (except those three) can be overridden. Jesus appeals to this understanding when he breaks the law against working on the Sabbath in order to heal a man. "Is it lawful to cure on the sabbath? . . . Suppose one of you has only one sheep and it falls into a pit on the sabbath; will you not lay hold of it and lift it out? How much more valuable is a human being than a sheep! So it is lawful to do good on the sabbath" (Matt. 12:10–12). The question we will need to pursue is the relative weight of various laws in the Old Testament.

Themes or Ideas: Use the Bible by Finding Key Ideas or Themes

Many Christians contend that it is more important to find the principle behind the command or law, rather than apply the commandment directly. We employ Scripture not by discovering exact rules or laws but by finding certain ideals by which to live. So, for example, rather than appeal to specific rules, we try to live by the ideal of "neighbor love." Such an appeal has scriptural support in Jesus' statement that all of the law and the prophets can be summed up in two commands: to "love the Lord your God with all your heart, and with all your soul, and with all your mind" and to "love your neighbor as yourself" (Matt. 22:37, 39).

Some of the other ideals found in Scripture are holiness or purity, liberation, justice, self-sacrifice, bearing the cross, repentance, and forgiveness. What is right about this approach is that we need to read particular laws within the larger movement of Scripture. But each of these ideals requires elaboration or specification. This is where the stories, parables, psalms, and other biblical literature can be of use, namely, in fleshing out the significance of neighbor love or other ideals. This approach has the benefit of taking into account not just laws but the entirety of the narratives of the Bible. For example, if we wish to specify what mercy is, we can look to the life and parables of Jesus. And if we want to flesh out the ideal of justice we can turn, among other places, to the prophets.

Circumstantial Use: Find Circumstances in the Bible Similar to One's Own

A third use of Scripture might be what some scholars call *circumstantial*. In this view, those actions are judged wrong that are similar to actions judged wrong (or against God's will) in Scripture. Likewise, those actions are judged right that are similar to actions judged right in Scripture. The strength of this approach is that we take into account all the complexities of a given situation, rather than simply searching for a general rule that might govern the situation.

However, this approach runs into some obvious snags. One difficulty is that it is notably hard to find situations in the Bible that match our particular situation. This is the case not simply because moral situations are quite complex and often unique but because we encounter situations today that were never conceived of in biblical times. Does one withdraw life support from one's permanently comatose parent? Should I download music even though doing so violates copyright laws? Should I support the building of nuclear power plants? These are simply beyond the scope of the biblical period; it is hard to find directly analogous situations.

A second difficulty is that it is not always clear how the Bible judges a particular action. For example, Jacob deceives his blind and aging father Isaac into giving him a blessing intended for his brother Esau. The Bible is simply silent on the morality or immorality of this action. Is this a warrant for lying? We find another example in the actions of King Saul, who commits suicide by falling upon his sword after being gravely injured in battle. Is this a warrant for committing suicide if one is gravely ill and dying? The Bible is silent on the morality of these actions. It simply reports them.

Character Imitation: Use the Bible by Finding Characters to Imitate

A fourth mode of using the Bible in ethics is to find characters and try to imitate them. This is the model behind the popular question "What would Jesus do?" (We shall discuss the imitation of Jesus in more depth in chapter 9.) This is an important way of using Scripture for ethics. It is probably true that our morality is shaped more by efforts to imitate or emulate our parents, mentors, heroes, and others than by any abstract ethical reasoning. We see people we admire and we want to imitate them.

The Bible is full of characters who can function as models for moral behavior. We can look to the obedience of Abraham, the bravery of Rahab the prostitute, the righteous anger of the prophet Amos, the humility of the Roman centurion. This way of using Scripture has the benefit of focusing not just on actions but also on virtue and character development. Moreover, it opens up vast portions of Scripture that would not be used if one focused merely on laws.

However, we are faced with a number of questions when character imitation is our primary use of Scripture in ethics. First, which characters are we to imitate? Sometimes it is not completely clear which characters are paradigms of virtue and which are examples of vice. Throughout Scripture, we run across characters that reveal both seemingly positive and negative traits. In fact, the Bible is unswervingly honest in its depictions of the ancestors of Jesus, even showing the faults of Noah, Moses, and David. David is often portrayed as the ideal king, and most Sunday school classes recount in colorful detail the amazing stories of David facing the giant Goliath or soothing King Saul with his harp. What few Sunday school classes cover is the story of David's sleeping with another man's wife and having that man killed. Solomon reigns over the most prosperous period of Israel's five-thousand-year history, but he takes foreign wives and enslaves his own people. Model or not? For a New Testament example, turn to Peter, the apostle of Jesus. In the book of Acts, Peter is portrayed as a faithful knight of Christ, preaching the good news fearlessly and tirelessly. However, this is the same Peter who had denied knowing Jesus three times and whom Jesus even called "Satan" at one point. What these examples tell us is that God does not call sinless saints but everyday human beings to be instruments for the divine kingdom. Nevertheless, such examples do raise difficulties concerning the use of the Bible for models of imitation.

That said, it is clear that we have yet to discuss the ultimate model, namely, Jesus of Nazareth. Jesus is the one truly human person who lived as God intended human beings to live. Therefore, he can and should function as the model for human living. Nevertheless, we should move with care in using Jesus as a model. Since we will discuss this later, I will only briefly raise some issues:

- It is noteworthy how little reference there is to the imitation of Jesus by Jesus himself. The notable exception is John 15:12: "This is my commandment, that you love one another as I have loved you." Other than this, there are few explicit references to imitation by Jesus.
- What are we to imitate about Jesus? His actual actions? His attitudes and emotions? His principles?
- Since Jesus is not only fully human but also fully divine, are there some actions of Jesus that we are not supposed to imitate?

We will discuss these and other issues more fully when we explore the teachings and person of Jesus.

Character Formation: The Bible Shapes Our Characters and Virtues

One might approach the Bible less as the *revelation of morality* and more as the *revelation of reality*.[6] To approach the Bible in this way is to claim that its function is only partly to give us a set of rules, models, or ideals. Its primary function is to describe who God is, what the world is like, and what human beings are like (revelation of reality). The Bible functions to shape our character by shaping the way we see the world. It forms our very beings by enabling us to experience the world through the interpretive lens of Scripture. For example, rather than simply finding a place in Scripture where it commands us to care for the poor and powerless, Scripture helps us to see these people differently. Through Scripture we begin to experience them as children of God, made in the image of God, and having a special place in God's heart. In Matthew 25:31–46, Jesus says that whenever you have fed the poor or visited the imprisoned you have done it to him. One might easily turn this into a law: Visit the imprisoned and feed the hungry. But this is to lose the depth of the message. It is not enough simply to feed the hungry and visit the prisoners; we need to reenvision them, seeing in them the face of Christ. This involves being totally transformed by the worldview of Scripture. It involves a radical reconfiguring of our moral imagination.

This is the model championed by Birch and Rasmussen when they say, "It is not claiming too much to say that scripture in the life of the Christian community has this moral vocation, to shape the personal moral identity of community members in keeping with the ways of God. Scripture encourages in myriad ways the internalizing of moral qualities which mirror who we are as a people of faith."[7] I think this is a particularly helpful model for the use of Scripture, and it dominates the rest of this book as we begin to examine the foundations of biblical morality.

Yet this way of using Scripture is less common among most Christians. Why? Because it is much more demanding and time-consuming than using the Bible as a rulebook or a sourcebook for characters to imitate. To use Scripture as a way of transforming our very experience of reality is neither quick nor simple. It involves a great deal of reading, study, and contemplation to begin to be shaped not by our culture but by the Bible. Most people would rather simply employ the Bible (selectively) as a rulebook. Not only is this less time-consuming, but it allows persons to remain comfortably within their own mindset without being challenged to be transformed by Scripture.

Summary of the Use of Scripture in Ethics

The Bible is the first and primary source for Christian ethics. It is authoritative and infallible for faith and practice. Even if one believes in natural law (that we can know the moral order naturally by human reason and observation), it is still the position of almost all Christians that the Bible is the fullest and clearest revelation of God's will for human beings. All of the above models have a place in Christian ethics. We might debate, discuss, and even disagree as to the merits and meaning of each method, but the very fact that we are doing so indicates that we agree that Scripture sets the parameters within which the debate will take place.

Guidelines for the Use of Scripture

Before moving to a discussion of the other sources of Christian guidance and wisdom, let me propose four guidelines for the use of Scripture.

No One Method for the Use of Scripture Is Adequate

James Gustafson contends that the best method for using Scripture may be to avoid any single method. While I will stress the role of character formation in the use of Scripture, I agree with Gustafson that no single method of using Scripture is adequate. The very diversity of the Bible itself warns us against a simplistic use. Scripture contains stories, songs, parables, riddles, histories, prayers, and laws, to name just a few of the many genres found in the Bible. To employ one and only one method for using Scripture is to oversimplify the complexity of both Scripture and the moral life.

Whenever Possible Scripture Should Be Read in Its Historical and Cultural Context

Scripture is the eternal and authoritative word of God for us. However, it was written in a particular time under particular cultural conditions. It would be both naive and arrogant to assume that we can come to the fullness of God's revelation to us without seeking to understand the political, cultural, military, and economic customs of the writers and original communities that created these witnesses to God.

Not All Scripture Carries the Same Normative Weight

We should avoid what Edward LeRoy Long calls the assumption of "flat equivalency," whereby all scriptural passages are treated as if they held the same authority. There is barely a single idea that is so ludicrous that we could not find some remote passage that appears to support it. In a book as large and diverse as Scripture, isolated passages can be used to support many positions and ideas that are clearly refuted by the more central movements of the Bible.

Therefore, while recognizing the importance of diverse voices in Scripture, we should seek to read minor themes or principles in the context of larger themes or principles. In particular, I would argue that we should interpret all Scripture in the light of the fullest revelation of God's being and will, namely,

Jesus Christ. Shirley Guthrie calls this the christological principle, which he finds embedded in some of the central creeds of the Reformed Christian faith:

> Jesus Christ is the clearest revelation of who God is and what God promises and wills for faithful Christian life. Therefore all Scripture is to be interpreted in light of "what Christ Jesus himself did and commanded" (Scots Confession, 18), "in light of its witness to God's work of reconciliation in Christ" (Confession of 1967, I.C.2). "When we encounter apparent tensions and conflicts in what Scripture teaches us to believe and do, the final appeal must be to the authority of Christ" (Declaration of Faith, 6.3).[8]

Whether or not we agree on the exact details of Jesus' message, our interpretation of Scripture must be christocentric—that is, Christ centered.

Scripture Is Normative and Primary, but It Is Not Our Only Source of Guidance and Wisdom

Scripture is our primary source for Christian ethics. But it is not our only source. Tradition, experience, and reason also guide and shape us, for the Holy Spirit is alive and working among Christians, inspiring and directing us. Moreover, we should seek out and listen to both historical and contemporary guides to the interpretation of Scripture.

Tradition

As noted above, in addition to Scripture, Christians recognize three other authoritative sources for guidance and wisdom: tradition, experience, and reason.

The word "tradition" comes from the Latin *traducere*, meaning "to hand down." It is the wisdom, knowledge, and methods of interpretation that have been handed down through the centuries. This is an important source of guidance. Modern Christians often (pridefully) assume that they have nothing to learn from the two thousand years of thinking about the Christian life, as if they are the first ones to ponder the central questions of Christian ethics. As a child, you did not have to rediscover the vast array of moral rules and virtues that make up your own moral existence; most of them were handed down to you by your parents, who themselves were the beneficiaries of a long history of moral reasoning and living. In much the same way, our spiritual ancestors have handed down a treasure of wisdom and guidance to the church.

When discussing many ethical issues, you will often see ethicists addressing the questions "What has the church said throughout the centuries?" or "What have the great religious thinkers of history said about this?" For example, what have Christians said throughout the ages about the morality of suicide, warfare, wealth, and government? This appeal to tradition is very important, because it reminds us that we are not the first Christians to struggle with such issues. We can rely on a long history of exploration by many very faithful and very intelligent Christian men and women. Yet we must also recognize that even if the church has been fairly uniform in condemning or condoning a practice or virtue, that, by definition, does not make it right or wrong. The tradition may be mistaken. (Recall the distinction between normative and descriptive ethics from chapter 1.) That said, if the church has been consistent in its treatment of a moral issue or consistent in its portrait of some aspect of the moral life, the burden of proof falls on those of us who wish to challenge that consensus.

Experience

The role of experience in Christian ethics is quite controversial. However, it remains an important source of guidance. Experience functions on two planes. First, our experiences shape our reading of Scripture. Second, experience might function as an independent source of knowledge. Again, no one comes to Scripture as a totally blank page; we come with a world of experience. Our experiences shape how we read Scripture. For example, if someone had a distant and cold father, the recurrent biblical image of God as "Father" will be shaped in her reading by that experience. If someone is rich and lives in a powerful nation, he will read Scripture through that general experience. If someone has been the victim of a violent crime, she might read with suspicion the command to "turn the other cheek." The very fact that one is a man or a woman, young or old, rich or poor shapes how one goes about reading the Bible. We all come to Scripture with a world of experiences. We have no choice but to read the Bible to some degree through the "lens" of those experiences. Experience helps us make the words of Scripture our own, to bring them into *our* lives. But because we have limited experience, it can also blind us to some degree. For this reason, it is helpful to listen to how people with very different experiences read Scripture.

Experience might serve another role in Christian ethics, namely, as a source of guidance in terms of evaluating our moral decisions and ideas. One danger of doing ethics is the ivory-tower syndrome, in which professional ethicists engage in intellectual inquiry far removed from the actual experiences of everyday people. Ethicists should bring their findings and ideas into conversation with people's experiences. They should check their findings and claims against people's lived experiences.

Let me briefly note some places where experience might be an element in moral considerations.

Example 1. Christians are commanded to care for the poor. But this command is situated in the context of trying to raise them up and respect them as children of God. Might we not want to ask those who are being helped what their experience of welfare programs is? Do they feel empowered and respected, or disempowered and condescended to by welfare programs?

Example 2. Many gay Christians have argued that the stance of many churches on homosexuality has completely ignored their experience. They claim that many gay couples experience fulfilling lives of Christian discipleship. To what degree should the reported experience of some gay couples of loving, long-term, fulfilling, monogamous relationship be a factor in our moral discussion, in light of the fact that some other homosexual Christians report less positive experiences with their sexuality?

As the above example demonstrates, the place of experience in moral decision making is hotly debated for a number of reasons. First, it is nearly impossible to refute someone's experience, and what we often run into is a clash of experiences. Don experiences a statement as offensive, but Sally does not. How do we adjudicate those experiences? A second reason that experience is a particularly unwieldy source of guidance is that human beings are so very sinful. Our sinfulness greatly affects our experience of the world around us. Just because someone intuitively experiences something as right or wrong, as permissible or prohibited, does not necessarily make it so. Our cultural upbringing as well as our own history of sinful action may blind us to the real moral quality of a particular situation or issue. These difficulties, notwithstanding, we should make an effort to bring Christian ethics into conversation with people's lived experiences.

Reason

Finally, we come to the source of guidance called reason. Like both experience and tradition, reason can mean a number of different things as a source of Christian wisdom.

Reason Can Mean "Reasonable"

If someone's moral position is internally contradictory, then that is a problem. God has provided human beings with a mind as well as a soul and body. While it is certainly true that God remains ultimately a mystery, this does not provide a warrant for assuming that all matters of faith and morals are beyond the scope of reason. On the other hand, our God is a God of unimaginable creativity and freedom. God often breaks through ways of thinking and being that we find perfectly "reasonable."

Reason Can Function as an Independent Source for Knowledge about God and the World

In particular, Roman Catholics contend that we can know much about who God is and what God wills by using our minds and our powers of observation and reasoning. This is often referred to as an appeal to *natural law*. The notion of a natural law has a long and complex history going back to the Stoics of ancient Greece. But at their core, most natural law theories hold to the following three ideas:

1. There is an objective moral order to the universe. Like the laws governing light, gravity, fluids, and so forth, there are laws that govern human behavior.
2. Human beings can discern these laws through observation and contemplation.
3. Human beings ought to live by these laws.

Christian natural law theorists argue that even without Scripture we can know a great deal about how human beings are supposed to behave toward God and one another. Most natural law theorists, such as Thomas Aquinas, argue that the moral laws revealed through observation of the world and through the use of human reason will never contradict Scripture (if properly interpreted), since the God who creates and the God who reveals God's self in Scripture are one and the same.

This use of reason and its resulting notion of natural law have been most prevalent in the Roman Catholic tradition. Protestants, with their emphasis on sin (note how this is an element of the Protestant tradition) have generally been suspicious of such appeals, arguing that human reason is too deformed by sin to function as a proper guide for human behavior.

Reason as Science

While most people envision a conflict between science and religion, the findings of scientists can provide valuable data for moral decision making.

Example 1. Biologists can inform us of the degree to which a proposed new oil refinery or oil rig may or may not affect the environment.

Example 2. Doctors can provide information on the brain activity of fetuses and the comatose to help with decisions about how to treat them.

Example 3. Sociologists might help in ascertaining whether capital punishment really does function as a deterrent to crime or whether capital punishment is applied unequally across racial lines.

Example 4. Psychologists can help us understand the psychological processes involved when spouses physically abuse one another.

Note that in each of these examples, the scientific data cannot determine the general ethical stance that Christians should take. Nevertheless, they do provide invaluable information that Christians can employ in making their judgments. While we should always read scientific data with an awareness of the limitations of the methods employed and with sensitivity to the origins and biases of the study, science can provide levels of information that are simply beyond the expertise of most Christians, even professional ethicists.

Relation between the Sources

Putting aside the source of human reason, let us briefly examine the relationship between the various sources of wisdom:

Experience » Tradition » Scripture/Christ » Tradition » Experience

This chart is designed to show the dialectical relationship between Scripture and other sources of guidance. Christ is the center of the Christian life. However, we do not have any unmediated experience of Christ. We come to Christ through the Bible. This is not to say that one cannot have a personal relationship with Christ. It is to say that our relationship with Jesus is mediated through the Bible; otherwise we would not know who Christ is. We come to know Jesus Christ through Scripture, but we do not come to Scripture as a blank slate. We read Scripture through both tradition and experience.

On the other hand, our relationship with Christ as met in Scripture shapes and transforms our traditions and shapes our experiences. As discussed above, we should seek to experience reality through the lens of Scripture. Our very experience of the world is transformed as we read and internalize the message, values, virtues, and worldview of the Bible, at the center of which is God's fulfillment of covenant history in Jesus of Nazareth.

Chapter 5

God, Humans, and Creation in Genesis 1–3

Biblical Reading

Genesis 1–3

As a way of guiding you through the Bible readings for the following chapters, I will provide a short "reading guide." Read this first, and then read the assigned Scripture. Doing so will make the rest of your exploration much more fruitful, as there is no substitute for a careful firsthand engagement with the foundation of Christian ethics.

Reading Guide

For some readers, these stories may be quite familiar. For others, this may be the first time you have ever opened a Bible. But whether you are familiar with these passages or not, you may be asking the same question: What do these first few stories have to do with ethics? Shouldn't we be turning to the many laws and commands for which the Old Testament is so famous? And since these stories don't really have any characters that we seem called to imitate, how would these stories relate to ethics?

Recall from chapter 4 that "laws" and "imitation" are only two of the ways in which Scripture might be used to shape the moral life. Another way is "character formation," an approach closely identified with virtue theory. We saw that the way we understand God, human beings, and the world will shape our vision of the moral life. For Christians, Scripture provides a lens by which we envision and interpret reality. And how we envision and interpret God and the world shapes who we are and how we behave.

The stories in Genesis 1–3 have been central to the shaping of that vision of reality. They have become core narratives through which Christians and

Jews make sense of the three elements that make up our lived universe: God, human beings, and the created world. As you read these stories, try to get a feeling for how God is described. What does this God do? How does this God act? Additionally, try to get a sense for how human beings are understood. How are they depicted in these stories? As weak? Powerful? Greedy? Virtuous? Why does God create them? Finally, what are these stories trying to tell us about the relationship of human beings to the created world around us?

Introduction

The description of creation in Genesis 1–2 and the portrayal of human disobedience found in Genesis 3 tell us serious and important truths about who God is and who we are in relationship to God and to one another. They reveal truths about our universe that act as "lamps" unto our feet (Ps. 119:105). By no means do these stories tell us everything we need to know in order to live the Christian life. In fact, there are few if any direct commandments in these opening stories. Yet these stories tell us important things about the three primary elements of the universe: God, human beings, and the created world. Any Christian ethical stance or perspective must take into consideration these foundational claims. Any moral position or ethical stance has the burden of proving that it does not violate these basic moral presumptions. In other words, the claims made in Genesis 1–3 provide the framework for the rest of Christian morality. They are the scaffolding upon which we will build our moral vision.

What Does Genesis 1–3 Tell Us about God?

God Is Sovereign Creator

Even though the Bible begins, "In the beginning . . . ," the story really starts somewhere in the middle. Although it starts with the beginning of the created world, it does not start with the beginning of God. God simply appears on the stage. But where did God come from? Who created this God? How did this God get the power to create a world? What was there before the world was created? You may think that these are silly questions, saying to yourself, "Nobody created God. That is why God is God. Of course it had to begin with God simply there. How else could it begin?" It is often difficult to see the implicit claims made about God in the opening chapters of Genesis because even secular Westerners have been significantly shaped by the Judeo-Christian depiction of God. Therefore, it might be easier to see the implicit claims about God in this story if we compare Genesis 1 to other creation narratives in the ancient Near East.

Because most scholars believe that the creation story in Genesis 1 took its final shape during a period when the Israelites were enslaved by the nation of Babylon, it is useful to compare Genesis 1 with the Babylonian creation narrative called the *Enuma Elish*. Composed sometime around 1200 BCE in Mesopotamia (modern-day Iraq), the *Enuma Elish* describes how the Babylonian god Marduk came to hold ascendancy over all the other gods. The *Enuma Elish* can be summarized as follows:

Before the creation of the heavens and the earth, the gods were created by the preexistent primordial force/god named Apsu. The story describes the births of multiple generations of gods. At one point, a goddess named Tiamat (depicted as a personification of the raging seas) and her cohort Kingu lead a rebellion against the other gods. A young God named Marduk is sent to do battle with Tiamat. When Tiamat opens her mouth to devour him, Marduk sends a great wind into her face so that she cannot close her mouth. Marduk shoots an arrow into her distended belly and then strangles her. He splits her body in two and with one half creates the heavens and with the other half creates the earth. He then kills Kingu and out of Kingu's blood he creates human beings, as slaves for the gods. Marduk is thus enthroned as the highest god in the Babylonian pantheon.

In comparison to the *Enuma Elish*, the theological claims made by Genesis 1 become much more stark. The *Enuma Elish*, as with many other ancient creation narratives, begins with a *theogony*, a description of the origin of the gods. Not only is there no discussion of the origin of the biblical God, there are no other gods even mentioned. God alone is the supreme actor on the stage. Note also that God does not have to do anything to achieve the creation of the world. In contrast to Marduk, who must battle other gods and then use the body of the defeated goddess Tiamat to create the heavens and the earth, Yahweh simply speaks the world into being. God creates merely by willing the world into existence. In fact, the Hebrew word for "create" (*bara*) is used exclusively of God. Human beings do not ultimately create. They simply rearrange what is already there, giving it new form. Only God creates out of nothing—*creatio ex nihilo*, to use the technical language.

What we learn from the very first pages of the biblical story is that there is only one God and that God is absolutely sovereign. To be "sovereign" is to be a lord and ruler over something. Genesis 1, with its all-powerful, creative

God, declares that God is the ruler and lord of the universe; there is no power greater than or even equal to God. Moreover, one of the very first things we discover about our God is that God's nature at its heart is creative and life giving.

In declaring the absolute sovereignty of Yahweh, Genesis 1 also tells us that God does not create out of necessity. God was not forced to create the world, nor does God need the world in order to be God. Christians believe in a God who already has love, community, and mutual self-giving within God's very self—in the relationship among Father, Son, and Holy Spirit. God, as three-in-one, already knows and experiences community within God's self, and so it is purely out of freedom that God chooses to extend that love and create human beings, bringing them into the circle of God's divine community of love. This is what the theologian Karl Barth was driving at by characterizing God as the "One who loves in freedom."[1]

Ethical Implications of God's Sovereignty

Of the many ethical implications of God's sovereignty as depicted in Genesis 1, we shall focus on two.

Nothing Else in the World Is Absolute or Worthy of Worship   Few of us in the twenty-first century are tempted to worship other gods such as Marduk, Tiamat, Baal, or any of the other gods of the ancient world.[2] But how often do we put our trust, hope, confidence, or ultimate concern in something that is not God? Self, money, family, job, technology, democracy, political party—the sovereignty of God who alone creates the world is the fundamental presumption that keeps us from placing our ultimate trust in any of these lesser goods. Since nothing is to be identified with God, all human values are relativized. This does not mean that nothing on earth is valuable; it means that its value is never ultimate.

Even life itself is not to be worshiped. Human life, while valuable, is not worthy of worship. As Karl Barth says, "Life is no second God."[3] The function or purpose of life is to worship that which is worthy of our ultimate allegiance, namely, God. This is why, contrary to popular opinion, the notion of the "infinite value of human life" is not a Christian concept. Nothing has infinite value except God—and that includes human life. The Christian acceptance of martyrdom (i.e., dying for one's beliefs) exemplifies the belief highlighted in Genesis 1 that God alone is worthy of our absolute confidence, worship, and allegiance. Any time we place earthly commitment above our allegiance to God we are implicitly creating a second and rival god. Genesis 1 proclaims that there is only one God to be worshiped. When the disciple

Peter says, "We must obey God rather than any human authority," he is proclaiming the sovereignty of God (Acts 5:29). We shall return to the ethical importance of monotheism and the sovereignty of God in chapters 6 and 7, as this is a central concern of the Torah and the prophets.

Nothing Is to Be Absolutely Feared   The first ethical implication of God's sovereignty as described in Genesis 1 is that we should worship nothing alongside of God. There is a related yet reverse danger, namely, fearing something absolutely. Genesis 1 tells us that there is no other power worthy of worship in the universe, but it also tells us that there is no other power that can ultimately thwart the will of God. Evil and sin clearly exist. But they are neither eternal nor ultimate. There is no evil, malicious god alongside of our good and loving God. Such a misconception has a long insidious history, going back almost to the beginning of Christianity. In particular, a mode of thinking called Manicheanism claimed that there were two forces in the universe, the force of light/goodness and the force of darkness/evil. In fact, one of the earliest Christian heresies was Marcionism, which falsely distinguished between the evil God of the Old Testament and the good God of the New Testament. This idea, called *dualism* continues to live today. People talk about the cosmic battle between good and evil, between God and the devil, as if there were an open question concerning the outcome, as if the devil had some kind of independent power alongside that of God. There may be a battle between God and the forces of evil that oppose God such as sin, death, evil, and Satan. But these forces, these "powers and principalities" as Paul calls them, have no real power *ultimately* to thwart the will of God. They exist only by God's permission. This is what Martin Luther was proclaiming in his triumphant hymn "A Mighty Fortress Is Our God":

> Though hordes of devils fill the land
> All threat'ning to devour us,
> We tremble not, unmoved we stand;
> They cannot over pow'r us.
> This world's prince may rage,
> In fierce war engage.
> He is doomed to fail;
> God's judgment must prevail!
> One little word subdues him.[4]

What Genesis 1 proclaims so elegantly is that there is *no* power outside of God. Evil certainly exists, but it only exists as a "shadow side" of what God wills. Evil, death, and disease have no independent existence, as if they were other gods that stood as real, viable, opponents of the true God. They "exist" only insofar as God wills their opposite.

One danger we must avoid is not taking evil seriously enough. But the opposite danger is to assume or imagine that evil might ultimately thwart the will of God.[5] From the very beginning of the Bible, the possibility of an ultimate opposition to God's will is depicted as an impossibility. God alone has true power. God alone creates. God alone truly *is*. Therefore, nothing is to be feared absolutely. Paul reminds us that the "new creation" in Christ has reiterated the message of the *first* creation in Genesis 1: "For I am convinced that neither death nor life, neither angels nor demons, neither the present nor the future, nor any powers, neither height nor depth, nor anything else in all creation, will be able to separate us from the love of God that is in Christ Jesus our Lord" (Rom. 8:38–39 NIV). One important ethical implication of this confession is that we can live lives of *hopeful trust*. We can live in the confidence that in the end God's will shall be done on earth as it is in heaven. We are thus set free to live, love, and serve, knowing that the forces of evil, despite their apparent momentary victories, have no ultimate power. They continue to seek to destroy God's good creation, but their efforts are futile. Therefore, Christians are free to serve God and others with faith, hope, and love, for we know that there is no other power that rivals God.

Finally, we should recognize that since God is the creator of all things, God is clearly *our* creator. Human beings are not self-created. We are absolutely and totally dependent upon God for our existence. This should elicit in us the dual virtues of humility and gratitude. None of us *had* to be; it is only out of God's free love that we are given life. Gratitude, thanksgiving, and humility are the proper responses to this gift.

God's *Hesed* (Steadfast Love)

The first confession we draw from Genesis 1 is that God is powerful and in complete control. Theologians refer to this as God's "sovereignty." But it would paint a skewed portrait if we were to stop there, for the creation stories in Genesis 1 and 2 depict not just a God who rules and controls but also a God who loves and cares for what God has created. Because God creates out of freedom, it is clear that God creates out of love. God is not merely *over* creation, but with and for it.

Alongside of God's sovereignty, we also witness the love and compassion of God in Genesis 1–3. This is particularly true of the creation narrative in Genesis 2. If Genesis 1 highlights God's transcendence (God "transcends" or "stands beyond" creation), Genesis 2 highlights God's closeness to and almost motherly care for creation.

Note some of the features of this narrative that highlight God's intimate care for creation, especially the human creature. Whereas in Genesis 1, God creates human beings simply by willing and then speaking them into existence, Genesis 2 portrays God carefully crafting the human creature. This is quite literally a more "hands on" portrayal of God. God molds the human creature and then blows the breath of life into it. This kiss of life, as it were, is one of the most strikingly tender moments in all of Scripture. God imparts God's very spirit (Hebrew, *ruach*) into the newly formed earth creature (the name "Adam" comes from the Hebrew for "earth": *adamah*). As one group of biblical scholars has commented on this narrative, "The image of a God with his hands in the dirt is remarkable; this is no naïve theology, but a statement about the depths to which God has entered into the life of the creation."[6] God has provided everything necessary for the human creatures to live. But in another moment of compassion, God anticipates that Adam will be lonely. Notice that Adam does not come to God with the request for a companion.[7] Rather, God says, "It is not good that the man should be alone; I will make him a helper as his partner" (Gen. 2:18). God is so attuned to the needs of the creation that God knows what Adam needs even before Adam himself knows what he needs. One cannot help but think of mothers who are so sensitive to the wants and needs of their children that they feel those needs themselves. This is literally what "compassion" means—to feel (*passion*) with (*com*). We will see this same compassion when God's chosen people, the Jews, are slaves in Egypt: "I have heard their cry on account of their taskmasters. Indeed, I know their sufferings, and I have come down to deliver them" (Exod. 3:7–8).

We see this same intimacy and closeness depicted in Genesis 3, where we hear about a God who is often found "walking in the garden in the cool of the day" (Gen. 3:8 NIV). Of course, we also find a God who punishes disobedience in this well-known story involving Adam and Eve. But we must not overlook the profound ways in which God continues to care for his creatures *despite* their rebellion and disobedience. At least by one interpretation, the punishment for their sin should have been immediate death. However, God allows them to live. And even after expelling the disobedient couple from the garden, God provides clothing for them, a sign of his ongoing care and protection. Finally, God is shown providing and caring for Adam and Eve by giving them children, as Eve recognizes when she says, "I have produced a man with the help of the LORD" (Gen. 4:1).

From the very first pages of Scripture we get a portrait of a God of steadfast love. The Hebrew term for this is *hesed*. It occurs hundreds of times throughout the Old Testament and is demonstrated in many places where it is not named. *Hesed* is often translated as "steadfast love" because it is a love that cannot be shaken. It is the kind of love that the New Testament writers call *agape*, a love that hopes for, but is not dependent upon, reciprocation. This is the kind of love expressed so powerfully in the incarnation of God in Jesus, who continued to love and forgive even when nailed to a Roman cross.

Ethical Implications of God's Hesed

God wills to be for us and with us in loving companionship.   Contrast this foundational belief with that depicted in the *Enuma Elish.* In the *Enuma Elish,* humans are not created to be in a loving relationship with one another or with the gods. Theirs is a relationship of master and slave. What Genesis 1–3 portrays is a very different kind of relationship. God creates out of love, and so human beings can trust that this God will neither abandon them nor mislead them.

What does this mean for the Christian life? At its most basic, it means that the Christian life should be one of praise, thanksgiving, and joy. The lives of Christians can never be characterized by complete pessimism and despair. Christians are not called to be naive about evil or unmoved by sin and misery, but neither can we be basically cynical, because from Genesis 1 onward, we find a God who creates out of love and is therefore with and for his creation. Christians can therefore live with assurance, hope, and joy.

God has a purpose for creation.   However the Christian feels about Darwin's theory of evolution, he or she is not at liberty to say that the creation of our planet and the human race is simply a chance occurrence. Whether the "six days" of Genesis 1 is literal or poetic, the message embedded in the story is central to our faith. God creates out of love and therefore creates with a purpose. Consequently, one of the foundational ethical presumptions of Christianity is that the world is orderly and purposive. It is our task, as creatures of a God who creates with a purpose, to discern God's will for us and for our fellow creatures. Complete relativism is therefore rejected. The manifestation of God's will might take different forms, but we are not at liberty, in light of Genesis 1–3, to say that all ethical rules are simply human creations. There is a purpose, or *telos,* for all things, including humans. We must seek that purpose and seek to live lives that rightly reflect God's purposes.

God Brings Order out of Chaos

The understanding of a God who brings peace, order, and comfort out of chaos and disruption is found in the very opening lines of the Bible. We have seen how the notion that God creates out of nothing reflects God's power and freedom. But within the creation narrative of Genesis 1 we get a hint of an additional understanding of the way God creates. An alternative translation of Genesis 1:1 is "In the beginning, when God created the heavens and the earth, the earth was formless and empty." By this translation, prior to creation, the world was formless and void, like a great raging sea over which God's spirit hovers. The Hebrew words for "formless and void" are a wonderful case of onomatopoeia (where the words sound like their meaning); they are *tohu wa bohu*. The words sound both ominous and confused. Prior to God's creative act, there is simply chaos, craziness, and disorder. There can be no life in such a world of *tohu wa bohu*. Into this confusing, crazy nonsense comes our God, creating order out of chaos and life where the possibility for life seems impossible.

Just as God brings orderly creation out of the chaos in Genesis 1, God also brings order into the chaos of our lives. How often do our lives feel *tohu wa bohu?* You have five papers due for school or four projects for work. Someone in your family is ill. You are not sure you have enough money to last out the month. Your car breaks down. Your life seems on the brink of spinning out of control, and there seems to be no hope of order being restored. For Christians, God is the one who brings order out of this chaos, hope out of hopelessness, and life out of death. This is the God we meet in Genesis 1, and this is the God we see in Jesus of Nazareth, the one who brings wholeness out of sickness, who brings forgiveness out of the chaos of sin, and who brings life out of death by undergoing death on the cross. He is the one who brings hope to the hopeless and preaches good news to the poor. The God who brings order and life into the chaos and death of the universe is the God who brings order and life to our own *tohu wa bohu*.

What Does Genesis 1-3 Tell Us about the World?

The creation narratives in Genesis 1-2 reveal two very important things about the way Jews and Christians understand the created world in which we live. And these two must be held together.

The World Is Good

Like the refrain of a song or the rhythm of a worship service, again and again God proclaims elements of our world "good." The Hebrew word used here is *tov*, which has the connotation not only of moral goodness but also of aesthetic beauty. God finds the world pleasing and delights in it.[8] But what does it mean to say that the world is delightful and good? As we begin to pursue this question, it might be helpful to identify once again what this foundational Christian belief is disclaiming (i.e., what are Christians rejecting when they profess that the world is good).

Much of the ancient world held to a type of metaphysical dualism. Metaphysics has to do with the nature of the reality of the universe. Metaphysical dualism is the belief that there are two great eternal forces at war in the universe: the force of good and the force of evil. We have already seen how the sovereignty of God depicted in Genesis 1 dispels the idea of an eternal force of evil that exists alongside of, and in true opposition to, God. But metaphysical dualism usually involves a second claim that whatever is spiritual and eternal is good and whatever is physical or temporal is evil. Therefore, the mind, spirit, and soul are viewed as good, but the world and the body and anything associated with them are either unreal or evil.[9] Such dualism was particularly strong during the early years of the Christian church, as most new converts were non-Jews who were heavily influenced by Plato, Aristotle, Zoroastrianism, and Near Eastern mystery religions. All of these belief systems held to some form of dualism that denigrated the temporal, material, created world in favor of the eternal, nontemporal, spiritual realm. One early Christian sect, the Manicheans, felt that the body was inherently evil and that the "spark" of true humanity was trapped in the prison of the body. Therefore, the goal of life was to deny the body and its pleasures in order to liberate the true spiritual self from the evil material body.

In stark opposition to such dualism stands the proclamation in Genesis 1: "And God saw that it was good." The Hebrew implies more than just satisfaction on God's part, as if God were saying, "It is OK." The connotation is that God is pleased with the creation. "It is wonderful" or "It is pleasing" might better capture the sense of delight that God expresses for God's creation. God takes pleasure in that which has been so lovingly created.

But what does all this mean, this proclamation on the part of Christians that the world is good? First, it means that the natural world is good. The trees, birds, fish, and sky are all beloved by God. While we need to avoid worshiping nature, we also need to recognize that the natural creation is not merely an object for human consumption and exploitation. Too many Christians have taken the statement that human beings are to "fill the earth and subdue it; and have dominion over the fish of the sea and over the birds of the air" as a warrant for exploiting the natural environment (Gen. 1:28). To invoke Genesis 1 as a justification for exploiting the environment is a clear misreading of the story. Genesis describes the human creatures not as exploiters of the natural world but as "caretakers."[10]

The Hebrew term translated as "rule over" really means "to direct or lead," as when a shepherd directs the flock. Moreover, even if human beings are meant to be "lords" over creation, their lordship should be modeled on Jesus Christ, who "came not to be served but to serve" (Matt. 20:28).

Second, when the Bible proclaims the goodness of creation it is saying that those things associated with created existence are good. One of those things is physical pleasure. Pleasure can all too easily become an idol or second god, the most obvious case being the idolatry of pleasure associated with drugs or alcohol. But it is equally un-Christian to claim or imply that pleasure is evil. Humor, beauty, and the physical pleasures that come from eating, drinking, and playing are all good gifts of God. God takes delight in the world and so should we. When we confess that the world is good we are saying that those things associated with the physical world are good. We should not worship or pursue them as gods, but neither should we treat them as demons.

The same is true of sexuality. It is not just a minor part of either Genesis 1 or 2 that the differentiation between male and female takes place. In Genesis 1, maleness and femaleness are actually connected, in some way, with the "image of God." And the very first commandment is to "be fruitful and multiply." In Genesis 2, God creates male and female as companions; they are "united" and "become one flesh." The pleasure inherent in sexual activity, both physical and emotional, is part of God's intention for creation. The playful and erotic quality of sexuality is celebrated in the biblical book called the Song of Songs, in which two lovers sing the wonders of their love:

> How beautiful your sandaled feet,
>   O prince's daughter!
> Your graceful legs are like jewels,
>   the work of a craftsman's hands.
> Your navel is a rounded goblet
>   that never lacks blended wine.
> Your waist is a mound of wheat
>   encircled by lilies.
> Your breasts are like two fawns,
>   twins of a gazelle.
>
> . . . .
>
> Your stature is like that of the palm,
>   and your breasts like clusters of fruit.
> I said, "I will climb the palm tree;
>   I will take hold of its fruit."
>   (Song 7:1–3, 7–8 NIV)

Remembering that sex is a good gift of God helps us avoid two dangers. While it warns us against viewing sexual activity and the pleasure it brings as inherently evil, it also warns against taking what we do with our bodies too lightly. What we do with our bodies really matters. God is concerned not merely with our spiritual well-being but also with how we treat the gift of the body and how we live out our faith in the physical realm. Too often human beings mistreat their bodies through the abuse of drugs and alcohol, overeating, or promiscuous sexual activity. To do so is to defile what Paul calls the "temple of the Holy Spirit." Rather, we are called to "glorify God in [our] body" (1 Cor. 6:19–20).

The confession that human bodies are good affects not only what we do with our *own* bodies but also how we treat *other* embodied persons. As such, one can see that the claim that the created world is good is foundational for Christian ethics, for a large part of Christian ethics has to do with how we treat other embodied selves. Abortion, warfare, health care, prison conditions, capital punishment, stem cell research, and adultery—all of these issues have to do with our treatment of human bodies (or potential human bodies). The Christian claim that embodiment is good is a warrant for taking care of human bodies. We must care for people not merely in their spiritual illness and need but in their material needs as well. Too often the Christian church has been so concerned about the spiritual welfare of people that it has ignored their physical welfare. For example, when Spanish Christians arrived in Central and South America, they would simultaneously convert the Native Americans and then enslave and exploit them.

This is just the kind of spiritual myopia that the biblical writer James describes: "If a brother or sister is naked and lacks daily food, and one of you says to them, 'Go in peace; keep warm and eat your fill,' and yet you do not supply their bodily needs, what is the good of that?" (Jas. 2:15–16). James knew what all Christians would do well to remember: that much of Jesus' ministry had to do with real, immediate, and physical human needs. The Gospels spend a great deal of time depicting Jesus engaged in two activities: healing and feeding. In fact, he is shown healing no less than twenty separate times, and his miracle of feeding five thousand people is the only miracle recounted in all four Gospels. Jesus' emphasis on caring for human bodies is apparent in one of the few places where Jesus talks about hell. He says that those who will inherit the kingdom are those who fed the hungry, gave drink to the thirsty, clothed the naked, cared for the sick, and visited the imprisoned. Those who are thrust into "the eternal fire prepared for the devil and his angels" are those who have failed to do these things (Matt. 25:31–46). All of these activities involve caring for embodied neighbors.

Finally, Christians have another reason to pay particular attention to the treatment of the flesh: God "became flesh and lived among us" (John 1:14). God took on a human body and lived, played, ate, and drank in that body. What Christians call the "incarnation" shows how highly God holds that which is physical. For Christians to abuse that which God values so highly is a serious sin.

The World Is Not God

Genesis 1 tells us that the world is good. But it also tells us that the world is not God; it is not divine. To say that the world is "created" is to reject two views of creation that were prevalent in the ancient world. First, the world is not eternal. Plato, Aristotle, and other ancient Greek philosophers held that the world was uncreated; it had no beginning or end. Genesis 1 refutes this claim. The world and everything in it, including time, had a beginning, and that beginning was an act of God. This universe will one day end; this heaven and this earth shall pass away and be replaced by a new heaven and a new earth. Second, the Christian doctrine of creation as narrated in Genesis 1-2 refutes pantheism. *Pantheism* is the idea that everything is divine (*pan,* "every" + *theos,* "God/divine"). Because God is the creator of the world, the world is neither eternal nor divine, and nothing in the world should be understood as divine or worthy of our ultimate allegiance. One ethical implication of this is that while the created world is good and to be cared for, it is not the ultimate value. This includes all parts of the created order. Environmentalists rightly call on human beings to be the stewards of creation. But when care for the natural environment becomes ultimate, Christians have fallen into a kind of pantheism where God is no longer beyond the creation but totally within it. The natural environment then becomes a kind of god.

It also implies that while taking care of human beings and their physical needs is good, such ministry is not the final or absolute good. We must not raise the physical to such a level that we make it divine. If we provide food and water to human beings and ignore their spiritual hunger and thirst, we are turning the physical world into something divine, implying that the physical world is all there is and thus raising it to ultimate importance.

Because the world is good, we are called to care for human bodies. However, we must also be careful to avoid reducing human beings to mere bodies. Treating other people as nothing more than bodies can take many forms. Sexual promiscuity reduces the other to a mere body. Exploitative labor practices in which people are overworked and underpaid reduce that which is made in the image of God to a machine. Of course, one of the most evil manifestations of this sin is racism, as if the color of the outer part were somehow more important than our relationship with God.

We must also beware of reducing *ourselves* to our bodies. This might involve the pursuit of physical pleasure with the abuse of drugs, alcohol, or sex. Ironically, what happens in such cases is both a reduction of life to the bodily and a kind of body worship. Bodies are creations, and like all other creations they are not to be worshiped. We must treat the body with care, but we must also remember that we are more than our bodies. Jesus reminds his listeners, "What good will it be for a man if he gains the whole world, yet forfeits his soul? Or what can a man give in exchange for his soul?" (Matt. 16:26 NIV).

What Does Genesis 1–3 Tell Us about Human Beings?

As we have seen, Genesis 1–2 makes two foundational claims about the world that need to be kept in dynamic tension: The world is good, but the world is not God. We find a similar tension in the depiction of human beings when we include the third chapter of Genesis. Just as the world is good but not divine, human beings are made in the image of God and yet sinful.

What does it mean to be made in the image of God? This question has occupied theologians and ethicists for centuries. At first glance, it may sound like a merely theological question and fairly remote from the main topic of Christian ethics. But it is not. As I have stressed, ethics and theology are almost indistinguishable. The way that Christians understand the nature of God, world, and human beings greatly affects how they will relate to God and other human beings. Our vision shapes our actions.

Human Beings Are Made in the Image of God

All of God's creation reflects the glory of God, but the Bible says that only human beings are made in the "image of God":

> Then God said, "Let us make humankind in our image, according to our likeness; and let them have dominion over the fish of the sea, and over the birds of the air, and over the cattle, and over all the wild animals of the earth, and over every creeping thing that creeps upon the earth." So God created humankind in his image, in the image of God he created them; male and female he created them. (Gen. 1:26–27)

While the exact language of "image of God" is not prevalent throughout the rest of Scripture, the underlying idea of humanity's creation in the image of

God is central to biblical faith. What does it mean to be created in the image of God? At the very least, it highlights the high view of human life held by God. Contrast the view of human beings in the biblical creation stories with the depiction of human beings in the Babylonian creation story, the *Enuma Elish*, where human beings are created largely as an afterthought. Moreover, Marduk creates them primarily as slaves for the gods. In contrast, the opening chapters of Genesis depict a God who is willing to give up some control, to share with human creatures the responsibility of caring for the world and achieving God's purposes.

Whatever else we may learn about human beings throughout the rest of the Bible, we must never forget that God holds human beings in particularly high regard. They alone are to be the clearest reflections of God's glory. The psalmist marvels that God would assign human beings such a vaulted position:

> When I look at your heavens, the work of your fingers,
>   the moon and the stars that you have established;
> what are human beings that you are mindful of them,
>   mortals that you care for them?
> Yet you have made them a little lower than God,
>   and crowned them with glory and honor.
> You have given them dominion over the works of your hands;
>   you have put all things under their feet.
>
> (Ps. 8:3–6)

The Bible has a profoundly high view of human life. Humans are "crowned with glory and honor" and are partners in God's cosmic plan. There are many ethical implications of this Christian view of human beings. First, it acts as a check against the arbitrary or capricious destruction or abuse of human life. All human life is valuable. Those who wish to take life have a strong burden of proof. Philip Wogaman calls the value of human life a "positive moral presumption" in Christianity: "The burden of proof falls against any action or policy or social movement that has as its rationale the alleged unimportance or disvalue of any individual life."[11] The "burden of proof" means that those who would argue for harming or taking human life have to overcome a very strong presumption in favor of maintaining life. In a world such as ours, where human life is held in such low regard, Scripture demands that any action which would violate the value of life, if it can ever be justified, must be seen only as an exception and must be undertaken with great humility and seriousness. Therefore, to use our earlier language, there is a very strong *prima facie* prohibition against actions such as capital punishment, warfare, euthanasia, and abortion, and a strong *prima facie* obligation to protect and nurture human life. Christians must never forget this foundational biblical claim: that all human life is valuable because human beings are made in the image of God.

In the Genesis story, *all* human beings are made in the image of God. This would have sounded strange to the ears of most ancient people. In many societies such as Egypt, people believed that the pharaoh (king) and only the pharaoh was made in the image of God. Despite the fact that Scripture is clear that all humans are created in the image of God, this central claim has been ignored throughout much of the history of Christianity in relation to groups such as women and blacks. For many centuries, some Christian theologians argued that women did not image God.[12] And during America's early years, many theologians, both northern and southern, held that black men and women were not made in the image of God. But against all such attempts to limit the "image of God" to certain persons or groups of persons stands the clear and radical biblical claim that *all* human beings are created in the image of God. Color, gender, race, or socioeconomic status are irrelevant when it comes to the equality of all persons who are made in the image of God.

What is meant by "image of God"? For centuries, theologians tried to isolate some quality that human beings have that makes them like God. Most often, they argued that this was rationality. Humans were like God in that they could reason. Other theologians, appealing to the Genesis story itself, felt that human beings image God by being "lords" over creation, just as God is Lord over humans. While this second interpretation has the benefit of some biblical evidence, too often its adherents have used it to justify a strict hierarchical worldview where domination and control are equated with imaging God. In so doing they have failed to take into account that the way in which God's lordship is revealed in Jesus Christ is that of *servanthood*.

An increasingly prevalent interpretation of the "image of God" draws on the close connection between the phrases "in the image of God he created them" and "male and female he created them." To be made in the image of God is connected with being created male and female. This does not mean that God has both male and female "parts." What it does mean is that human beings "image" God when they enter into mutual relationships with an "other," relationships of care, service, and love. In human life, the primary model of such fellowship with an "other" is the male-female relationship. We encounter persons of the opposite sex and enter into mutually self-giving relationship with them. When we do so we reflect the God who created us, the God who has chosen not to live only for God's self but to turn outward and encounter and relate to a creature that is distinct from God. While the male-female relationship is a model of relationality in the image of God, it is only one of the many ways that we enter into a fellowship of care, love, and self-giving with an "other." Whenever we risk encountering another person as a "Thou" and not just an "It," to use Martin Buber's language, we are imaging God.[13]

The idea that the image of God is understood in terms of the ability to enter freely into fellowship with another is particularly appropriate for Christians, who understood God not as a lonely singularity but as a community of three persons (Father, Son, and Holy Spirit). God is not alone; there is love and fellowship within God's very being. As Karl Barth puts it, "In Himself he does not will to exist for Himself, to exist alone. On the contrary, He is Father, Son and Holy Spirit and therefore alive in His unique being with and for and in another."[14] Therefore, when we enter into relationships of self-giving love with other human beings, it is then that we are imaging God. We are reflecting God's perfect triune love back to God, like a mirror.

This helps make sense of the very first commandment to "be fruitful and multiply" (Gen. 1:28). When men and women love one another, they seek to share that love. Like God's creation, the couple does not need an "other" to have love; they already experience love between themselves. But their love overflows to such a degree that they wish to expand their circle of love and bring in others. They create life out of their love. While procreation is the archetype of this fruitful love, it is not the only type. Whenever human beings seek to create new relationships out of love and for love, they are being fruitful. They are reflecting the image of a God who creates out of an overflow of divine love.

To sum up, being created in the image of God means that God holds human beings in very high regard. No human life is disposable. No human life can be used merely as a means to some other end. Moreover, to be created in the image of God means that we are created to be in fellowship with God and human beings.

Human Beings Are Sinful and Disobedient

We have seen that human beings are created in the image of God. They image God by loving God and one another, by creating relationships of harmonious coexistence and support. Christian ethics takes this as a starting point. But we must balance this vision of human beings with a second claim. Human beings are not what they were intended to be. Christians and Jews confess that human beings are sinful and disobedient creatures. This is a prevalent theme throughout the entire Bible. Turn to practically any page in the Bible and you will find examples of human greed, pride, disobedience, lust, envy, and hunger for power. Cain kills Abel out of jealousy and anger. God's chosen people, the

Jews, are constantly complaining about their situation and worshiping other gods. David, the greatest of Israel's kings, takes another man's wife and has her husband killed when she becomes pregnant. Even the chosen disciples of Christ are shown as weak, bickering, and unfaithful in many situations. But the sinfulness of human beings is brought out most vividly in the story of the garden of Eden. It is the prototype of all human sinfulness.

God has given the first human beings everything that they could want or hope for. The garden is full of those things that make life not only possible but delightful. Most of all, Adam and Eve are given an intimate relationship with their maker, who is uniquely present with them, "walking in the garden in the cool of the day" (Gen. 3:8 NIV). God has given them one command: not to eat of the tree of the knowledge of good and evil.

Yet they disobey God. Why? Why would they do such a thing? The story seems intentionally ambiguous about this. On the one hand, there is the tempter (who is not identified here as Satan but simply the most cunning of God's creatures).[15] It is interesting that the Bible simply remains silent as to the status or motives of the tempter. It is as if the narrator recognizes that the temptation to evil cannot be fully explained. Evil by definition defies rational explanation, as Guthrie writes:

> The Genesis story is very profound in its simplicity at this point. It makes no attempt to explain where the Tempter came from or how he could exist at all in God's world. Satan is a hideous intruder who does not belong in the picture but is nevertheless there. Logically, evil is impossible in a world created and ruled by God, for it is just what God did *not* create and does *not* will. That is the parasitical power of evil. . . . It is a lie, a contradiction and denial of the truth. That is why it is so dangerous.[16]

For Christians, sin must be understood not simply as what human beings do, but as a kind of power or force that exists in the world. Sin exists in the world as more than the sum of human failure, ignorance, and disobedience. Sin is not merely the result of human action, but the cause of it. It is often described in the Bible as having a will of its own. God tells Cain that "sin is lurking at your door" (Gen. 4:7), and Paul says that "sin sprang to life and I died" (Rom. 7:9 NIV).

We must resist falling into a kind of flippant optimism about sin, thinking that with enough education or moral fortitude we can completely overcome evil. Evil exists as an inexplicable, irrational force in the world. This is why it is important to continue thinking about evil in terms of a person. To do so keeps us from explaining evil simply as a weakness of will or knowledge. Thinking about evil in personal terms also keeps us vigilant about the sin and evil in our own lives. It helps us to keep watch for it lurking at our door or hiding in some unexpected form.

But the presence of the serpent does not explain everything. The snake only tempts; he does not force. There is something in the human pair that leads them to disobey. While most people identify this as pride, I think it is more accurate to say that it is pride mixed with independence and *lack of trust*. The serpent is able to instill doubt in the minds of Adam and Eve. Recall that his first words to the woman are "Did God really say . . . ?" Instead of turning to God for reassurance and strength, the human couple tries to handle the situation alone. What they want is to be like God, able to decide for themselves what is right and what is wrong, how best to be human in this world. They have already been made in the image of God. But by acting independently and without concern for others, they have distorted the very image of God in themselves. They want to be more than a creature; they, like so many of us, wish to be God, or at least God as they imagine God must be.

In terms of overall theological and ethical vision, the results of the disobedience are more critical than the reasons why. What happens as a result of the humans' refusal to live out their place as creatures of God? Besides the introduction of shame (they clothe themselves), deceit (they hide from God), and blame (they all point the finger elsewhere), there is a series of punishments that ensues, three of which are most important for our purposes:

1. Adam and Eve are put out of the garden.
2. Man will rule over woman, while woman will have an inordinate desire for man.
3. Man must work the ground for food.

What all of these punishments have in common is that they represent a disruption of the original harmonious relationships between humans, God, and the natural creation. Prior to this act of disobedience by Adam and Eve, all things were in harmony. God was present to Adam and Eve in a special and immediate way. There was perfect harmony between humans and the natural world; the earth yielded its fruit easily, and there was no killing of animals for food (Gen. 1:29–30). Human beings lived in right relationship with one another, as symbolized by the relationship of Adam and Eve, united together as one flesh (Gen. 2:24).

But with the disobedience came a disruption of the original harmony. The relationship between God and human beings was disturbed. In trying to be "like God" the human beings overstepped their creaturely status. In so doing they also disrupted interhuman relationships. What Genesis 3 reveals in brilliant narrative fashion is the state of the human condition. We are estranged from God and in competition with our neighbor. Who among us has not felt the truth of Genesis 3 in our own lives? We wonder, "Where is God? Why does God feel so distant?" Or we think, "Why do human beings treat each other so awfully? Why don't I feel the kind of love for my fellow creatures that I know I should?"

One of the foundational claims of Christian theology is that we live in a condition of brokenness, sickness, and disruption in our most basic relationships—those with God and with fellow humans. This is the very nature of sin. Alienation and brokenness are both the sin itself and the result of sin. But this is not the end of the story. God will constantly be seeking to heal the disruption that sin causes. He will give the law (Torah) and he will send the prophets, all in an effort to fix broken relationships. And as Paul will make so brilliantly clear, Jesus of Nazareth, as God made flesh, has come to heal the rift we experience with God and our neighbors.

Conclusion: Covenant and Creation

One of the unifying themes throughout the Bible is the notion of covenant. A covenant is an agreement or promise between two or more persons. We shall examine this concept more closely in the next chapter when we discuss the Mosaic covenant in detail. But at this juncture it is helpful to see that the creation stories in Genesis function as a foundation for the covenant relationship between God and human beings.

Karl Barth calls creation the "external basis of the covenant."[17] It is the stage on which God will play out God's purposes. God creates with a purpose: to glorify God's self through covenantal relationship with the world and through the "being for" human creatures, that is, their salvation. That the Word was with God in creation (John 1) reflects the Christian confession that *God's creation has as its goal the joining together of God with humanity, by which the human creature may one day join in the divine community of Father, Son, and Holy Spirit.*

Creation is the stage or groundwork for the working out of the covenant between God and human beings. God has chosen the created order as the means for establishing and developing a history with human beings (and animals) through which God's free love can be demonstrated and God's glory revealed. As Barth explains, "Creation is the external basis of the covenant. It can be said that it makes it technically possible; that it prepares and establishes the sphere in which the institution and history of the covenant take place; that it makes possible the subject which is to be God's partner in this history."[18]

Creation is not established without a purpose. Its very structure and nature is determined by God for the establishment of the covenant. God is like a great architect who has a vision of and for his creation. Barth puts it:

> Hence what God has created was not just any reality—however perfect or wonderful—but that which is intrinsically determined as the exponent of His glory and for the corresponding service. What God created when He created the world and man was not just any place, but that which was fore-ordained for the establishment and the history of the covenant, nor just any subject, but that which was to become God's partner in this history, i.e. the nature which God in his grace willed to address and accept and the man pre-destined for His service.[19]

The purpose for which God creates is covenant life. This belief stands as the very foundation of Christian ethics, because it tells us why human beings were created. It tells us that human beings have a twofold end or purpose in life: *to be in relationship with one another and to be in relationship with God.*

As God says, "It is not good that the man should be alone" (Gen. 2:18). Humans were created to be in fellowship with God and with one another. Sin is therefore characterized by either a refusal to rightly worship God or a refusal to live in proper relationship with our fellow creatures. If humans are meant to be with and for others, then sin can be characterized as self-centeredness, a refusal to live out God's purpose for our lives. Sin, at its core, is a rejection of what it means to be a human being. This is why, later in the Bible, Paul calls sin a kind of "death," for sin represents a denial of our true humanity. Physical death is separation from self, others, and God. But spiritual death is the "wages of sin," because the results of such sin are broken or fractured relationships—separation from God and others. In Genesis 3 we saw how the sin of Adam and Eve led to a disruption of their relationship with one another and with God. In the next chapter we shall see how God seeks, through the Mosaic covenant, to mend those two primal sets of relationships—between human beings and between God and human beings.

Ultimately, we shall see that it takes *God* to heal or mend the brokenness of our relationships. We are incapable of doing so on our own. Therefore, God takes on human flesh to enact the healing, to set us back into right relationship. This is what Paul means when he says that we "all have sinned and fall short of the glory of God . . . [and] are now justified by his grace as a gift, through the redemption that is in Christ Jesus" (Rom. 3:23–24). Jesus' *death* puts us back into right relationship, but his *life* also reveals what we were created to be. Jesus is the embodiment and fulfillment of what God intended you and me to be. Jesus is the true image of God in that he is in perfect harmonious relationship with the Father and with his fellow creatures (see Col. 1:15).

Genesis 1–3 sets the stage for the rest of the history of God's covenant relationship with human beings. It does so by introducing the tension that will only be resolved at the end of time—the tension between what we were intended to be (in harmonious relationship with God and others) and what we are (sinful creatures who refuse to live as God created us). Genesis 1–3 begins "in the beginning" with the creation of heaven and earth. Only with the creation of a new heaven and a new earth (see Rev. 21) in which God's will is done on earth as it is in heaven will we experience the complete resolution of the contradiction between what we were meant to be and what we presently are. Christian ethics seeks to give guidance on how to live the Christian life in this "in between" time.

Chapter 6

The Mosaic Covenant

New Guidelines for a New People

Biblical Readings

Exodus 20–24
Deuteronomy 5–8
Leviticus 11–13; 18–19; 25

Reading Guide

These sections of Scripture contain a great number of commandments; some of them may be familiar and others very strange. As we read these commandments, it is important to try to understand the setting in which these laws were formulated. The laws in the Old Testament may have eternal significance, but they were still formulated at a particular time in a particular social and religious context. These laws were not just arbitrarily imposed restrictions or obligations. They embody a particular theological and social worldview. Therefore, if we are to understand the many laws of the Old Testament and their significance in our own lives, it is not enough simply to pull a law out and begin applying it. It is absolutely essential that we understand how these laws functioned in the lives of our ancient religious ancestors.

As you read, do not try to remember all of these commandments and laws. Simply try to get a flavor for Old Testament law. Ask yourself these three questions: What does this law say about the religious/ethical worldview of this community? What is the principle behind the law? How might it apply today?

Introduction: A Covenant Community

According to the Bible, about 1300 years before the birth of Jesus Christ, a small band of people called Hebrews was enslaved by one of the two great centers of power of the ancient world, Egypt. This was not particularly noteworthy. Empires such as the Babylonian, Sumerian, Akkadian, and Egyptian had been enslaving less powerful groups since the dawn of civilization. But according to the biblical book of Exodus, this was not just any enslaved people. God had made a promise (or covenant) with these people to protect them, give them land, and bless them (Gen. 12:1–3). True to God's promise, God sent a messenger named Moses to the Pharaoh of Egypt, demanding that he release the Hebrews so that they might worship their God freely. When Pharaoh, the supposed embodiment of the Egyptian god on earth, refused to release the Hebrew slaves, the true God sent plagues upon the nation of Egypt. The final plague was the death of the firstborn son of all Egyptians, a plague so devastating that the Egyptians finally freed the enslaved Hebrews. This last plague and the freeing of the Hebrews (known as the "exodus") are commemorated during the Jewish festival of Passover. God then led the Hebrews into the wilderness of the Sinai Peninsula, a land so barren and desolate that God had to provide food and water for the people along the way. When the people reached the mountain where God first commissioned Moses to rescue the people, God entered into a new covenant with the people.

We touched on the term *covenant* briefly in the previous chapter, but let us examine it more closely since it plays such a pivotal role in understanding the commandments of the Old Testament. A covenant is a formal agreement or arrangement between two or more parties. The term is used in the Old Testament to describe the agreement between two individuals, for example, between Laban and Joseph (Gen. 31:43–55) or between David and Jonathan (1 Sam. 18:1–8). A covenant can also be an agreement between groups of people such as the Jews and the Gibeonites (Josh. 9:15). But most often it describes the agreement or relationship between God and God's people. It is somewhat analogous to a contract in that two parties enter into an agreement. However, God-human covenants and human contracts differ in a number of ways. Contracts are normally bilateral and assume that the two parties are generally equal. God-human covenants are often unilateral, and the parties are never on equal footing. God initiates and determines the nature of the covenant.

While covenants are somewhat analogous to contracts, a better analogy is that of wedding vows. During a wedding, two persons make a commitment to each other. It is not merely a quid pro quo arrangement. Rather, out of love and devotion, the couple desires to be bound exclusively to each other. They become bound by their vow and therefore take on special obligations and commitments in light of their new relationship. In fact, the Hebrew term for covenant (*berit'*) comes from the word for "bind." A covenant is the way in which God binds God's self to human beings and human beings become bound to God. In that sense, a covenant is more like a wedding vow than a commercial contract. In a wedding vow, the participants themselves are transformed. Their identities are now largely defined in terms of their relationship.

All of the laws that we find in the Old Testament must be understood in light of this concept of covenant. God is entering into a special relationship with the Jews. Like a great divine wedding vow, God is proclaiming God's steadfast love for the people and a desire that they be God's exclusively. When we hear God say, "I will walk among you, and will be your God, and you shall be my people" (Lev. 26:12) or "I will take you as my people, and I will be your God" (Exod. 6:7), we hear echoes of modern wedding ceremonies.

Covenant is the dominant and unifying motif in the Old Testament; in fact, "testament" comes from the Latin word for "covenant." While the exact term may not always be used, the *Bible is essentially a story of God's covenantal relationship with Jews and that branch of Judaism that later became Christianity.* Prior to their liberation from the Egyptians, God had already entered into two covenants:

1. *Noachic.* After the great flood, God entered into a covenant with Noah, his descendants, and all the creatures on the earth. God vowed to never again completely destroy the earth (Gen. 9:1-17).
2. *Abrahamic.* God promised Abraham land, descendants, and blessings. In fact, it is because of God's agreement with Abraham that God later rescues the Hebrews (later known as Jews) from their slavery in Egypt. "Out of the slavery their cry for help rose up to God. God heard their groaning, and God remembered his covenant with Abraham, Isaac, and Jacob" (Exod. 2:23b–24).

For our purposes, the covenant that God established with the people through Moses at Mount Sinai is the most important one, because it is in this covenant that God established some conditions for the people. The Noachic covenant and the covenant with Abraham were essentially one-sided promises on God's part. But with the *Mosaic, or Sinai, covenant,* in addition to God's promises, the people take on certain obligations and responsibilities in light of their new covenant identity. These obligations for covenant life with God are what we know as the Old Testament law.

God is entering into a new relationship with this people. In fact, by doing so God is creating a new people, with a new identity, out of this band of liberated slaves. This is a new act of creation on God's part, symbolized by the dividing of the waters at the Red Sea (Exod. 14). Just as God had created the world by dividing the watery chaos in Genesis 1, God creates a new people at the Red Sea.

But this people will not be just any people. They are to be God's special people, God's chosen ones, a "priestly kingdom and a holy nation" (Exod. 19:6), witnesses throughout the world to Yahweh's power and steadfast love. And so God calls them to be different, to be what Walter Brueggemann calls an "alternative community." They are to be unlike all the peoples and nations around them, including the nation they once called home, Egypt:

> The reality emerging out of the Exodus is not just a new religion or a new religious idea or a vision of freedom but the emergence of a new social community in history, a community that has historical body, that had to devise laws, patterns of governance and order, norms of right and wrong, and sanctions of accountability. The participants in the Exodus found themselves, undoubtedly surprisingly to them, involved in the intentional formation of a *new social community* to match the vision of God's freedom.[1]

Yahweh is unlike any of the other so-called gods, and because Yahweh is different, Yahweh's followers must be different. They simply cannot worship this God in the same way that the people around them worship their gods. Integrally connected with this transformed relationship with God is the creation of an alternative *social* community. No longer will the old ways of relating to one another be appropriate. Nor will they be able to simply take over the customs of the peoples with whom they will coexist in and around the promised land of Canaan.

As Brueggemann points out, the Mosaic covenant represents a new way of loving God and loving neighbor. These are new laws for a new people. The old ways of Pharaoh and Egypt are inadequate. The way of life in Egypt was primarily one in which "might makes right," where violence and control were the norm and where everyone had to look after his own needs. Laws were structured to protect the interests of the wealthy, the powerful, and the privileged. After such a long period of slavery in Egypt, the Hebrew community was in danger of adopting this worldview.

The ancient world was not so different from our modern one in its focus on materialism, the acquisition and maintenance of possessions and wealth. Since the powerful and the wealthy tended to make the laws, ancient customs and practices often functioned to support the status quo, protecting the rich and keeping power in the hands of a few. All around them, individual life was held in low regard. Children were sacrificed. Slaves were killed. The old and the sick were left to fend for themselves.

In the laws of the Old Testament, we see God's desire that the Israelites live differently from the nations around them. The Jews must resist worshiping multiple gods, as their neighbors do: "You shall not bow down to their gods, or worship them, or follow their practices" (Exod. 23:24). And they must avoid the temptation of following the customs of their neighbors. God is insistent that "you shall keep all my statutes and all my ordinances. . . . You shall not follow the practices of the nation that I am driving out before you" (Lev. 20:22–23). God is calling this frightened band of liberated slaves to live differently from the world around them. He is calling them to a separate and holy existence, telling them, "If you obey my voice and keep my covenant, you shall be my treasured possession out of all the peoples. Indeed, the whole earth is mine, but you shall be for me a priestly kingdom and a holy nation" (Exod. 19:5–6). God is setting conditions upon the relationship. God is saying that if the Israelites truly wish to be God's special bride, they must love and worship only Yahweh. Moreover, to be a covenant people, they must live lives that reflect their devotion to God by demonstrating the kind of justice and mercy that characterizes the very nature of God. Ignoring what the world thinks, they must become an alternative community of love, mercy, equality, and devotion to one God. We might speak here of the *two pillars of covenant faith—exclusive worship of Yahweh and the practice of compassionate justice among one another.* The whole of covenant life boils down to these two basic tenets. To be God's people is to uphold these two pillars.

The ancient Israelites did not view the Old Testament laws as harsh or arbitrary requirements by a domineering and demanding God. The promises that the people made at Sinai (and that Jews and Christians have repeated throughout the ages) are like the promises that lovers make on their wedding day. They are not seen as impositions, but as joyous expressions of their love for one another. This is why for Jews the law is the most wonderful of all of God's gifts:

> Happy are those
>   who do not follow the advice of the wicked,
> or take the path that sinners tread,
>   or sit in the seat of scoffers;
> but their delight is in the law of the LORD,
>   and on his law they meditate day and night.
>   (Ps. 1:1–2)

> I delight in the way of your decrees
>   as much as in all riches.
> I will meditate on your precepts,
>   and fix my eyes on your ways.
> I will delight in your statutes;
>   I will not forget your word.
>   (Ps. 119:14–16)

The Israelites rejoiced in the law because it allowed them to know how to please their God. The law was seen as a gift because the Jews were privileged to know how to stand in proper relationship with God and with one another. It was an expression of their love for Yahweh and Yahweh's love for them.

Even the punishments that accompany the laws are a sign of God's love and concern. Take parenting as a model. You drive home at 2:00 a.m. smelling of alcohol. You stumble through the door and your parents say, "I know you've been drinking and driving, but it is no big deal." That is not love; that is indifference. God punishes because God loves and has high expectations, in light of the relationship that has been established and the promises that have been made: "You only have I known of all the families of the earth; therefore I will punish you for all your iniquities" (Amos 3:2). Of course, not all the bad things that happen to people are a punishment from God. But the fact that Old Testament laws come with punishments reflects how seriously God takes human beings and the covenant by which God and humans are mutually bound together. (We shall see that God takes human sin so seriously that God is willing to experience alienation and death on the cross to overcome it.)

Ten Commandments (Decalogue)

Prologue

Let us now take a closer look at the specifics of what the Jews held as their greatest possession, namely, the Torah. *Torah* means "instruction," "teachings," or "commandments," and according to Jewish tradition, there are 613 such instructions in the Hebrew Scriptures. It is appropriate, however, to begin with the Decalogue, or Ten Commandments, since these represent a basic foundation on which all other commandments are built, as Jesus himself attests (Mark 10:17–19).

The astute reader will notice that the Decalogue actually begins not with a command but with a statement: "I am the LORD your God, who brought you out of the land of Egypt" (Exod. 20:2). This statement is often referred to as the "prologue" to the Decalogue. It is as important as any of the commandments. In fact, Jews consider it part of the first commandment. This prologue is so important because it reinforces everything I have said about the function of the law. The law is not simply an arbitrary set of commands dropped from heaven by some unknown God; it is part of the overall, ongoing relationship between God and the Jews (and later, the Christians). Bruce Birch rightly notes, "Obedience to these commands will not establish relationship with God; they but spell out the framework of *response in community to a relationship already initiated by God.*[2] This is not just any god giving these rules for living; this is the God who did what the Hebrews were unable to do for themselves, namely, liberate them from bondage to the Egyptians. Therefore, the prologue functions as a reason for obedience. It reminds the Jews of their ongoing relationship with a God who loves, protects, and liberates God's special people. The Israelites can adhere to these laws in gratitude for what God has done and in assurance of what God will do. Once again we see the close connection between a statement of faith (indicative—what God has done) and a norm or commandment of action (imperative—what the Jews should do). Theology and ethics go hand in hand. The recital of God's mighty deeds comes first; obedience is simply a response to God's actions and character.

The prologue also reminds the people of the context for the law, which is God's calling the people out of Egypt and into the promised land, where they will live out a unique type of existence, one in which they remember their own slavery (as a reason to demonstrate mercy and justice to the powerless) but leave behind the ways of Egypt. Walter Brueggemann describes the nature of the covenantal life in relation to the exodus:

> Reference to the Exodus suggests that the theological intention of the Ten Commandments is to institutionalize the Exodus: to establish perspectives, procedures, policies and institutions that will generate Exodus-like social relationships. The reason the commandments are so urgent and insistent is that they are Yahweh's (and therefore Israel's) strategy for fending off a return to pre-Exodus conditions of exploitation and brutality within the community.[3]

The prologue establishes a context for the commandments by highlighting God's call for a radical break with the ways of Egypt, Pharaoh, and slavery. The Jews are called to live out "Exodus-like social relationships," relationships that reflect the nature of their God as one who loves justice, mercy, and freedom from bondage. Yahweh is calling them out of Egypt not just geographically but spiritually and morally. They are challenged to leave behind not simply the old location, but to leave behind old ways of acting and being, while always remembering that they were once slaves themselves (see Deut. 5:15; 24:21–22).

The prologue places the entire law in a larger theological context by reminding the people who Yahweh is (the one who liberates) and who they are as a people (ex-slaves, called to leave behind the ways of Egypt). And they are being challenged to transform their relationships with God and one another. This can be seen in the very structure of the Decalogue, which is traditionally divided into two "tables." The first table, consisting of the first four commandments, concerns the relationship between God and human beings. The second table addresses human-human relationships.

First Table: Human Relations with God

You shall have no other gods before me.

The claim that there is only one God worthy of worship is the very foundation of Jewish and Christian life. Many scholars consider monotheism (*mono*, "one" + *theos*, "God") to be the greatest contribution of Judaism.[4] Egypt briefly toyed with the idea of belief in a single, all-powerful deity in the fourteenth century BCE, but this was a short-lived and isolated case in a world where polytheism (or henotheism) was the rule.[5] The first commandment given on Mount Sinai makes it clear that the Israelites are no longer permitted to divide their loyalty between Yahweh and other gods. It is difficult for modern Christians to appreciate the significance of such a command. Ancient peoples were largely polytheistic; they worshiped multiple gods. Particular gods were often associated with particular natural forces such as rain, fertility, a river, or the sun. More often than not these gods were also limited geographically. A god was sovereign over a particular region, and so a visitor to a foreign land would worship the god of that land. The more gods one could worship, the safer one would be since the worship of the gods was often viewed as a way of appeasing that god to attain benefits for the worshiper. Through magic, sacrifice, and ritual, the god was manipulated into acting in ways beneficial to the worshiper.

But with Jews, the story is a different one. They must forgo all other gods in favor of this single deity. They must cast their lot entirely with Yahweh. No longer can they hedge their bets; they must trust Yahweh alone. Total and unqualified commitment is demanded. This commandment represents the foundation of all other commandments. It is only in light of a total commitment to this one God that the importance of the other commandments can be fully appreciated. If the people are to follow this *one* God, they must live under *one* set of rules that reflects the nature of this God. No longer will they be permitted to adhere to the various rules and laws of the people among whom they live. Just as they can worship only one God, they can only abide by one set of God-given laws.

This commandment is so important that Jews are commanded to recite their undivided loyalty to God when they "lie down and when [they] rise up" (Deut. 6:7). Even today, observant Jews recite the most important prayer in Judaism upon awakening and before going to bed: "Hear, O Israel: The LORD is our

God, the LORD alone. You shall love the LORD your God with all your heart, and with all your soul, and with all your might" (Deut. 6:4). This prayer, known as the *Shema,* draws the logical conclusion that because God is one and there are no other gods, divided loyalty is prohibited. If there are no other gods, then one must devote oneself totally to Yahweh.

Few Christians are drawn to the worship of such ancient gods as Marduk, Isis, or Baal. But how often are our loyalties divided between God and something else? We turn things that are less than God into God. And so the most basic commandment in Christian ethics is to worship God alone, never placing our loyalty even to family, nation, or friend above our love of God (for a fuller discussion see chapter 7).

You shall not make for yourself an idol, whether in the form of anything that is in heaven above, or that is on the earth beneath, or that is in the water under the earth. You shall not bow down to them or worship them; for I the LORD your God am a jealous God.

This sounds very similar to the first commandment, and there are indeed certain overlaps, particularly in our modern context. To worship some non-god such as money, youth, or success is to turn that thing into an idol. It is to take something that has no power to create, deliver, or reconcile and to pretend that it does. The prophet Jeremiah mocks those who "say to a tree, 'You are my father,' and to a stone, 'You gave me birth'" (Jer. 2:27). But this does not keep us from identifying all kinds of human creations with God.

But while there are overlaps between the first and second commandments, there are also differences. The prohibition against making idols is grounded in the human desire to control. Ancient idol worshipers certainly understood that their gods were not to be identified with the images made in wood or stone. Nevertheless, as Gerhard von Rad points out, non-Jews saw idols as the way in which their gods became present and available to them: "The crucial thing was that the deity became present in the image. But with the presence of the deity, there was at the same time given the presence of its power, for it could now become effective, with its particular blessings, for man and in the world of man."[6] As such, an idol represented one way in which the people could appease and ultimately manipulate their god. If their god is now present in the idol, that god's presence can be controlled. If a god can be reduced, no matter how symbolically, to a human creation, then that god remains, at least partially, within human control.

In contrast, the God of Christians and Jews is totally free. This God becomes manifest not in lifeless objects but in the very relationship God creates with God's people. This is why Jesus of Nazareth is the ultimate of God's revelations. Because God is personal, God's true revelation takes place in a *person*, not in an object.

This is a God who cannot be manipulated or controlled for human purposes. This is a God who refuses to be co-opted for the interests of any group of believers. The freedom of this God crashes through any attempt to identify God unreservedly with any human creation. This freedom of God is another way of referring to the sovereignty of God that was illustrated so clearly in the creation narratives. God should not be "idolized" by identifying God with any human creation. In our case, that includes race, nation, political ideology (even democracy or capitalism), or social program. When we hear both sides in a war declaring that God is on their side, we risk turning nation and national interests into idols. When we assume that God can be unequivocally identified with some human project, we make an idol of God. The prohibition against creating idols warns us to maintain constant vigilance against manipulating God for our own interest and benefit.

You shall not make wrongful use of the name of the LORD your God, for the LORD will not acquit anyone who misuses his name.

The very fact that this prohibition is grouped with such serious issues as idolatry, murder, and theft leads one to suspect that more is involved here than merely "cursing." While that is clearly included in misusing God's name, there are certainly other, more serious ways of misusing the name of the Lord. As Walter Harrelson rightly notes, "The prohibition against the misuse of divine name . . . seems particularly designed to prevent the misuse of the power of religion, the numinous power of the holy, to further one's own ends at the expense of the life or welfare of others."[7] With this broader interpretation, we can readily imagine other cases of "misusing God's name." Whenever the name of "God" is employed to harm or manipulate others, we encounter an abuse of the name of the Lord. Whenever we invoke the name of God in order to build ourselves up at the expense of others, we are probably violating the third commandment. Some examples of this are

- when the Spaniards oppressed, enslaved, and forced the conversions of the natives of the Americas in the sixteenth and seventeenth centuries, all done in the name of God
- when televangelists bilk pensioners out of their social security checks in the name of the Lord
- when Palestinian suicide bombers kill civilians in the name of God
- when people hide behind the name of God in order to feel self-righteous and superior

These are all ways in which the name of God has been misused. We must be very careful about taking the gift of God's revelation to us and using it for our own glory rather than God's.

Remember the sabbath day, and keep it holy.

Because the observance of the Sabbath day and the Sabbath year play such a central role in the life of the covenant community, I shall discuss them at length below.

Second Table: Relationships between Human Beings

Honor your father and your mother, so that your days may be long in the land that the LORD your God is giving you.

As we move into the second table of the Decalogue, describing how members of the alternative covenant community are to treat one another, we encounter commands that sound simple and explicit. Yet when we look at them more closely, there is considerable room for debate as to their meaning and weight. "Honor your father and your mother" is one such command. The first thing to note about this command is that it has a rather utilitarian rationale. God tells the Israelites to honor mother and father so that "your days may be long in the land."

But what exactly does "honor" mean? Does it mean strict obedience? Imagine the following scenarios. You are a college student pursuing your dream of becoming a schoolteacher. Your mother calls you one day and says, "Your father and I have decided that you should be a doctor." Is your refusal to begin taking premed classes a case of dishonoring your parents? Or imagine that you grew up in a Democratic family and fall in love with a Republican whom you plan to marry. Your father comes to you and says, "How can you bring such disgrace upon this family? You will be dishonoring me if you marry that man." Does "honor" mean "obey"?

While obedience might be one aspect of honor, it seems clear that this commandment should not be reduced to mere obedience. What else might it mean? One possibility is that it commands us to act in such a way as to bring honor to our parents; we should not act in such a way that brings disgrace and shame upon the family. For ancient Israelites, this would have meant holding tightly to the worship of the true God and doing those things that God commands as a way of upholding the unique identity of the covenant community. Similarly, we bring honor to our own Christian parents by continuing the worship of their God and seeking to live lives that reflect the God-given values that have shaped their Christian journey.

Another possibility is that this commandment calls upon us to take care of elderly parents who need our help. In fact, most biblical scholars think that this commandment primarily concerned adult children and elderly parents. If this is the case, then underlying this commandment is a particular and profound understanding of what it means to be a member of the worshiping community. Like Sabbath observance, this law "insists that one's labor and the products of one's labor are not everything. When persons grow old and are no longer able to carry their load, their place within the community has not come to an end."[8] Such an understanding of community is in sharp contrast to the brick pits of Pharaoh, where people were largely reduced to their productivity.

In fact, such an understanding of what it means to be a valuable member of a community stands in contrast to the contemporary emphasis on productivity. We see this in the debate about euthanasia, in which people say that they want to die peacefully when they can no longer contribute to society. We see this in the criticism of the homeless and unemployed as being a "drag" on society. If this commandment is really about caring for the elderly who can no longer work, it represents an alternative vision of the worth of human beings.

You shall not murder.

Even a cursory reading of the Old Testament makes clear that this commandment is not an absolute prohibition against the taking of human life. There are abundant crimes for which death is the sentence (e.g., murder, kidnapping, homosexual acts, striking mother or father, sorcery). Moreover, warfare is not only permitted in the Bible, but it is occasionally commanded by God.[9] Killing in self-defense is implicitly condoned in the Old Testament. Since not all killing is murder, the question then becomes, What counts as murder and what counts as justifiable killing? Christians continue to debate this question in the realms of abortion, capital punishment, euthanasia, and warfare.

At its core, this commandment reinforces the key Judeo-Christian notion that *life belongs to God.* It is to be respected. Human beings are made in the image of God. Therefore, taking life can only be done in great seriousness and for significant reasons. This means that there is always a strong negative presumption against taking life. The burden of proof always falls upon those who would take life, and the burden is a very heavy one.

John Calvin goes further than this. He says that it is not enough simply to avoid taking life. This commandment, he argues, reflects the Christian conviction that because life is a gift from God, we must go out of our way to protect the life of the neighbor: "We are accordingly commanded, if we find anything of use to us in saving our neighbors' lives, faithfully to employ it; if there is anything that makes for their peace, to see to it; if anything harmful, to ward it off; if they are in any danger, to lend a helping hand."[10] Is it too much to say that we murder when we support oppressive regimes in other nations, or when we fail to struggle against unjust social and economic systems that lead to starvation, political killing, and death by easily preventable disease?

You shall not commit adultery.

The prohibition against adultery is unequivocal and consistent throughout Scripture. There is no example of excusable adultery. Jesus calls it a "sin" (John 8:11) and restates the prohibition when asked about guidelines for the moral life (Luke 18:20). Given that most cultures have rules forbidding adultery, how should we understand the biblical prohibition within the larger Jewish and Christian worldviews?

First, as we saw in the previous chapter, what we do with our bodies matters to God. Sexuality is a gift from God, and the misuse of that gift affects our relationship with God. Moreover, the dishonesty and betrayal that accompany adultery almost always cause pain for the spouse and children. Sexual expression is far from a private matter. Communities of faith, like the early Israelite community, can and should establish guidelines and expectations regarding the sexual activities of their members.

Second, many scholars believe that the prohibition was directed primarily at women as a way for men to be sure that their children were truly theirs. In other words, the command was a way of protecting men. In the world of Pharaoh, protecting men and their property (children) was probably the main rationale for rules against adultery. But unlike many of the law codes of the ancient Near East, the Torah mandates death for both the adulterous man and woman (Lev. 20:10). What we begin to see is that the law is set up not merely to protect the interests of the powerful and wealthy, but to protect the relationship itself. Even in this widely held law, we find a unique twist, as God sets up a new kind of community.

In the canonical context of the Sinai covenant, the command not to commit adultery takes on a deeper meaning. In the surrounding cultures, immediate gratification of one's desires may be acceptable and natural. But God is creating an "alternative community," a people that is willing to sacrifice for the good of others. It is not surprising, then, that prefacing an entire series of laws concerning sexual activity, God says, "You shall not do as they do in the land of Egypt, where you lived, and you shall not do as they do in the land of Canaan, to which I am bringing you" (Lev. 18:3). Standing behind this prohibition is God's insistence that pleasure and self-gratification are not the highest ideals. "If it feels good, do it" is diametrically opposed to God's insistence that we must often forgo personal pleasure for the sake of our commitment to others. Adultery is often justified in the popular imagination because one partner has fallen out of love with the other. But Scripture gives us a different view of marriage, as a lifelong covenant of loyalty and commitment even if the ardor of romance wanes. We subordinate our own personal desires for the good of others—spouse, children, and wider community.

This is why both the prophets and Jesus (Matt. 12:49) often compare the nation of Israel to an adulterer, someone for whom loyalty and commitment are less important than immediate gratification. Yet God does not abandon Israel, even when there might well be a better covenant partner in whom God would find a new and more passionate relationship. Like a faithful spouse God maintains God's steadfast love and the covenant promises that God has made.

You shall not steal.

To take the possessions of another person is recognized as immoral in practically all cultures. I shall simply raise a number of questions for consideration. One has to do with the weight of the law, and the second has to do with its meaning. First, in regard to the weight, is the prohibition against stealing absolute, or merely *prima facie?* In other words, are there instances of justifiable stealing? Second, what is the meaning of "stealing"? We all know the obvious examples: breaking into a family's house and taking their goods. But what about other types? Are there types of "stealing" that are legal and yet immoral? When the United States, with 5 percent of the world's population, uses 25 percent of the earth's fossil fuels, is this a kind of stealing? When giant corporations set up headquarters on tiny islands to avoid paying U.S. taxes, is this stealing? When government unfairly taxes one set of its citizens, is this not stealing?

Underlying the commandment not to steal lie three important ideas. First, private property is not inherently evil or prohibited; the work of one's labor is one's own and should not be unjustly taken. Second, as we shall see in more detail in chapter 8, Christians and Jews are to "be on . . . guard against all kinds of greed; for one's life does not consist in the abundance of possessions" (Luke 12:15). We live in a society where greed and acquisitiveness have become virtues and where people are judged not by their character but by their "success" in accumulating wealth. In some ways our society encourages stealing by placing such a high value on material possessions. The sixth commandment reminds us to be on guard against falling into the rampant materialism of our culture.

Third, the command not to steal acts as a positive warrant for helping others. We saw above how John Calvin felt that the prohibition against killing includes actually seeking to protect the life of the neighbor. We might say the same about the prohibition against stealing. If we are prohibited from taking other people's goods, might we also be called to protect their goods and rights? If so, then the prohibition against stealing creates a positive duty to help others. This important commandment reminds us that we are to seek to build a world that protects the products of everyone's labor. It also reminds us to seek a world where stealing is less of a temptation because there are fewer desperately poor people and less materialism and acquisitiveness by those of us who are not poor.

You shall not bear false witness against your neighbor.

Speech is a vital component of human relationships. It is the way in which we reveal ourselves to others and enter into common projects with them. To misuse speech in order to deceive is to hide ourselves from others and to disrupt the harmony of our relationships with them. Lying and untruthfulness entail manipulating and using other people for our purposes. So while most of us would consider lying to be only a strong *prima facie* prohibition, it is nonetheless important to maintain truthfulness in our interactions with others.

Lying is certainly an extension of the seventh commandment. But in its original form, the commandment meant quite literally, "Do not give false testimony in a court of law." In a world without fingerprints, DNA, and taped confessions, the eyewitness was the most important component in criminal cases. In Judaism, a man could be put to death on the testimony of two eyewitnesses (Deut. 17:6). Therefore, to testify falsely in a court of law was a most serious offense. It perverted justice and undermined the integrity of the community. False testimony was taken so seriously that, if discovered, the perjurer himself would receive the punishment he intended for the defendant (Deut. 19:16–19).

As we shall see more fully when we turn to the prophets, the courtroom is the last resort for the poor and powerless. If the judicial system fails to function fairly and equitably, and therefore as an advocate for the marginalized of society, then the alternative community envisioned by God has become like all the other nations where the interests of the rich, popular, and powerful are supported institutionally and the poor and marginalized are left defenseless.

You shall not covet your neighbor's house; you shall not covet your neighbor's wife, or male or female slave, or ox, or donkey, or anything that belongs to your neighbor.

Whereas the first nine commandments have to do with observable actions, the final commandment concerns a matter of the heart. No longer is it enough simply not to steal or murder someone. Now members of the Mosaic covenant are being called to change their very desires. This commandment is the prime example of the call to live as an alternative community. The Jews are called to be a people among whom materialism, power, and status are *not* the driving forces. Covetousness of the good fortune of another person is the symbol of all that God tells the Israelites to leave behind. This commandment is particularly relevant in a time and culture such as ours, in which we are inundated with images and messages trying to convince us to be dissatisfied with what we have. Television, glossy catalogs, billboards, and magazines all tell us that happiness is just one purchase away. And so we covet.

In some ways this commandment acts as a nice bookend to the first commandment prohibiting multiple gods. As the first commandment acts as a foundation for the first table, the last commandment is the culmination of the second table. Murder, false witness, adultery, and stealing are almost always the result of greed and covetousness. If we can put away some of our lust for things, people, and people's things, then the other commandments might be more easily followed.

Connection between the First and Second Tables of the Decalogue

Besides being a summary of Jewish law, the Decalogue is a paradigm of the Jewish understanding of covenant morality. First, the two tables represent the two pillars on which the foundation of covenant life is built. If the people are to be holy, set apart as a new and different kind of community, they must abandon the worship of many gods and cast their lot solely with the Lord. Therefore, the first table of the Decalogue represents this first pillar. But exclusive worship of Yahweh is not sufficient; the people must also treat one another with justice, mercy, and love. This is the second pillar of covenant faith.

We are so accustomed to seeing these two pillars together that we might easily miss the importance of the very fact that they are united in a single set of commandments. As much as the content of the commands themselves, this close connection between God-human relations and human-human relations lies at the core of Jewish and Christian ethics. The unity of these two sets of commandments reflects the understanding that the relationship you have with your neighbor and the relationship you have with God are closely bound. You cannot love God and mistreat your neighbor. Nor is it enough to deal justly with your neighbor, if you ignore the proper worship and reverence of God.

This may sound obvious. But this close connection was not self-apparent to Israel's neighbors, nor is it to many people in our society. In some religions, your relationship with God and your relationship with your neighbor were only distantly connected. For example, in Baalism, if you made the right sacrifices and performed the proper rituals, you would remain in good relationship with Baal. How you treated your fellow human beings was an important but unrelated matter.

Such thinking continues unabated among many Christians today. On the one hand, we all know people who are ardent churchgoers. They say the right prayers and sit on church committees and put money in the collection plate. They feel that their relationship with God is secure. Yet when it comes to how they treat their children, or how they conduct their business affairs or their sex lives, they live in ways that do not reflect a relationship with God. On the flip side, there are those who claim that it is enough to be a "good" person. "I follow the golden rule. God knows what is in my heart. I do not need to go to church or pray or read the Bible." This second type of disconnection between one's relationship with God and one's relationship with others is also a distortion of Jewish and Christian faith. To fail to seek a personal relationship with God is a failure to live up to why God created us. No matter how morally good we are, to live as if there were no God is to live a less than fully human life. As Karl Barth so eloquently put it:

> Real man lives with God as His covenant partner. For God has created him
> to participate in the history in which God is at work with him and he with
> God; to be His partner in this common history of the covenant. He created
> him as His covenant partner. Thus real man does not live a godless life—
> without God.[11]

It is not enough to simply be a good moral person; one must seek a relationship with the true creator of the universe. One must worship, pray, praise, and glorify God.

Love of God and love of neighbor are intricately connected in the Decalogue. In this way, the Ten Commandments are ideally representative of the Jewish and Christian understanding of what it means to be faithful.

Key Theme in the Torah: Protection of the Powerless

The Decalogue deals in rather broad categories. This leaves many questions as to the exact meaning of a commandment. The many other laws found in the Old Testament "flesh out" the skeleton of the Decalogue. To discuss each of these commandments or laws would require a great deal of space. In fact, the great Jewish work called the Talmud, which seeks to interpret all the Old Testament laws, runs to almost six thousand pages in some editions. It is worthwhile, however, to point out a major theme that runs throughout the Torah—the emphasis on protection of the vulnerable and weak.

Many of the laws that God gives to God's alternative community seek to maintain justice in the community. One notion of justice being upheld in these laws is a commonly held one, namely, that if someone does something wrong, he or she must be punished. They must be put to death, be put out of the community, or pay the injured party. This is called *retributive justice,* because retribution is made. What lies behind this conception of justice is the common notion that people should get what they deserve. If you do something wrong, you "deserve" to be punished. For example, if you own an ox or donkey and someone carelessly digs a pit into which it falls, you deserve to be compensated (Exod. 21:33–34). The Bible presents a picture of personal responsibility that is often missing in our own society, where people spend a great deal of time passing the blame and avoiding responsibility for their actions.

The Bible is particularly concerned about ensuring that those persons without economic or political power get what they deserve and are not cheated by those in power. Thus, there is a large number of passages that seek to protect the rights of the orphan, the widow, and the foreigner, all of whom represent the most vulnerable members of society:

> You shall not oppress a resident alien; you know the heart of an alien, for you were aliens in the land of Egypt. (Exod. 23:9)

> You shall not abuse any widow or orphan. If you do abuse them, when they cry out to me, I will surely heed their cry; my wrath will burn, and I will kill you with the sword, and your wives shall become widows and your children orphans. (Exod. 22:22–24)

The logic of this last commandment is arrestingly simple. Mistreat widows and orphans and your wife will become a widow and your children orphans. Widows and orphans represent the most vulnerable members of society. In an age where only adult males could hold land, testify in trials, engage in business, and so forth, widows and orphans were almost completely at the mercy of others. Yahweh is a God who cares deeply about the widows and the orphans; to mistreat these members of the community whom God loves so deeply is a rejection of God.

The Bible calls us to stand up for those who cannot stand up for themselves, to ensure that they get what they deserve. As individuals and as a society we must not show favoritism to the rich and powerful: "You shall not pervert the justice due to your poor in their lawsuits" (Exod. 23:6). "You shall not follow a majority in wrongdoing; when you bear witness in a lawsuit, you shall not side with the majority so as to pervert justice" (Exod. 23:2). The Israelites were once slaves and aliens themselves, as the prologue to the Decalogue reminds them. They should thus seek justice for the slave, the alien, and other vulnerable members of society. As you think about these passages, you may want to explore ways in which our nation or other nations structure themselves to protect the rights and privileges of the rich and powerful rather than the poor and powerless.

But the biblical conception of justice is radically more profound than "getting what you deserve." A remarkable number of laws in the Old Testament display a different understanding. It is not enough for this new alternative community simply to give people what they deserve; they must give them more than they have earned. The Torah contains a number of laws that call God's people not simply to protect the rights of the weak and marginalized, but to actively provide for them, to give them more than they deserve or can contract for:

> If you take your neighbor's cloak in pawn [i.e., as collateral for a loan], you shall restore it before the sun goes down; for it may be your neighbor's only clothing to use as cover; in what else shall that person sleep? And if your neighbor cries out to me, I will listen, for I am compassionate. (Exod. 22:26–27)

> When you reap your harvest in your field and forget a sheaf in the field, you shall not go back to get it; it shall be left for the alien, the orphan, and the widow. . . . When you beat your olive trees, do not strip what is left; it shall be for the alien, the orphan, and the widow. (Deut. 24:19–20)

To show kindness and mercy to those who are vulnerable is not considered voluntary charity by God; it is mandatory. It is just. To take advantage of a poor person by keeping his cloak overnight is an act of injustice. And to greedily squeeze every last dime out of our investments is prohibited because we are actually *obligated* to care for the widow, the orphan, and the alien.

Note the vision of community that lies behind such laws. Too many modern Christians contend that the poor don't "deserve" anything and that people get what they can bargain for. (For example, when was the last time you heard a sermon about unfair labor practices or trade policies?) So often in our society, we are judged by what we produce, by the amount of output we can generate. But this stands in stark contrast to the biblical vision. Unlike the land of Egypt, where a person was defined by what he produced and contributed, in the alternative covenant community a person is defined by his relationship with God, simply by his presence in the faith community. Just because someone is poor and cannot support herself does not make her less worthy or less human.

We see this same concept in the prohibition against lending money at interest to a poor person:

> If any of your kin fall into difficulty and become dependent upon you, you shall support them; they shall live with you as though resident aliens. Do not take interest in advance or otherwise make a profit from them, but fear your God; let them live with you. You shall not lend them your money at interest taken in advance, or provide them food at a profit. (Lev. 25:35–37)

We should not take advantage of those persons who require a loan to live, even if they entered into the loan contract freely. We are prohibited from ever benefiting from the misfortune or poverty of others. We must treat them as human beings by giving their cloaks back at night and by not seizing what they need to live if they must default on a loan (Deut. 24:6).

Caring for the weakest, the marginalized, and the powerless is a characteristic mark of this new community. As Old Testament ethicist Christopher Wright observes, "The economic system was geared institutionally and in principle towards the preservation of a broadly based equality and self-sufficiency of families on the land, and to the protection of the weakest, the poorest and the threatened—and not to the interests of a wealthy, landowning élite minority."[12] People should not always get what they deserve; they should get more than they deserve. Is not this the heart of the good news proclaimed by Jesus? Is not this exactly what Paul means when he preaches that "all have sinned and fall short of the glory of God, and are now justified by his grace as a gift through the redemption that is in Christ Jesus" (Rom. 3:23–24)? The God who gives the Jews more than they deserve, the God who commands us to care for the seemingly undeserving, this same God gives us what we do not deserve—forgiveness and everlasting life. How often do we hear, "It is not fair that I must give up some of my money to other people who aren't working; it is unjust"? Yet we are all too willing to accept what we do not deserve before the throne of God, namely, forgiveness and reconciliation.

Such thinking may appear strange in our larger society, but the Jewish and Christian community is called to be what Stanley Hauerwas calls "resident aliens."[13] We are residents in the larger world, but we are called to live by a different code, to embody an alternative vision of reality. The Mosaic covenant is the charter document for this alternative community.

Sabbath Day, Sabbath Year, and Jubilee Year

Sabbath Day

In the observance of Sabbath day, Sabbath year, and jubilee year we find some of the most profound examples of God's effort to create a radically different kind of community. Let us begin by exploring the command to observe a day of Sabbath:

> Remember the sabbath day, and keep it holy. Six days you shall labor and do all your work. But the seventh day is a sabbath to the LORD your God; you shall not do any work—you, your son or your daughter, your male or female slave, your livestock, or the alien resident in your towns. For in six days the LORD made heaven and earth, the sea, and all that is in them, but rested the seventh day; therefore the LORD blessed the sabbath day and consecrated it. (Exod. 20:8–11)

> Observe the sabbath day and keep it holy, as the LORD your God commanded you. Six days you shall labor and do all your work. But the seventh day is a sabbath to the LORD your God; you shall not do any work—you, or your son or your daughter, or your male or female slave, or your ox or your donkey, or any of your livestock, or the resident alien in your towns, so that your male and female slave may rest as well as you. Remember that you were a slave in the land of Egypt, and the LORD your God brought you out from there with a mighty hand and an outstretched arm; therefore the LORD your God commanded you to keep the sabbath day. (Deut. 5:12–15)

Christians do not take Sabbath observance particularly seriously anymore. But for Jews, the commandment to honor the Sabbath was paradigmatic of their entire covenant faith. It was a vitally important aspect of their faith, for it reflected both their relationship with God and how they were called to relate to one another. We see this in the two reasons given for observing the Sabbath in Exodus and Deuteronomy. In Exodus, the Israelites are called to imitate God who rests on the Sabbath. But what does it mean that God rests on the Sabbath? It is not as if God is tired and needs a break. When God rests on the Sabbath we get a sense of the completeness of creation. God is at peace with the world. There is a fullness or wholeness about the relationship between God and the created order. Jews have a word for this peace and wholeness: *shalom*. Humans are to try to imitate this *shalom* where the compulsive busyness of life, especially the making and consuming of goods can momentarily cease and we can rest in the trust of God's sovereign *hesed* (steadfast love). As Brueggemann notes:

The conduct of Yahweh on the seventh day is in sharp contrast to the world of pharaoh, in which there is no rest but only feverish productivity. The command on Sabbath also looks forward: to a human community, an Israelite community peaceably engaged in neighbor-respecting life that is not madly engaged in production and consumption, but one that knows a limit to such activity so has at the center of its life an enactment of peaceableness that bespeaks the settled rule of Yahweh. . . . Jewishness is indeed an alternative way of being in the world; alternative to the exploitative ways of the world that begin in self-serving idolatry and end in destructive covetousness.[14]

In imitating a God who is different from Pharaoh and other gods, the Israelites "visibly enact" their status as an alternative community. Jews would have stood out very clearly from the rest of the world in their refusal to work on the Sabbath. If nothing else, modern Christians can learn from the worldview that underlies such a practice. What Sabbath observance says is that work, while good, is not the sole purpose of human life, nor is the never-ending acquisition of goods. Sabbath, coming at the end of the week, reflects the Jewish understanding that the end or "goal" of human life is peaceful and worshipful communion with God.

The second reason given for the Sabbath is to remember the slavery in Egypt. In the version of this command given in Deuteronomy, the emphasis is on the equality of all persons. Slaves, foreigners, servants, and even the animals are given the day to rest. In a world of strict hierarchies this would have been an expression of radical egalitarianism.

Sabbath therefore represents both an echo of the *shalom* of the garden of Eden and a foreshadowing of the coming kingdom of God, envisioned by prophets such as Isaiah and proclaimed joyously by Jesus. On the Sabbath, all of the primary relationships that were disrupted by the disobedience of Adam and Eve are temporarily set right. Humans are not exploiting and lording over one another (slaves, children, and women are resting). Humans and the natural order are at peace (no working of the fields, and the animals are given rest). Most importantly, humans are to imitate and rest in God, taking this day to worship God and reflect on God's goodness. On that one day each week, we are to look forward to the peaceable kingdom in which

> the wolf shall live with the lamb,
> the leopard shall lie down with the kid.
>
> . . . .
>
> The nursing child shall play over the hole of the asp,

and the weaned child shall put its hand on the adder's den.
They will not hurt or destroy
on all my holy mountain.

(Isa. 11:6, 8–9)

The observance of this Sabbath day proleptically anticipates the kingdom of God. It marks this community of people as radically different from the world around them in their treatment of one another and their assurance of God's sovereign control over history.

Sabbath Year and Jubilee Year

If the Sabbath day was radical, the Sabbath year was revolutionary. Every seventh year was to be a Sabbath year, and every seventh Sabbath year was a jubilee year. During the Sabbath year:

1. *No crops are planted.* "For six years you shall sow your land and gather in its yield; but the seventh year you shall let it rest and lie fallow, so that the poor of your people may eat; and what they leave the wild animals may eat" (Exod. 23:10–11).[15]

This Sabbath year provision reflects three key faith claims of the Israelites. First, the land is really owned by God, not by human beings (Lev. 25:23). The land that the Israelites have been given is an instrument for the establishment of an alternative community; it is not simply a resource to be used for their own enrichment. Second, business practices themselves should take into account the poor of the land. We might ask ourselves what our modern world would look like if corporations and businesses took an active concern for the poor, if they were as focused on the welfare of their workers as they are on the profits of their shareholders. Third, the observance of the command not to plant in the Sabbath year would require an amazing trust in God's provision on the *sixth* year. In this single Sabbath-year provision, we again see an effort to embody a shalomic reconciliation between human beings, between humans and the earth, and between humans and God.

2. *All debts are to be forgiven.* "Every seventh year you shall grant a remission of debts. And this is the manner of the remission: every creditor shall remit the claim that is held against a neighbor, not exacting it of a neighbor who is a member of the community, because the LORD's remission has been proclaimed" (Deut. 15:1–2). With this law, the Israelites attempted to break the vicious cycle of poverty whereby the rich got richer and the poor poorer. The goal was that the burden of debt would never be so crushing as to create a permanent underclass. As Richard Lowery describes it, the worldview

behind this law is that "God wills that everyone have enough to survive and flourish. Homelessness, starvation, and degrading labor are not 'the way of the world,' immutable laws of the universe that cannot be overturned. Poverty and degradation are unnatural in the sabbath and jubilee view."[16] Besides the implications of this for treatment of poor individuals, the most telling comparison is with debtor nations. In some cases, third-world countries are saddled with crushing debt, sometimes spending up to a third of their entire GNP to pay their debt to first-world nations. What might it mean for a supposedly Christian nation to live by the vision of the Sabbath year in relation to forgiveness of debts?

3. *All Hebrew slaves are set free.* "If a member of your community, whether a Hebrew man or a Hebrew woman, is sold to you and works for you six years, in the seventh year you shall set that person free" (Deut. 15:12). The slaves discussed here are "debt slaves," people who have sold themselves into slavery to pay off a debt. Once again, we see the Hebrew emphasis on mercy and justice; perpetual slavery (for fellow Hebrews) is prohibited.

The jubilee year was to occur every fifty years. In addition to the Sabbath year provisions, in the jubilee year all land that was bought or sold had to be returned to its original, ancestral owners. In ancient Palestine, people were often forced to sell their land because of onerous taxation or simply misfortune. In those days, losing one's land forever almost always entailed a spiral into abject poverty, as land was the primary source of capital and sustenance. Once again, as with the forgiveness of debts, we see that it is not part of God's intention that people be left without means of sustaining themselves so that they fall into dehumanizing poverty. With the jubilee year we find a mechanism by which the community seeks to shield against the winds of misfortune and to mitigate the blind forces of the marketplace. While Scripture upholds the legitimacy of owning private property (as modern-day Christians should, against radical forms of socialism), such ownership is not absolute. For the good of the community, property may need to be redistributed, in keeping with Isaiah's eschatological vision that each person will have a house and a vineyard to call one's own (Isa. 65:21–22).

With the Sabbath day, Sabbath year, and jubilee year we have a manifestation of some of the key themes seen in Genesis 1. The fact that all humans are made in the image of God means that all human beings are essentially equal before God. This is embodied in Sabbath observance that treats male and female, slave and free as equal before God. We also see that, contrary to the portrait in the *Enuma Elish* where humans are created as "slaves" for the gods, Jews and Christians proclaim that unending labor is not the end of human life. Rather, humans are created to be in peaceful and worshipful relationship with their God. Sabbath observance was a unique characteristic of the Jews because they worshiped a unique God.

Holiness and Purity Laws

The observance of the Sabbath day and year would have distinguished Jews from their non-Jewish neighbors. Another set of laws would have done so even more markedly: the ritual purity laws. These laws dealing with purity and holiness are undoubtedly some of the strangest-sounding laws to our modern ears. Found primarily in the book of Leviticus, these commandments demand that the people be "holy" and "pure." In Jewish life, a person is either ritually pure/clean or ritually impure/unclean. Any number of things can make a person ritually impure: eating or touching certain animals, such as pigs, shellfish, rats, flying insects that walk on all fours, birds such as eagles, vultures, and owls; sexual intercourse; childbirth; blood of any kind, including menstrual; dead bodies; skin diseases.

Anyone who comes into contact with one of these things or touches someone who is ritually unclean becomes ritually impure. It is important to recognize that impurity here has little to do with being *physically* dirty. To be ritually pure means to be in a condition whereby one can approach that which is holy. It is to be ready to come into contact with God because one has "separated" oneself from those things that are unclean. Because God is holy and pure,[17] only those things that are ritually pure may approach God: "For I am the LORD your God; sanctify yourselves therefore, and be holy, for I am holy" (Lev. 11:44). Ritual impurity meant that one could not eat with his or her family or have contact with any strictly observant Jew. One could not go out to battle. One could not offer sacrifices to God or enter the temple (when that was built around 950 BCE). In other words, a ritually impure person was temporarily cast out of the covenant community.

What is going on with this very strange set of commandments that involve ritual purity? Should Christians just chalk these up to ancient superstition? It is important to go behind these laws and see what they represent, to move from the law to the principle behind the law. First, we must recognize how the holiness laws depict the *total* claim made by God upon the lives of believers. Everything that people do concerns God: what they eat, what they wear, what they touch. So at minimum the holiness laws reflect the Jews' recognition of God's all-encompassing, all-pervasive concern for their lives. Contemporary Christians might learn from this emphasis on God's claim upon the totality of our lives, as too often we have a tendency to compartmentalize those aspects of life that are "religious" from those that are "secular."

Second, as with so much of the covenant, these laws reflect the Jewish emphasis on becoming an alternative community. To be holy is to be set apart. Part of the concern of these holiness laws is to distinguish the Jews from everyone else. During the period of the Old Testament, you would have known Jews when you saw them because they would eat different things than non-Jews, dress differently, not work on Saturday, and most of all because they would avoid contact with non-Jews, since all non-Jews were considered ritually unclean.

We can see, then, how the holiness laws are an effort to maintain the unique and distinct identity of Israel by prohibiting intermingling with non-Jews (Gentiles) and by not following the ways of the nations around them:

> Do not defile yourselves in any of these ways, for by all these practices the nations I am casting out before you have defiled themselves. . . . So keep my charge not to commit any of these abominations that were done before you, and not to defile yourselves by them: I am the LORD your God. (Lev. 18:24, 30)

Thus, these very strange-sounding laws are one way in which the people of Israel embody their existence as an alternative covenant community. The upholding of ritual purity reflects the importance of maintaining one's religious identity.

Modern Christians are too often indistinguishable from non-Christians. We no longer act differently or speak differently. Even more troubling, we often no longer view the world differently. Too often, American Christians have bought into the militarism, consumerism, cult of youth/beauty, and the individualism of a marketplace mentality that so characterizes our larger culture. In other words, we are no longer an alternative community with a distinct voice and vision.

How Should Christians Employ the Torah?

How should Christians incorporate Old Testament law into their Christian journey? This is a very difficult question. We must avoid two traps. On the one hand, we must avoid simply ignoring or dismissing Old Testament law. Since many of the Torah laws seem very strange and no longer relevant, many individuals ignore the Torah altogether. They read, study, and preach almost exclusively out of the New Testament.

The other danger is to claim that all the Torah laws are still valid. Not only does this ignore the particular context of many Old Testament laws, such a position also fails to appreciate the significance of the life, death, and resurrection of Jesus. According to Paul, Jesus came to liberate us from the bondage of the law. We no longer must fulfill all of the Torah to be found "just" in God's eyes.

Cultic, Civil, and Moral Law

How can Christians faithfully employ the Torah while avoiding these two traps? There are several possible options. The first is to say that some laws still apply while others do not. How are we to do this without simply choosing the ones we like and jettisoning those we do not? A common solution is to divide Old Testament Law into three types: cultic, civil, and moral. *Cultic* (ceremonial) laws are those that have to do with the particular way in which God was worshiped. Laws about sacrifice, temple worship, and holy days are clear examples of cultic laws. Most people place the holiness laws discussed above into this category. The second category of law is *civil* law. These laws have to do with punishments for crimes committed. For example: "When someone causes a field or vineyard to be grazed over, or lets livestock loose to graze in someone else's field, restitution shall be made from the best in the owner's field or vineyard" (Exod. 22:5). The third category is that of *moral* law. This has to do not simply with ritual purity or with civil matters, but with issues of moral behavior.

Many Christians contend that the moral laws are still applicable for all Christians but the civil and cultic laws are not. They argue that civil laws are no longer in effect because the church is not in a position to enforce such laws. Similarly, according to this way of thinking, cultic laws are no longer applicable because they have been abolished with the coming of Christ.

There is certainly some truth to this proposal. First, Christ's sacrifice on the cross is the act by which we are put back into right relationship with God; we no longer are required to remain pure to approach God since Christ has become our mediator and we have been made pure through his sacrifice (Heb. 9:1–10:10). Second, Christ's own actions seem to warrant some distinction between moral laws and the laws of ritual purity. Jesus often criticized those who followed ritual purity laws at the expense of real human welfare, and he himself often violated Jewish cultic law if the need arose.

While the distinction between cultic, civil, and moral requirements is helpful and generally valid, we must not overlook some problems with this hermeneutic (method of biblical interpretation). First, many scholars criticize this distinction as foreign to Jews. In the Old Testament, there does not seem to be such a distinction drawn between different types of law. A quick glance at lists of Old Testament laws reveals that cultic, moral, and civil laws are mixed together (for example, see Lev. 19). A second problem is an offshoot of the first: How are we to decide which laws are moral and which laws are cultic or civil? For example, most people immediately assume that the prohibition against homosexuality is a moral law. However, some scholars argue that it is a cultic law, meant primarily to distinguish the Jews from other nations that practiced homosexuality.[18] While I believe that the distinction between moral and cultic laws is an important one, we must be careful lest we simply assign any law we do not like to the category of laws that we feel are no longer applicable.

Looking for Meaning behind the Law

Rather than trying to apply the commandments directly, some ethicists argue that we should look for the larger principle behind the law and try to live by that. This would correspond, in our discussion of the use of Scripture, with the hermeneutic of "ideal." For example, the following commandment is in Exodus 23:4–6: "When you come upon your enemy's ox or donkey going astray, you shall bring it back. When you see the donkey of one who hates you lying under its burden and you would hold back from setting it free, you must help to set it free." We could easily dismiss this commandment as irrelevant to our lives, since few of us will ever encounter the burdened donkey of our enemy. However, if we seek the larger vision or principle behind this law, it might still be significant for us. In this law we see active concern and love, not just for one's friends but also for one's enemies. This commandment is enmeshed in a view of the world that seeks to break down boundaries between friend and enemy, an approach to the moral life in which my obligation to care for and assist others is enlarged beyond what many would consider "natural justice."

This is only one small example. But as we continue our exploration of Christian ethics, you might want to ask yourself the important question of how Christians should go about using the laws/commandments in the Old Testament. How can we utilize this part of God's word but still recognize that some commandments and laws are context dependent and may have been made obsolete by the coming of Jesus or by changing times? How do we make a sensitive and nuanced use of these commandments without simply picking and choosing the ones we like while discarding those we do not?

Chapter 7

Prophets

Spokespersons for God and Troublers of Israel

Biblical Readings

1 Kings 18–19; 21
Amos (entire book)
Isaiah 65:17–25

Reading Guide

Reading 1: Elijah and the Prophets of Baal

After entering into covenant with the Israelites at Mount Sinai, God led them into the land that God had promised their ancestors (Abraham, Isaac, and Jacob). When the Israelites settled in Israel (then called Canaan), many of the original inhabitants remained there and continued to worship their own gods. Chief among these was a god named Baal. Despite what they were told in the first table of the Decalogue, the Israelites began to worship not just Yahweh but also Baal and other gods such as Asherah. Ahab, a king of Israel, had married a foreign wife named Jezebel and allowed her not only to worship foreign gods but also to build temples to them in Israel, in violation of explicit prohibitions against such actions (Deut. 17:14–17). Elijah, the prophet of Yawheh, is very upset about this and challenges the priests of Baal to a contest. A key line in this account is "How long will you go limping with two different opinions? If the LORD is God, follow him; but if Baal, then follow him" (1 Kgs. 18:21).

Reading 2: Elijah and Naboth's Vineyard

Later in 1 Kings, Ahab takes the land of a man named Naboth and has Naboth killed. Elijah, again, is extremely upset about this event and confronts the king. Naboth refused to sell his land because it was his ancestral inheritance. According to Jewish law, one should not permanently sell the land that God has provided.

Reading 3: Amos

Amos is one of the earliest prophets from whom we have an entire book of writings or "prophecies" (individual sayings or pronouncements). Amos, a simple shepherd and "dresser of sycamore trees," goes to the people of the northern kingdom and strongly criticizes them. When you read the book of Amos, try to identify some of the things that make Amos so angry. Try to connect Amos's criticisms to the laws of the Mosaic covenant that we explored in the previous chapter.

Chapter 1 begins with a denunciation of the nations or cities that surround Israel (Damascus, Gaza, Tyre, Edom, Ammon, Moab). Think about how Amos's readers or hearers would have applauded his criticisms of Israel's enemies. But then Amos drops a bombshell when he turns his wrath upon Israel. Pay special attention to Amos 2:6–7.

Introduction: The Spokespersons for God

Standing behind the Sinai covenant between God and the Israelites was God's desire to establish an alternative community, a community of people that lived as God's special chosen bride, a community where equality, justice, and mercy between people reflected the nation's worship of their God. Because the Israelites worshiped a different kind of God, they were called to be a different kind of nation, a nation unlike all the other nations. But in the decades and centuries following the exodus from Egypt and the Sinai covenant, the nation of Israel failed to live up to its unique calling.

After settling in Canaan (c. 1250 BCE), the land that God had promised them, the people of the covenant become increasingly tempted by the ways and the gods of the nations around them. In an ironic twist, the very land that symbolizes the covenant relationship between God and the Jews leads to a sense of security and self-sufficiency among the Israelites, such that they no longer feel a total and constant need to keep God's commandments. This is especially true as the people demand that God give them a king: "We are determined to have a king over us, so that we also may be like other nations, and that our king may govern us and go out before us and fight our battles" (1 Sam. 8:19–20). This request represents not only a rejection of God who had governed them and fought for them (1 Sam. 8:7) but also a rejection of their special status as an alternative community, as they desire to "be like other nations."

Out of this situation emerge some of the most compelling figures in the Old Testament—the Hebrew prophets. The prophets are not ethically significant because they set new standards or established new laws but because *they call the community back to covenantal faithfulness.* When you think of prophets, you may immediately imagine someone who predicts the future. Certainly this is one aspect of prophecy. But as we shall see, these men and women are not fortune-tellers who look into crystal balls to see the future. Rather, it is better to think of them as "forth-tellers," men and women who speak forth God's words directly to the people. In fact, they are less concerned with the future than with the present and the past. They call individuals and the nation to repent, literally to "turn back," and return to the life of covenant existence outlined by God through Moses on Mount Sinai.

The Hebrew word for prophet is *nabi.* A *nabi* is a messenger or spokesperson. Earlier in the Bible, because of Moses' supposed slowness of speech, God assigns Aaron as his *nabi* (Exod. 4:14–16). The same connotation emerges from the Greek *prophetes,* from which we get the word "prophet": *pro* (for) + *phetes* (is called) = prophet. In both cases, the term is identified as one who "speaks for" another. The most basic understanding of a Hebrew prophet is someone who *speaks for God.* Prophets are God's messengers or spokespeople.

What is the message that God sends through the Hebrew prophets? The actual details of the messages differ according to the time and place of the prophet. However, the core of their message can be summarized quite simply as a call to return to covenant faithfulness. They call the people to return to the kind of relationships that gave them their unique identity as a people of God. Because they are God's chosen people, they must act like it. They must live out the covenant promises they made when they said to Moses, "Everything that the LORD has spoken we will do" (Exod. 19:8).

The call to repentance, not surprisingly, focuses on the two foundations of covenant faith: a call to justice and mercy among the people, and a call for exclusive worship of Yahweh. We shall shortly see how these two are closely connected. For now, let us turn to the two episodes we read concerning Elijah, because these two stories clearly illustrate the central concerns of Hebrew prophets.

Exclusive Worship of Yahweh: Elijah and the Prophets of Baal

It would be wrong to view this story as a battle between Elijah and the prophets of Baal. The real contestants, according to the story, are the true God Yahweh and the "no-god" Baal. Elijah, in some of the most humorous and sarcastic lines in the Bible, plays upon the silence and impotence of Baal by taunting his frenzied prophets: "Cry aloud! Surely he is a god; either he is meditating, or he has wandered away, or he is on a journey, or perhaps he is asleep and must be awakened" (1 Kgs. 18:27). The Hebrew is even more sarcastic, since the words the NRSV translates as "wandered away" are a euphemism for going to the bathroom. Elijah is ridiculing Baal by comparing him to a human being who has to sleep and relieve himself. In other words, Elijah is highlighting how ridiculous it is to worship a god who is really just an image or projection of human beings.

As such a projection, he has no real power. This is brought out dramatically in the story. After Elijah's taunts, the prophets of Baal go into a frenzy of prayer, dance, and self-mutilation. When they stop to see if their frantic efforts have borne fruit, the silence is deafening. The story says, "But there was *no* voice, *no* answer, and *no* response" (18:29). Baal is shown to be unworthy of worship, not a god at all. Then Elijah calls upon Yahweh, the God of "Abraham, Isaac, and Israel [Jacob]," and the response is immediate and overwhelming. The fire is so hot that it even burns the water-soaked ground around the offering.

The key passage in this story actually occurs at the beginning when Elijah addresses the people: "How long will you go limping with two different opinions? If the LORD [Yahweh] is God, follow him; but if Baal, then follow him"(18:21). Here we see one of the two central themes of the Hebrew prophets: exclusive worship of Yahweh. This is not a new theme. We also saw it expressed in the creation narratives' emphasis on the sovereignty of God. We saw it in the first commandment of the first table of the Decalogue. Elijah is not creating a new moral or religious law; he is calling the people back to their original promise to worship Yahweh and Yahweh alone. This is what we mean by a return to covenant faithfulness. The problem is not that the people have abandoned Yahweh for some other god, but that they want to worship "Yahweh and . . . ," in this case, "Yahweh and Baal." Because they lack trust in Yahweh, they want to hedge their bets by making sacrifices to other gods in addition to Yahweh.

Many other Hebrew prophets echo Elijah's call for a return to true and exclusive worship of Yahweh. Hosea, writing a few centuries after Elijah, employs a common prophetic image for Israel—the whore:

> They shall eat, but not be satisfied;
>> they shall play the whore, but not multiply;
> because they have forsaken the LORD
>> to devote themselves to whoredom.
>
> .   .   .   .
> My people consult a piece of wood,
>> and their divining rod gives them oracles.
> For a spirit of whoredom has led them astray,
>> and they have played the whore, forsaking their God.
>
>> (Hos. 4:10–12)

Hosea portrays Israel as a prostitute, whoring herself to any old god that promises her something. For the promise of a little rain or a good crop or protection against her enemies, the people of Israel will lie down and give themselves to any god who happens to come along. Of course, the great irony is that those gods are incapable of providing anything, while throughout history the true God of Israel has provided the Israelites abundantly.

One of the most colorful of Hebrew prophets, Jeremiah, lived several hundred years after Hosea, but he confronted the same problem: the people were dividing their loyalty between Yahweh and other gods. So whereas Jeremiah also compares Israel to a prostitute, he takes the image a step further. In the following passage Jeremiah confronts and mocks the people's love for foreign gods:

> How can you say, "I am not defiled,
>> I have not gone after the Baals?"
> Look at your way in the valley;
>> know what you have done—
> a restive young camel interlacing her tracks,
>> a wild ass at home in the wilderness,
> in her heat sniffing the wind!
>> Who can restrain her lust?
> None who seek her need weary themselves;
>> in her month they will find her.
> Keep your feet from going unshod
>> and your throat from thirst.
> But you said, "It is hopeless,
>> for I have loved strangers,
>> and after them I will go."
>
>> (Jer. 2:23–25)

Jeremiah compares the people to a sex-crazed camel in heat. Israel not only worships the gods that come to her, but she actually seeks out new gods to whom she can give herself. These gods, like male camels, "need not tire themselves" in pursuit of her. She is so unfaithful that she will seek out and find them.

Does the same kind of divided loyalty characterize the contemporary worshipers of Yahweh known as Christians? Few of us are tempted to explicitly worship other gods. But how often is our loyalty divided between God and lesser "gods"? We do not want to abandon the true God, but we want to split our loyalty between God and something else.

The number of other gods in our society is as numerous as the gods of the ancient world. Political party, nation, race, fame, denomination, sex, youthfulness, beauty, popularity, power—all of these can and have been gods that entice us to worship them, to pursue them, to place our trust in them. But all of these gods that we are tempted to call upon are really "no-gods," like the non-god Baal. We spend time pursuing them, we place our trust in them, and what do we get? No answer, no response. These things that we depend upon, that we look to for meaning and significance, have no power. Like Baal, they are unable to do anything; they are incapable of giving our lives meaning. No matter how frantically we dance around and devote ourselves to our job or to money or to our nation, we will be left feeling empty and alone, like the priests of Baal.

Justice, Mercy, and Equality among People: Elijah and Naboth's Vineyard

A second episode out of Elijah's life has the same main characters: Elijah, Ahab, and Jezebel. Once again we see Elijah coming into conflict with the king and his foreign wife. Ahab covets the land of a fellow Israelite named Naboth and offers to buy the land from him for more than it is worth. Kings, in all of their manifestations (industrialists, dictators, CEOs), tend to think that anything and everything is for sale; like Ahab, they simply cannot understand that some things are not to be commodified. But Naboth refuses to sell. He understands that the land that God provided is not a mere commodity to be bought or sold.[1] Ahab then acts like a spoiled child that is "resentful and sullen" (1 Kgs. 21:4) until his wife Jezebel takes charge and cunningly has Naboth brought up on false charges and killed.

In one fell swoop Ahab and Jezebel have violated four of the Ten Commandments. Ahab covets another man's property, Jezebel brings false witness, and both of them commit murder and steal. Such blatant abuse of power may have been commonplace back in Egypt or in the royal courts of Tyre where Jezebel was raised. But Israel is to be an alternative community that practices equality, justice, and mercy among the people. Such behavior cannot be tolerated in Israel. As God's spokesperson, Elijah functions to critique violations of covenant faith. At Mount Carmel he stood up for the first pillar of covenant faithfulness, the exclusive worship of Yahweh. With the story of Naboth's vineyard we see the second central concern of Hebrew prophets—*the practice of justice and mercy among the people*—with particular emphasis on those who are less powerful, less capable of standing up for themselves. Through Elijah, God pronounces a death sentence on both Ahab and Jezebel, a sentence matching the crime.

In these two stories we see the essence of Hebrew prophecy. The primary concern of the Hebrew prophets is to call the people to *repent*. To repent (Hebrew, *shub*) is more than to be "sorry." It literally means to turn back, "retracing one's steps in order to return to the right way."[2] It is as if God sees God's beloved people walking toward a great dark chasm and sends the prophets not simply to warn them but to call them back to the right path, back to a right relationship with their God and with their neighbors.

As we saw in chapter 6, the two pillars of a covenantal relationship are exclusive worship of Yahweh and practicing justice, mercy, and equality among one another. So it is not coincidental that the two central concerns of the Hebrew prophets are the two pillars of covenant faith, since their primary role is to get the people to turn back to God and the covenant.

Amos of Tekoa: "Troubler of Israel"

The function of Hebrew prophets, especially those prior to the exile, is often described as "afflicting the comfortable."[3] In other words, they serve to stir up people who have become complacent, lazy, or lukewarm about their covenantal commitments to God and to neighbor. We see this characterization of prophets in Ahab's address to Elijah: "Is it you, you troubler of Israel?" (1 Kgs. 18:17). The prophets are indeed "troublers of Israel." They are sent to awaken the people from their stupor of comfort and complacency. It is worth quoting at length one of the greatest descriptions of the prophets ever penned, by the Jewish theologian Abraham Heschel:

> We and the prophets have no language in common. To us the moral state of society, for all its stains and spots, seems fair and trim; to the prophet it is dreadful. . . . Our standards are modest; our sense of injustice tolerable, timid; our moral imagination impermanent; yet human violence is interminable, unbearable, permanent. . . . The prophet makes no concession to man's capacity. Exhibiting little understanding for human weakness, he

seems unable to extenuate the culpability of man. Who could bear living in a state of disgust day and night? The conscience builds its confines, is subject to fatigue, longs for comfort, lulling, soothing. Yet those who are hurt, and He Who inhabits eternity, neither slumber nor sleep.[4]

God, who neither slumbers nor sleeps, sends prophets who function as the conscience of the people, stirring up their moral imagination for new ways of living and loving. God sends them to stir up those who are lulled, soothed, and comfortable. They are indeed troublers of Israel.

One of the greatest troublers of Israel was Amos of Tekoa. Amos preached (c. 750 BCE) during a time in which the nation of Israel (by then divided into a southern and northern kingdom) had grown wealthy, secure, and complacent about following the covenant. Into this situation of comfort and satiation came Amos, spokesman for God, prophesying against Mount Zion (which symbolizes Jerusalem, the capital of the southern kingdom) and Mount Samaria (which symbolizes Samaria, the capital of the northern kingdom): "Alas for those who are at ease in Zion, and for those who feel secure on Mount Samaria" (Amos 6:1).

Imagine the following scene. Amos, dressed in his simple, dusty, country clothes, enters into the bustling marketplace of Samaria. He begins preaching on a street corner as people go about their buying and selling. He starts off by criticizing the enemies of Israel, calling down doom upon the heads of the people of Damascus (v. 3), Philistia (v. 6), and Phoenicia (v. 9). By now people are beginning to listen. Amos is preaching what they want to hear; he is ranting about the wickedness of the enemies of Israel. "For three transgressions and for four" God is not going to hold back God's holy wrath but will destroy these wicked peoples. As more Israelites gather around, Amos continues his denunciation of Israel's neighbors. The Ammonites will be destroyed (v. 13) and the Moabites will be wiped out (2:11–12). Amos then claims that the people of Judah are objects of God's wrath. This begins to hit a little closer to home because Judah is the southern section of the once united nation of Israel.

Then Amos drops the bombshell. Just as his audience is ready to proclaim him a true and wonderful prophet of the Lord, he brings down judgment upon them! "Thus says the LORD: For three transgressions of Israel, and for four, I will not revoke the punishment" (Amos 2:6). It is as if Amos is saying that Israel is no better than all those pagan nations that do not know the true God and therefore do not follow the ways of Yahweh. And he immediately begins to bring charges against them, outlining the nature of their sins. Let us now take a look at some of these charges that he levels against them.

Luxurious Living and Injustice toward the Poor

Amos preached during a time of relative prosperity for the Jewish people. Archaeological evidence from that period reveals splendid houses with ornate decorations.[5] In comparison to the rather simple lifestyle of their earlier life in the promised land, Israel has now become fat on "lambs from the flock" and drunk on "wine from bowls":

> Alas for those who lie on beds of ivory,
>> and lounge on their couches,
> and eat lambs from the flock,
>> and calves from the stall;
> who sing idle songs to the sound of the harp,
>> and like David improvise on instruments of music;
> who drink wine from bowls,
>> and anoint themselves with the finest oils,
>> but are not grieved over the ruin of Joseph!
> Therefore they shall now be the first to go into exile,
>> and the revelry of the loungers shall pass away.
>> (Amos 6:4–7)

Amos's complaint is not necessarily that the nation has become wealthy, for God had promised great blessings to the descendants of Abraham. Rather, the problem is that wealth, and the comforts it brings, have led the people to forget or abandon the promises they made concerning justice, mercy, and equality. In their luxurious living, they are blind to the moral and religious disintegration of "Joseph" (Amos uses Joseph, one of the founding fathers of the nation of Israel, to represent the entire nation). This is the heart of Amos's harsh condemnation. The people no longer practice justice and mercy, particularly toward the poor and powerless. It is not coincidental that the very first charge he brings against the people is injustice and lack of compassion:

> They sell the righteous for silver,
>> and the needy for a pair of sandals—
> they who trample the head of the poor into the dust of the earth,
>> and push the afflicted out of the way.
>
> . . . .
> They lay themselves down beside every altar
>> on garments taken in pledge;
> and in the house of their God they drink
>> wine bought with fines they imposed.
>> (Amos 2:6–8)

> Therefore because you trample on the poor
>> and take from them levies of grain,
> you have built houses of hewn stone,
>> but you shall not live in them;
> you have planted pleasant vineyards,
>> but you shall not drink their wine.
>
>> (Amos 5:11)

During the period of prosperity in which Amos preached, not everyone shared equally in the good fortunes of the nation. Both the biblical record and archaeological evidence suggest that, much like our own nation, the rich were getting richer while the poor were getting poorer. More than any previous period of Israel's history, there emerged a greater and greater gap between the haves and the have-nots.

Amos says that the Israelites "sell the righteous for silver, and the needy for a pair of sandals." Increasingly, poor persons had to borrow money from the rich to survive. And in many cases the poor person was forced to leave some collateral, such as her cloak or sandals. If the person could not repay the debt, the lender could keep the collateral or even sell the person into bondage. Amos denounces those who would sell their own neighbor into bondage over the cost of a pair of sandals. Gone is the kind of concern for the poor and the powerless witnessed to in the Mosaic covenant. Now other people's misfortune and poverty are just one more opportunity to enrich oneself.

The keeping of the Sabbath day and the Sabbath year was originally intended to anticipate and symbolize the equality of persons and shalomic harmony between humans, God, and the world. On the Sabbath day, all persons are equal; this includes women, children, and slaves. No one is to work, not even the animals. And during the Sabbath year, the land is to lie uncultivated so that the poor may reap whatever grows naturally. In addition, slaves are set free and debts forgiven. But now the Sabbath, once a symbol of equality and mercy, has become simply an impediment to commerce:

> Hear this, you who trample on the needy
>> and bring to ruin the poor of the land,
> saying, "When will the new moon be over
>> so that we may sell grain;
> and the sabbath,
>> so that we may offer wheat for sale?
> We will make the ephah small and the shekel great,
>> and practice deceit with false balances,

> buying the poor for silver
>> and the needy for a pair of sandals,
>> and selling the sweepings with the wheat"
>
> (Amos 8:4–6)[6]

The people can hardly wait for the worship of Yahweh during the Sabbath and the new moon festival to end so that they can get back to what they truly worship, namely, the making of money. Amos continues his harsh denunciation by leveling strong criticism against the people for unfair business dealings. The merchants cheat with dishonest scales. They boost the price, especially to the poor who have no other options. They even sell the sweepings off the floor along with the wheat.

Amos's harsh condemnation of these business practices may strike many American ears as strange, because what Amos implies is that we are God's people at work as well as in church or synagogue. We cannot divide our lives into discrete segments: our personal lives that are a concern of God and our business-economic lives that are not. Yet how often do we hear the notion that what we do in our jobs and with our money is a separate issue from our worship of God? "I can't run my business using Christian principles." "It's a dog-eat-dog world." Just like Amos's audience, there is a tendency among modern Christians to distinguish what we do with our money or at our jobs from our religious obligations. It is just this kind of hypocrisy that the prophets denounce so stringently.

Finally, Amos is critical of those who live luxuriously because they often do so at the expense of others. This too strikes Americans as unfair. "Look, I worked hard for what I have; it is not my fault if others are poor." What many Americans fail to understand is that much of our wealth is not merely the result of our own hard work but the backbreaking labor of third-world workers. The cheap prices we enjoy for such items as sneakers, coffee, bananas, and clothing are often the result of child labor, cheap immigrant labor, unfair trade practices, and the exploitation of the natural environment in third-world countries. As we can now see, Amos stands in a long Old Testament tradition of understanding justice not merely in terms of marketplace economics ("Those workers agreed to that wage, so it is fair") but in terms of respecting the dignity of persons in recognition of their common humanity—treating them as being made in the image of God. Justice involves creating social systems and practices that protect the poor, the powerless, and the vulnerable from both the whims of bad fortune and the whims of bad people. As we shall shortly see, Jesus himself clearly echoes this prophetic condemnation of luxurious living at the expense of others.

Bribery and Injustice in the Courts

In our time, studies have shown that the most important factor determining whether someone gets sentenced to death in America is how much money he has. There are simply very few wealthy people sitting on death row. The second most important factor is the race of the person killed. You are seven times more likely to be sentenced to death if found guilty of killing a white person as you are for killing a black person.[7]

Despite the fact that America has one of the most just and fair judicial systems in the world, there are still great inequalities. In many countries, bribes and corruption are the rule rather than the exception. In most such cases, it is the powerful and wealthy who are blind to the injustices, because they have the money and power to demand justice for themselves. This seems to have been the situation during Amos's lifetime and in the following centuries, for justice in the courts is a central theme in the message of the Hebrew prophets:

> They hate the one who reproves in the gate,
>   and they abhor the one who speaks the truth.
>
> . . . .
>
> For I know how many are your transgressions,
>   and how great are your sins—
> you who afflict the righteous, who take a bribe,
>   and push aside the needy in the gate.
>   (Amos 5:10, 12)

The city "gate" is where the judge sits to hear civil and criminal cases. But the needy are not able to get their case heard at the gate. They have no voice and therefore no justice. Isaiah, a contemporary of Amos, makes the same charge against the people of Judah (the southern kingdom), accusing them of perverting justice for money:

> Ah, you who are heroes in drinking wine
>   and valiant at mixing drink,
> who acquit the guilty for a bribe,
>   and deprive the innocent of their rights!
>   (Isa. 5:22–23)

By the time of Jeremiah, 250 years later, the situation has not changed. The rich and powerful use their position to grow "fat and sleek," while the widow and orphan are refused justice in the courts:

> Like a cage full of birds,
>   their houses are full of treachery;

therefore they have become great and rich,
    they have grown fat and sleek.
They know no limits in deeds of wickedness;
    they do not judge with justice
the cause of the orphan, to make it prosper,
    and they do not defend the rights of the needy.
                    (Jer. 5:27–28)

Observe how both Jeremiah and Amos exhibit particular concern over the lack of justice for the poor and the fatherless. In all other arenas of life, people on the margins of society are powerless. The widow, the orphan, the sick, the very poor—these people lack political power. Nor can they depend upon their wealth. The only means of defending themselves against the greed and injustice of others is the courtroom. In all other social arenas they are voiceless. In the courtroom their voice ought to be heard; they must receive a hearing. This is why the prophets are so unflinchingly critical of bribes and false witnesses. As we saw in the case of Naboth, if the wealthy and powerful are able to manipulate the court system, then the last refuge for the powerless and poor is corrupted. Their last safeguard against the greed and indifference of the socially and economically powerful is removed. Bruce Birch rightly notes, "It was the judicial system, both the local justice in the gates and the larger judicial apparatus of the monarchy, that should have provided the place for redress of injustice and protection for those who might be exploited by the self-serving interests of others."[8] If the widow and the fatherless can no longer get a fair shake in the courtroom, then the nation has essentially returned to its pre-exodus days. They have returned to Egypt, where power is the only rule and justice is bought and sold.

Justice and Worship Integrally Connected

Amos's primary concerns center around the failure of the people to adhere to the second pillar of covenant faith—justice. As we saw in our exploration of Jewish law, justice involves not simply giving people what they deserve, but caring for those on the margins of society. Does this mean that Amos is not concerned with the first pillar of covenant faith, namely, exclusive (and proper) worship of God? By no means! While Amos does not focus on strict monotheism as much as some other prophets (e.g., Hosea or Malachi), he clearly demonstrates that when it comes to the nature of covenant faith, the two pillars of justice and monotheism cannot be separated. It is simply impossible to be a follower of the true God and not show concern for one's neighbor. Those who worship Yahweh and fail to do justice are, in a very real sense, failing to worship

Yahweh. If they are unconcerned with the fact that widows are starving, if they are deaf to the cries of orphans who are being denied justice in the courts, if they are getting rich at the expense of the poor, then they are worshiping some other god, since our God cares deeply about those people who are considered the outcasts of society. Our God is one who "hates evildoers" and "abhors the bloodthirsty and deceitful" (Ps. 5:5–6). Our God is "merciful and gracious, slow to anger, and abounding in steadfast love and faithfulness," especially for the widow, the orphan, and the lowly (Exod. 34:6). To abuse or disregard such people is to worship some other god whose heart is unmoved by the suffering of the least and lowest. As a piece of ancient Jewish wisdom notes, "He who turns his back away from almsgiving is as if he worshipped idols."[9] As a more recent Jewish scholar puts it, for the prophet, "the frankincense of charity fails to sweeten cruelties. Pomp, the scent of piety, mixed with ruthlessness, is sickening to him [the prophet] who is sleepless and grave."[10]

All of those practices and symbols of human devotion that should be pleasing to God are, in fact, rejected by God because of the people's failure to do justice:

> I hate, I despise your festivals,
> and I take no delight in your solemn assemblies.
>
> . .   . .
>
> Take away from me the noise of your songs;
> I will not listen to the melody of your harps.
> But let justice roll down like waters,
> and righteousness like an everflowing stream.
>
> (Amos 5:21, 23–24)

It is important to note that there is no indication that these songs, assemblies, and feasts were not being properly practiced. Unlike the passage we saw earlier, in which the people are anxiously awaiting the end of the Sabbath and the new moon festival so that they may sell grain and "offer wheat for sale" (Amos 8:5), there is no hint here that the people are performing these acts of devotion to God reluctantly or halfheartedly. Nevertheless, God rejects their worship because justice and righteousness do not flow forth from them. No matter how devoted to God the people are, if they ignore the *second* pillar of covenant faith (justice and mercy), then their worship means nothing. We see this same idea echoed in Isaiah:

> What to me is the multitude of your sacrifices?
> says the LORD;
> I have had enough of burnt offerings of rams
> and the fat of fed beasts;

I do not delight in the blood of bulls
   or of lambs, or of goats.
. . . .
Bringing offerings is futile;
   incense is an abomination to me.
New moon and sabbath and calling of convocation—
   I cannot endure solemn assemblies with iniquity.
Your new moons and your appointed festivals
   my soul hates;
they have become a burden to me,
   I am weary of bearing them.
When you stretch out your hands,
   I will hide my eyes from you;
even though you make many prayers
   I will not listen;
      your hands are full of blood.
Wash yourselves; make yourselves clean;
   remove the evil of your doings
   from before my eyes;
cease to do evil,
   learn to do good;
seek justice,
   rescue the oppressed,
defend the orphan,
   plead for the widow.

(Isa. 1:11, 13–17)

What powerful language! The very feasts that Yahweh had previously commanded the people to keep are now a burden to God. The people lift up their
hands in prayer, but those very hands are covered in the blood of their neighbors, and so God rejects their supplications. We can imagine a modern-day
prophet saying something similar:

I have no pleasure in all your Sunday worship services.
The drone of your sermons only annoys me,
and the smell of your candles is a stench in my nose,
because you pray to me on Sundays
and then worship the gods of money, glory, and power the rest of the
   week.
Your Sunday school classes are a travesty,
for on Sunday you teach your children about love and forgiveness,
but then the rest of the week you demonstrate only greed,
self-interest, indifference, and immorality.

What the prophets' message boils down to is that the people of Israel have failed to live as an alternative community. They have slipped into the ways of the people around them. They have become "like the other nations." Walter Brueggemann argues that the people have fallen into what he calls a "royal consciousness." By this he means a particular way not just of acting but of *being*. The royal consciousness is a total perspective and mode of life. It is characterized by the idea that "might makes right" and that power is the ultimate arbiter of morality. There is an emphasis on maintaining the status quo so that those in power and comfort can remain undisturbed. God is used simply as another mechanism by which those on top justify and consolidate their status. What the prophets do, according to Brueggemann, is to subvert, challenge, and undermine the royal consciousness by calling the people back to their election as a covenant people.[11]

In addition to the concrete issues of social, economic, and judicial justice, the larger message that modern Christians should take from the Old Testament prophets is the warning against accommodating themselves too easily to the ethics of the wider culture. Have we given in to the "royal consciousness" of American culture, viewing the world in terms of conflicting rights where every individual seeks to get as much of the pie as possible? Have we bought into the consumerism, violence, relativism, and marketplace morality of our larger culture? Are Christians at all distinguishable by what they do, say, think, or feel? Or have we become complacent and comfortable in our moral superiority and our assurance that we have God on our side?

Prophecies of Doom and Prophecies of Comfort

I have intentionally waited until now to discuss the role that is most commonly associated with the prophets—foretelling the future. We have now seen that the primary concern of the prophets is not telling the future but calling the people back to covenant faithfulness by pointing up their present failures to live as an alternative community. With this in mind, we should not forget that the prophets often did engage in predicting the future.

We can divide the future predictions of the prophets into two broad categories, depending upon when they preached. In 722 BCE the northern kingdom was overrun by an ancient superpower called the Assyrians and assimilated into the Assyrian Empire. In 586 BCE another superpower, the Babylonians, destroyed the southern kingdom. In so doing, they burned Jerusalem, destroyed the temple, and took most of the leaders and skilled workers back to Babylon. This latter event is known as "the exile." Prophets who preached prior to this watershed event are called "preexilic prophets." Those who came afterward are called "postexilic prophets."

Prophecies of Doom

For those prophets who prophesied in the northern kingdom (Israel) prior to 722 or who came before the exile of the southern kingdom (Judah), the primary prediction concerned the coming destruction of the nation. These preexilic prophets predicted that if the people did not turn aside from their wicked ways, God would use other nations as instruments of punishment. Amos predicted that the people of the northern kingdom would be sent into exile if they continued on their current path. First, he says, their failure to worship Yahweh exclusively will lead them to destruction:

> You have lifted up the shrine of your king,
>> the pedestal of your idols,
>> the star of your god—
>> which you made for yourselves.
> Therefore I will send you into exile beyond Damascus.
>> (Amos 5:26–27 NIV)

Beyond Damascus, the capital of Syria, lies Assyria, waiting to pounce like a bear from her lair (Amos 5:19).

Not surprisingly, it is not just idolatry that Amos warns against but injustice and a failure of mercy:

> Alas for those who lie on beds of ivory,
>> and lounge on their couches,
> and eat lambs from the flock,
>> and calves from the stall.
> . . . .
> Therefore they shall now be the first to go into exile,
>> and the revelry of the loungers shall pass away.
>> (Amos 6:4, 7)

This is a very different kind of ending than the people had expected. Most Israelites, including most of the religious leaders, believed that the "finish line" for the nation would be a great and glorious day. They called this the "day of the LORD," and believed that on that day God would take all of Israel's troubles away and destroy its enemies. But Amos paints a very different portrait of the day of the Lord that awaits an unrepentant Israel:

> Alas for you who desire the day of the LORD!

Why do you want the day of the LORD?
It is darkness, not light;
  as if someone fled from a lion,
  and was met by a bear;
or went into the house and rested a hand against the wall,
  and was bitten by a snake.
Is not the day of the LORD darkness, not light,
  and gloom with no brightness in it?

(Amos 5:18–20)

This all sounds extremely harsh. And it is true that the prophets were unrelenting in their criticism of the people and their leaders. Prophets are not characterized by a tendency toward compromise and meekness, but their harshness grows out of their love for their fellow pilgrims in the faith. Condemnation and love go hand in hand. The prophets' denunciations have a purpose, namely, to get the people to repent. The prophets come in hope that the people will turn away from their wickedness and reorient themselves toward God: "Seek the LORD and live. . . . Seek good and not evil, that you may live" (Amos 5:6, 14). Let us not forget that the prophets are spokespeople for God. It is God who so desperately desires that the chosen people will return. This unrelenting love on God's part reaches its ultimate manifestation in the incarnation of Jesus Christ. God refuses to let people continue in their self-destructive sin. God refuses to accept the "no" that each of us inevitably expresses in our words, actions, and thoughts. God refuses to allow us to live lives of dehumanizing isolation, violence, and self-absorption. God has sent a prophet unlike any prophet before to call us to repent: "For God so loved the world that he gave his only Son, so that everyone who believes in him may not perish but may have eternal life" (John 3:16).

Prophecies of Comfort

But the people of Israel did not turn back; they did not repent and return to the exclusive worship of Yahweh and the practice of justice and mercy among themselves. And so they received a devastating punishment. In 586 BCE, the nation of Babylon wiped out what remained of the original nation of Israel. The Babylonians destroyed Jerusalem, razed to the ground the temple (the most important of Israel's symbols of God's presence), and sent most of the important and skilled people into exile in Babylon. For all intents and purposes, the people returned to the slavery out of which God rescued them. It is as if God were saying that if the people refused to live as an alternative community, unlike nations such as Egypt, then God would allow them to return to their pre-exodus condition.

This turn of events was inconceivable to the people. They believed they were so special and so much more faithful than other nations that nothing like this could happen to them. In fact, all of God's original promises were called into question: land, protection, blessings, and countless descendants.

With the Babylonian exile, the tone of Israelite prophecy changed. The prophets no longer needed to criticize and warn of impending disaster, for disaster had already come with cataclysmic consequences. The tone shifted from one of "afflicting the comfortable" to "comforting the afflicted." Instead of stirring the people out of their complacency, God sent prophets to bring hope and comfort to a devastated people.

The message shifted from the unfaithfulness of Israel to the faithfulness of God. The prophets reminded the people that God had not completely abandoned them. They told the Israelites in captivity (as well as those who remained in Israel to till the ground) that things would eventually get better, that they had paid for their disobedience and therefore God would bring their suffering to an end:

> Comfort, O comfort my people,
>   says your God.
> Speak tenderly to Jerusalem,
>   and cry to her
> that she has served her term,
>   that her penalty is paid,
> that she has received from the LORD's hand
>   double for all her sins.
>
> (Isa. 40:1–2)

For the days are surely coming, says the LORD, when I will restore the fortunes of my people, Israel and Judah, says the LORD, and I will bring them back to the land that I gave to their ancestors and they shall take possession of it. . . . On that day, says the LORD of hosts, I will break the yoke from off his neck, and I will burst his bonds, and strangers shall no more make a servant of him. But they shall serve the LORD their God and David their king, whom I will raise up for them. (Jer. 30:3, 8–9)

In this last prophecy, we begin to glimpse a prophetic role that becomes increasingly important in the New Testament, namely, the foretelling of the coming of a savior or messiah. As a means of comforting the people and bringing them hope in a time of despair, God promises, through the mouth of the prophets, to raise up a king who will usher in a new era in the life of Israel; a time without suffering, death, or hunger; a time when all nations will come to worship the true God in Jerusalem. These prophecies become central to the

New Testament Gospel writers, who declare that Jesus is the savior foretold by the ancient prophets.

Ethical Significance of Prophecies of Doom and Comfort

What can we take away from our discussion of prophecies of doom and prophecies of comfort? What is the ethical significance of the ways in which prophets tell the future? First, in the prophecies of doom, we see how seriously God takes human sins. God will not simply look the other way and allow sin to go unpunished. This is actually an indication of how much care and respect God has for human beings. God does not treat us merely as children who cannot be held accountable for our actions. Because we are free beings, God holds us responsible for what we do and say. If God takes human sin this seriously, so should we. Christians must never take a flippant attitude toward sin. We must not assume that because we are weak that sin is "natural." Nor must we be too quick to rationalize our own sinful actions or those of others. Forgiveness is a core virtue of the Christian life, but forgiveness is not to be equated with indifference. God forgives human sins, but that forgiveness comes at a very high cost for God—the death upon the cross of God's only Son. To fail to take sin seriously is to fail to take the crucifixion of Christ seriously. God holds us accountable; we should hold ourselves and others accountable as well.

If the ethical significance of the prophecies of doom is to take sin seriously, the ethical significance of the prophecies of comfort is to recognize that sin is not the final word. Despite five thousand years of unimaginable persecution, the Jewish people have never failed to maintain their belief that God remains with them and will rescue them. Christians, too, must never fall into the kind of rampant pessimism that so characterizes our society. The postexilic prophets remind us that hope is one of the central virtues of the people of God, not because we are capable of saving ourselves but because our God is faithful, "slow to anger and abounding in steadfast love." Christians must never lose their sense of breathless anticipation of the time when the will of God "will be done on earth as it is in heaven." Even in the midst of the darkness and despair of the exile, God sent prophets to proclaim the good news that the present hardships are not the final word. The people must live into the vision of a new heaven and a new earth:

> For I am about to create new heavens
>   and a new earth;
> the former things shall not be remembered
>   or come to mind.
> But be glad and rejoice forever

in what I am creating;
for I am about to create Jerusalem as a joy,
and its people as a delight.
I will rejoice in Jerusalem,
and delight in my people;
no more shall the sound of weeping be heard in it,
or the cry of distress.
No more shall there be in it
an infant that lives but a few days.

. . . .

They shall build houses and inhabit them;
they shall plant vineyards and eat their fruit.
They shall not build and another inhabit;
they shall not plant and another eat.

. . . .

They shall not labor in vain,
or bear children for calamity;
for they shall be offspring blessed by the LORD—
and their descendants as well.
Before they call I will answer,
while they are yet speaking I will hear.
The wolf and the lamb shall feed together,
the lion shall eat straw like the ox;
but the serpent—its food shall be dust!
They shall not hurt or destroy
on all my holy mountain.
says the LORD.

(Isa. 65:17–25)

This remarkable vision of hope is a confession of faith in the power of God to bring life and newness out of death and darkness. So, too, during the dark days when Israel was occupied and oppressed by the Romans did God send a light shining in the darkness who, like the prophets before him, proclaimed the good news of the kingdom of God. And the resurrection of Jesus from the dead is the ultimate victory of God over the forces of evil. It is the victory of the empty tomb over the cross. To fail to live lives of hopeful anticipation is to live as if the tomb really was not empty on that third day.

Chapter 8

Discipleship and the Teachings of Jesus

Biblical Readings

Mark 1
Gospel of Luke
Matthew 5–7; 25
John 8:1–11; 11:38–44

Reading Guide

Although you may be familiar with stories from the Gospels, it is important that you reread them with fresh eyes. Read the first chapter of Mark to see one account of Jesus' first days of public ministry. Follow this by reading the Sermon on the Mount in Matthew 5–7. Then read the Gospel of Luke. Try to cover at least half of Luke in one sitting, reading the second half in another sitting. This will help you get a better sense of the overall picture and how the entire story hangs together.

In all your reading, try to read the Gospels in light of our subject, ethics. Look for places where Jesus references themes or ideas from the Old Testament. Identify those passages that you feel are most significant for living the Christian life. Highlight things that Jesus does and says that might influence how Christians are to act, live, think, and feel.

Introduction

In one of the earliest stories in the book of Mark, Jesus calls his first disciples:

As Jesus passed along the Sea of Galilee, he saw Simon and his brother Andrew casting a net into the sea—for they were fishermen. And Jesus said to them, "Follow me and I will make you fish for people." And immediately they left their nets and followed him. As he went a little farther, he saw James son of Zebedee and his brother John, who were in their boat mending the nets. Immediately he called them; and they left their father Zebedee in the boat with the hired men, and followed him. (Mark 1:16–20)

Andrew, Simon, James, and John are called to leave everything they know. Jesus asks them to give up their old ways, their financial security, the relative comfort of their homes and friends. In the case of John and James, following Jesus means leaving their father and the rest of their family. All four men are called to give up family, home, and security in order to follow a traveling preacher from a remote village in the north of Israel. To follow Jesus means a total reorientation of their lives.

This event has been reenacted in the lives of millions of believers in the two thousand years since Jesus. To be a Christian means to be a disciple or follower of Jesus Christ. Being a disciple of Jesus Christ means leaving one's "boat" and journeying with Jesus. It is a journey into a new life. We forgo old ways of thinking, being, and doing and we walk beside and behind this preacher from Nazareth. Our lives become transformed when we forgo our old ways and become "new creations," to use Paul's language.

Here we come to the very heart of Christian ethics. In these next few chapters we will explore the place of Jesus Christ in Christian ethics. In doing so, there are several hermeneutical approaches that we could take. We might approach the question of how Jesus Christ shapes the moral life by focusing our attention on:

1. *His teachings.* We could focus on what Jesus taught, seeking to determine the core of Jesus' ethical teachings.
2. *His life and ministry.* We might examine what Jesus did and try to imitate his life in some way. If so, then we would need to determine which aspects of his life should be imitated and how.
3. *His life, death, and resurrection.* Finally, we might place the primary emphasis not simply on what Jesus taught or on what he did, but on the larger significance of his death and resurrection for the lives of Christian believers.

Certainly, these three foci are interrelated. What Jesus taught and how he lived are closely connected. And his death and resurrection are a vindication of his life and teachings. However, for the purposes of our exploration, we will divide our examination of the ethics of Jesus into three parts. The next three chapters will each treat one of these elements: his teachings (chapter 8), his life and ministry (chapter 9), and the significance of his death and resurrection (chapter 10).

Gospels

We begin our exploration by looking at the way in which Jesus is portrayed in the Gospels. A Gospel is a written account of the birth, life, death, and resurrection of Jesus. The Gospel writers all wrote in Greek, and the Greek word for "Gospel" is *euangelion*, which means "good news" or "good message": *eu* (good) + *angelion* (news or message) = good news.[1] This word reflects the attitude and purpose of the Gospel writers. The Gospels are not biographies in our modern sense of the word. The authors are not trying to be totally objective, unbiased reporters of the events they describe. Rather, Matthew, Mark, Luke, and John already believe that this man represents "good news," and they present his life in ways that most clearly depict their understanding of who Jesus is. The writer of the Gospel of John is the most explicit about this, for he clearly indicates the purpose of his writing: "But these are written so that you may come to believe that Jesus is the Messiah, the Son of God, and that through believing you may have life in his name" (John 20:31).

In this chapter we will focus primarily, but not exclusively, on the Gospel of Luke in order to explore Jesus' ethical teachings. This chapter is divided into two main parts. The first part examines Jesus' proclamation of the reign of God. The second focuses on specific ethical issues addressed by Jesus: wealth, sexuality, and the law.

The Core of Jesus' Preaching: The Reign of God

One of the first things we notice when examining the Gospels in search of resources for ethics is the scarcity of commandments and laws, especially in contrast to the many explicit commandments in the Old Testament. Jesus seldom gave direct commands. Instead he spoke primarily in parables, which are short stories in which Jesus compares two things. In fact, Mark says that Jesus *always* spoke to the crowds in parables (Mark 4:11). While this might be an overstatement, since the Gospel of John does not contain a single parable, it does indicate the degree to which Jesus generally avoided replacing the old law with a new set of specific and elaborate commandments. He certainly gave direct commandments at times, some of which we will examine in the coming chapters. But replacing the Torah with a new set of commandments was not the core of his teaching and preaching.

If establishing a new set of commandments was not the heart of Jesus' message, then what was? Some possible answers to this question might be: discipleship, love, liberation, forgiveness, or repentance. While all of these are vital to the teaching of Jesus, a careful examination of his message reveals that what holds all these themes together is the core of his preaching—namely, the reign of God, also known as the kingdom of God or the kingdom of heaven.

The importance of the reign of God is reflected in the sheer number of times that it is mentioned in the Gospel accounts. References to the reign of God occur 14 times in Mark, 37 times in Luke, and 51 times in Matthew. Jesus' very first sermon, according to Mark, concerns the kingdom of God: "Now after John was arrested, Jesus came to Galilee, proclaiming the good news of God, and saying, 'The time is fulfilled, and the kingdom of God has come near; repent, and believe in the good news'" (Mark 1:14–15). Jesus states that the primary purpose for which he was sent is the proclamation of the reign/kingdom of God: "I must proclaim the good news of the kingdom of God to the other cities also; for I was sent for this purpose" (Luke 4:43). Jesus not only preaches about the kingdom himself, but he instructs his disciples to preach about it also: "As you go, proclaim the good news, 'The kingdom of heaven has come near.' Cure the sick, raise the dead, cleanse the lepers, cast out demons" (Matt. 10:7–8).[2]

But what is this reign of God that Jesus preaches so fervently? First, it is an eschatological concept. *Eschatology* is a technical term for the doctrines, beliefs, or study of what happens at the end of time. When Jesus speaks about the reign of God he is talking eschatologically. The reign of God represents what will happen when God brings the present age and the present world to an end. At its most basic, the reign of God is exactly that—it is when God will reign supreme.

You might be thinking, "But doesn't God already reign supreme?" Certainly. As we saw in our discussion of the sovereignty or lordship of God in chapter 5, there is no other god besides the one true God. Nor is there any power that *ultimately* overcomes the will of God. But at present, there are forces and powers that continue to fight against what God desires for the world. Sin, evil, destruction, death, disease, hatred, chaos—these are all forces that futilely attempt to thwart God's plan for the world. Think about how this happens on a more personal level. Most Christians have had the experience of wondering, "Why do I continue to sin, to rebel against God even after I have given my life over to Jesus Christ?" Despite the fact that we turn our will over to God, we continue to press our own will (our desires, goals, and needs) upon God rather than allowing ourselves to be ruled by the will of God. The same is true on a more global level, as the powers of chaos, sin, and evil continue to fight against God.

The Jews of Jesus' time were neither blind nor naive. They knew that the world was not as God had intended it. However, the ancient Jews held on to a hope for the day when God's rule would be completed and fulfilled. Ancient Jews anxiously awaited and expected a time when God would destroy Israel's oppressors, restore the nation of Israel, and bring the entire world under God's absolute and unopposed rule.

This was their *eschatological* hope. We saw this hope in the postexilic prophets, especially in Isaiah, who envisioned a "new heaven and a new earth" where no one will die young, people will live in the houses they build, and where no one will "hurt or destroy on all my holy mountain" (Isa. 65). Jesus stands directly in the line of Old Testament postexilic prophets in his proclamation of the coming of the kingdom of God, a time when God's eternal purposes for human beings and the world will finally come to completion.

The Reign of God: Already Here but Not Yet Complete

Before we take a closer look at the characteristics of the kingdom as proclaimed by Jesus, we might pause to ask, "When will this event occur? When will God create a new heaven and a new earth and establish God's will on earth as it is in heaven?"

This is a very difficult question that has occupied both theologians and everyday believers for millennia. Some people view Jesus as proclaiming that the reign of God had already arrived during his lifetime.[3] Others believe that Jesus was proclaiming a future event. As strange as it might sound, many scholars (including the author of this book) are convinced that both of these are right; it is both already here and not yet complete.

There are places where Jesus refers to the kingdom of God as having already arrived. For example, in Luke 4 Jesus is shown reading a passage from Isaiah in the synagogue in Nazareth. This passage is part of Isaiah's vision of the kingdom of God in which the poor have good news preached to them, prisoners are set free, the oppressed are released, and the blind receive sight. Everyone who heard Jesus read this passage believed that this was a vision of a *future* event. Jesus' brief commentary on this reading could not have been more startling to his audience. Rather than saying, "That time will be wonderful" or "Prepare for that time," Jesus tells them, "Today this scripture has been fulfilled in your hearing" (Luke 4:21). Today. Not tomorrow or next week or next year. The kingdom of God described by Isaiah and awaited so anxiously by all Jews has arrived!

Yet there are other places where Jesus talks about the kingdom of God as a future event. He often tells people to "prepare for" the kingdom of God, an admonition that would be rather strange if the reign of God were already completely here. In fact, when some people ask Jesus when the "end of the age"

will come, Jesus replies, "But about that day and hour no one knows, neither the angels of heaven, nor the Son, but only the Father. . . . Therefore
you also must be ready, for the Son of Man is coming at an unexpected hour"
(Matt. 24:36, 44).

The scriptural evidence points to the conclusion that Jesus held what scholars call an *inaugurated eschatology.* This means that Jesus proclaimed that the
kingdom of God has broken into the world but is not yet complete. The world
has been transformed with the coming of Jesus, but the completion of that
transformation remains in the future. With the birth of Jesus the Messiah,
something radically new has broken into the world. God is with us in a new
way; there is a new covenantal relationship. The victory of God over the sin,
evil, and destruction of human lives is assured, even though more battles are
left to be waged. In the famous formulation by New Testament scholar Oscar
Cullmann, the reign of God is like the D-Day invasion of Normandy during
World War II. After this Allied invasion, the war was essentially over. Nevertheless, there were still objectives to be met and battles to be fought. Only on
V-Day was the victory over Hitler and the Axis powers fully accomplished.
In a similar way, Christians live in an in-between time, between D-Day (the
life, death, and resurrection of Christ) and V-Day (the time when God's reign
on earth is fully and completely established).[4] Ultimately, Christian ethics is
the exploration of how we are to live in response to the inbreaking of God's
kingdom, which has *already* occurred, and in preparation for the final coming of God's reign on earth, which has *not yet* been accomplished.

Characteristics of the Kingdom: What Will This "Reign of God" Look Like?

We have already seen the general outline of the reign of God. It will be a time
when God's will is completely done "on earth as it is in heaven." And we
touched on some characteristics when we saw how Jesus stands in the line of
prophets who proclaimed the coming of a "new heaven and a new earth." But
let us pause to explore this "kingdom" more carefully.

First, the kingdom is a real time and event. It is not merely an attitude or
an ideal. Too often, preachers and scholars talk as if the kingdom is really just
a state of mind. If we simply have Jesus in our hearts, then the kingdom is
here. But most often, Jesus describes the reign of God as a real event, especially its final consummation. The kingdom of God may be hard to recognize
at present, in our world of sin and disobedience. But when it comes to final
fulfillment, it will be a real event and easily recognized. It might look small
right now, like a mustard seed. But when it is complete, it will be clearly visible, like the mustard bush, which "when it has grown . . . is the greatest of

shrubs and becomes a tree" (Matt. 13:32). It is not merely a "spiritual" trans-formation. It will involve the observable transformation of relationships among human beings and between human beings and God. It is the creation of a new heaven and a new earth, as visible and recognizable as the creation of the "old" heaven and earth.

Second, the kingdom of God is related to the notion of heaven but is not identical with it. In some places, the kingdom of God is called the kingdom of heaven and is similar to our current conception of heaven as a place where believers go upon their death. Heaven and the kingdom of God on earth are similar because God's will is completely done in both. However, there are some clear differences between the way we often think about heaven and the way Jesus discusses the kingdom of God. The clearest difference is that whereas we think about heaven as a place where *we go* after we die, the king-dom of God *comes to us*. The kingdom of God is less individualistic than our notion of heaven. It is not merely a place where individuals go, but *a trans-formation of the entire earth*. Christ is going to return and enact a complete establishment of God's sovereign will. So although the two concepts overlap, the kingdom of God is a transformation of this world, not an escape from it.

This relates to a third feature. The kingdom of God is not a result of human efforts; it is an act of God. Human beings can and should prepare themselves for it, but we cannot "bring it in." We can anxiously await it, hope for it, and pray for it, as we do in the Lord's Prayer, but the final coming of the kingdom of God is a unilateral act on the part of the Lord.

Some Jewish communities around the time of Jesus believed that if they were faithful enough and strictly followed Jewish law, then they could help inaugurate the kingdom of God. In the eighteenth and early nineteenth cen-turies, many Christians felt that the kingdom of God was achievable on earth if only advances in education, politics, and social welfare were pursued vig-orously. But nowhere does Jesus make such claims. For Jesus, the completion of the kingdom of God is strictly the work of God.

Fourth, the kingdom of God is revolutionary. It marks a real and dramatic change in the status quo. In the "age to come," Jesus tells us that "many who are first will be last, and the last will be first" (Mark 10:31). In Matthew 21:31, Jesus shocks his listeners when he tells the chief priest and elders, "Truly I tell you, the tax collectors and the prostitutes are going into the kingdom of God ahead of you." The chief priests and elders were the most respected reli-gious leaders of their day. They were the "good church folk." It is as if Jesus were to walk into one of our churches on Sunday morning, point to the dea-cons, elders, and ministers, and say, "The crack addicts and the prostitutes will enter the kingdom of God before you."

The kingdom of God represents a great reversal of the status quo. It is not just a continuation of the current situation but marks a revolutionary and unimaginable reversal. Richard Hays describes it this way: "The appearing of the kingdom of God in Jesus ruptures the status quo, just as new wine bursts old wineskins."[5] Jesus embodies the kingdom of God, and much of his ministry involves subverting the status quo by raising up the outcast, oppressed, and downtrodden and bringing down the rich, proud, and comfortable:

> For all who exalt themselves will be humbled, and those who humble themselves will be exalted. (Luke 14:11)

> Blessed are you who are poor,
>   for yours is the kingdom of God.
> Blessed are you who are hungry now,
>   for you will be filled.
> Blessed are you who weep now,
>   for you will laugh.
> (Luke 6:20–21)

In one of the most compelling of Jesus' parables, he invokes a common image for the kingdom of God—a great wedding feast. His listeners would have immediately recognized this image of the coming kingdom as a time of great celebration and fellowship. But Jesus puts a new twist on the old image. In this parable a man throws a great banquet and invites many guests, all of whom make excuses for not coming. The man then orders his servant: "Go out at once into the streets and lanes of the town and bring in the poor, the crippled, the blind, and the lame." The parable ends with the host saying, "For I tell you, none of those who were [originally] invited will taste my dinner" (Luke 14:15–24).

Jesus himself goes to the lepers, the prostitutes, the tax collectors, and the sinners. His harshest words are reserved for the religious leaders and the apparently "righteous" folk of his time who are too self-righteous to come to the feast that Jesus is preparing. As such, Jesus practices what he preaches about the unexpected reversals in the kingdom of God.

The Kingdom Is Closely Connected to Jesus Himself and His Activity

Jesus proclaims the coming reign or kingdom of God. But Jesus is more than just a messenger for the kingdom. He is also a sign and instrument of the inbreaking kingdom. The elements of Jesus' life and ministry represent the start of the kingdom of God on earth: associating with outcasts, healing, casting out demons, forgiving sins, and resurrecting from the dead.

Jesus Eats with Outcasts and Sinners

One of the characteristics of the kingdom is that unexpected people will be there. Another is that it is often compared to a great wedding banquet. So when Jesus associates and eats with sinners, prostitutes, tax collectors, the unclean, and the unloved, he is embodying the very kingdom that he describes, one in which the first shall be last and the last first. He is living out the notion that divisions and hatreds have no place in the kingdom of God. When God reigns supreme there will be no more divisions between rich and poor, male and female, Gentile and Jew, slave and free. This is why Paul can say that with the coming of Jesus "there is no longer Jew or Greek, there is no longer slave or free, there is no longer male and female; for all of you are one in Christ Jesus" (Gal. 3:28).

Jesus Heals the Sick

A central aspect of Jesus' ministry involves healing. The Gospels depict Jesus healing at least twenty different times in the New Testament. In the ancient world, the sick and handicapped were often ostracized by the community. They were social and religious outcasts, no longer viewed as part of the people of God.

So when Jesus heals these people, he is doing two things, both of which foreshadow the kingdom of God. First, he is demonstrating that there will be no illness in the coming kingdom. This is what Isaiah envisions when he says that in the kingdom of God, "no more shall the sound of weeping be heard in it, or the cry of distress. No more shall there be in it an infant that lives but a few days" (Isa. 65:19–20). When Jesus heals the sick and gives sight to the blind, he is anticipating and initiating the coming kingdom of God in which illness and injury are abolished. Moreover, when Jesus heals, he is also reconstituting the people of God; he is bringing the sufferer back into relationship with the wider community. He is healing not just the individual person but also the community of God.

Jesus Casts Out Demons

We have already seen that the kingdom of God is most clearly characterized by the fact that God's will is completely done; there will no longer be any powers that battle against the sovereign and righteous will of the Lord. While the outcome of the war was never in question, the kingdom of God represents the final victorious battle with evil, destruction, and sin.

Demons are the ultimate representation of those "powers and principalities" that battle against the plan of God. So when Jesus casts out demons he is anticipating, and acting to bring in, the kingdom of God, in which there is no place for any power but God's. Jesus' defeat of demons is a microcosmic representation of Jesus' ultimate defeat of evil on the cross. As Richard Hays puts it:

> The cries of the demons are the sure sign of a cataclysmic disturbance in the cosmic order: "What have you to do with us, Jesus of Nazareth? Have you come to destroy us?" ([Mark] 1:24) The answer is yes: in the coming of Jesus, God has mounted a decisive campaign against the powers of evil that oppress humanity. But the campaign is waged in a mysterious way that no one could have expected, culminating in the cross.[6]

Jesus' defeat of the demons is a foretaste of the final victory of Jesus over the powers of evil that futilely fight against God's kingdom.

Jesus Forgives Sins

The Gospels tell us that Jesus often forgave the sins of people he met. In fact, one of the first miracles described by Luke involves the forgiveness of sins. While Jesus is preaching to a large crowd and healing the sick, a paralyzed man is brought to him. Jesus says to the man, "Friend, your sins are forgiven you." The Pharisees and teachers of the law are astonished, asking, "Who is this who is speaking blasphemies? Who can forgive sins but God alone?" (Luke 5:17–26; see also 7:47). Jesus as both fully God and fully human has the authority to forgive sins on earth. And this, once again, represents a foretaste of the kingdom of God, because the forgiveness of sins represents the reconciliation of humans with their Creator and Lord, which will take place when the kingdom comes. To be forgiven is to be put back into right relationship with God; it is the healing of broken relationships—a brokenness we saw illustrated so vividly in the punishments in the garden of Eden. As in our own human relationships, until there is forgiveness there is no healing between humans and God. The kingdom of God will be an event/time/place in which the all-encompassing and transformative love of God bridges the abyss caused by human rebellion and disobedience. Forgiveness will reconcile humans with God and humans with one another. Jesus models the kingdom and provides a foreshadowing of the final reconciliation through his acts of forgiveness.

Jesus Resurrects from the Dead

In the kingdom of God, death will no longer have a voice, for true death is eternal separation from God. In the most profound of all of Jesus' miracles, he resurrects from the dead. This is the ultimate symbol of his power to bring the kingdom of God into fruition. Certainly, the people he resurrects (Lazarus in John 11:38–44; Jairus's daughter in Luke 8:41–42, 49–56; the widow's son in Luke 7:11–15) die again. The kingdom is not yet fully here. But one day, the resurrected will live forever, never again tasting the unimaginable agony of separation from God. Instead, the kingdom will be a time and place for eternal enjoyment and praise of God.

All of these activities—eating with sinners, healing, casting out demons, forgiving sins, and resurrecting—are closely associated with the coming Messiah. This is made quite clear when John the Baptist sends several of his followers to ask Jesus, "Are you the one who is to come, or are we to wait for another?" (Luke 7:19). In the Greek, "one who is to come" is a single word, *erkomenos*. Many scholars believe that this is a technical term for the Messiah. If that is the case, then what John wants to know is, "Are you the Messiah, or should we expect another?"

Jesus' reply is quite telling. Instead of saying either yes or no, Jesus answers, "Go and tell John what you have seen and heard: the blind receive their sight, the lame walk, the lepers are cleansed, the deaf hear, the dead are raised, the poor have good news preached to them" (Luke 7:22). Jesus understands that John will recognize the signs of the Messiah because they are the same signs as the inbreaking kingdom. Thus, Jesus is giving John his answer: The activities of Jesus are the activities of the Messiah, who initiates the reign of God.

God's Reign as the Foundation of Jesus' Other Teachings

What does all of this kingdom talk have to do with ethics?[7] I contend that the kingdom of God is the foundation for nearly all of Jesus' ethical commands. Certainly, it is not by human effort that the kingdom will arrive. All of Jesus' parables about the kingdom point to an event beyond human control: A master returns unexpectedly, a king returns after giving his servants money to care for, a thief comes in the night. But we are called to prepare for the kingdom. Christians are called to live into, and in light of, the present and future reign of God on earth. We cannot bring it in, but we can live into it. We cannot cause the kingdom of God to come, but we can live in anticipation of it, preparing ourselves for it and living in the assurance that it is breaking in all around us and will one day be completed. As Wolfgang Schrage notes:

> This means that the kingdom of God . . . evokes conduct appropriate to the eschaton [the end time]. The kingdom of God is the foundation of ethics in the sense that it has already irrupted into the present as a joyfully acknowledged discovery, as something that even now brings salvation, joy, and direction.[8]

How do we prepare for the kingdom? The answer to this question is found in two of Jesus' sayings:

> The time is fulfilled, and the kingdom of God has come near; repent, and believe in the good news. (Mark 1:15)

> Keep awake therefore, for you do not know on what day your Lord is coming. . . . Therefore you also must be ready, for the Son of Man is coming at an unexpected hour. . . . Blessed is that slave whom his master will find at work when he arrives. (Matt. 24:42, 44, 46)

To prepare for and live in the light of the kingdom we must repent and do the "work" of the kingdom.

Repentance

Repentance is a central theme of the ethical teaching of Jesus. Luke 13:1–3 records this incident:

> At that very time there were some present who told him about the Galileans whose blood Pilate had mingled with their sacrifices. He asked them, "Do you think that because these Galileans suffered in this way they were worse sinners than all other Galileans? No, I tell you; but unless you repent, you will all perish as they did."

The Greek word used here for repentance is *metanoia*. It comes from the words *meta*, "to change," and *nous*, "mind, attitude, vision." To repent is not merely being sorry for one's deeds or thoughts but rather involves a total reorientation of life toward God. Schrage describes repentance as "an uncompromising, fundamental and ultimate reorientation before God." It is not "just a change of mind but also a change of attitude, of intention, of will, if not a total transformation of one's conduct and orientation."[9]

The kingdom of God is upon us. Jesus urges his disciples to prepare for the reign of God by giving over their lives to God, by repositioning God into the very center of their actions and thoughts. In other words, what Jesus calls for is a "conversion," not from Judaism to Christianity, but from a life of self-righteous self-centeredness to a life of God-centered neighbor love. Repentance, by definition, involves two elements: (1) turning away from the old self and asking forgiveness, and (2) turning toward God and doing God's will.

Turning Away from the Old Self

According to Jesus, repentance involves turning away from one's narrow self-interest and doing the will of the Father. To repent is to put oneself in a position of vulnerability. It is to recognize the need for forgiveness. It is an acknowledgment that we are not truly worthy of acceptance into God's kingdom. The light cast by the glory, beauty, and perfection of God's coming kingdom casts into stark relief the sinfulness and weakness of our old lives.

Jesus' proclamation of forgiveness of sins went hand in hand with his call for repentance. As Schnackenburg explains, "God's readiness to forgive, never preached on such a wide scale in Judaism, and in fact only promised for the last days, is limited by only one condition, repentance."[10] This is why Jesus reserves his harshest words for the proud and self-righteous, those who are unable or unwilling to recognize their own sinfulness. These are the men and women who feel no need to repent and are therefore unwilling to receive the free gift of forgiveness offered by Jesus. We might ask ourselves how similar those scribes and Pharisees are to many people in our day, both inside and outside the church. In our culture, humility and a willingness to admit one's sinfulness and need are not widespread virtues. This is why "guilt" has gotten such a bad reputation. But guilt is a proper emotion when one is indeed guilty and when it results in repentance.

Turning toward God and Doing God's Will

But guilt is not an end in itself. It is a step on the journey. It is not enough simply to turn from the old hatreds, sins, greed, and pride. In his call for repentance, Jesus echoes the sentiment of John the Baptist. Both men urge their listeners to turn their backs on wickedness. But both men also call for visible manifestations of repentance. John warns the crowds who come to him in the desert, "Bear fruits worthy of repentance" (Luke 3:8; see Jesus on "bearing fruit" in Luke 13:6–8 and Matt. 7:15–20). Note how this forerunner of Jesus connects the moral language of virtue ("bear fruit") with the theological language of repentance. John proclaims that it is not enough simply to be sorry for past behavior; repentance involves a metamorphosis from the "old self" to the "new self."

Similarly, Jesus tells the following parable about repentance.

"A man had two sons; he went to the first and said, 'Son, go and work in the vineyard today.' He answered him, 'I will not'; but later he changed his mind and went. The father went to the second and said the same; and he answered, 'I go, sir'; but he did not go. Which of the two did the will of his father?" They said, "The first." (Matt. 21:28–31)

The ones who demonstrate true repentance are not those who merely *say* they are willing to do the will of the Lord, but those who actually bring forth fruits of repentance.

Repentance involves a total transformation of oneself in light of the coming kingdom. It is not simply a transformation of actions but a sanctification and transformation of the heart. The will, the mind, the emotions, the attitudes—all of these are involved in the process of repentance.

Following Jesus and Doing the Work of the Kingdom

Keep awake therefore, for you do not know on what day your Lord is coming. . . . Therefore you also must be ready, for the Son of Man is coming at an unexpected hour. . . . Blessed is that slave whom his master will find at work when he arrives. (Matt. 24:42, 44, 46)

The way to prepare for the coming reign of God is to do the work of the master, to follow the one whose life represents the inbreaking of that reign. For this reason, Jesus calls upon his listeners to help with the work of bringing in the reign of God by *following him*, by becoming disciples. Jesus explicitly connects discipleship with himself and the work of the kingdom.

To another he [Jesus] said, "Follow me." But he said, "Lord, first let me go and bury my father." But Jesus said to him, "Let the dead bury their own dead; but as for you, go and proclaim the kingdom of God." (Luke 9:59–60)

If we want to be in the service of the kingdom, we must give up old ways of living and acting and be ready to make a total commitment to Jesus Christ. The coming reign/kingdom demands total dedication. And since Jesus is now and will be the king of this kingdom, commitment to the kingdom means commitment to Christ.

What is the work that the slaves should be doing in preparation for the return of the master? In other words, how do we, the slaves, prepare for the kingdom? The answer is that we do those things that the master did when he acted to inaugurate the kingdom. The work of the kingdom is the battle against all of those forces that oppose the will of God.

Ministry of Jesus	Overcomes opposition to the will of God in the form of:
Healing the sick	Sickness
Eating with outcasts	Hatred, ostracism, inequality
Casting out demons	Forces of evil
Forgiving sins	Sin
Proclaiming the good news	Despair and hopelessness
Resurrecting from the dead	Death as separation from God[11]

We get ready for the kingdom by battling sickness, hatred, evil, sin, despair, and death. We do all of those things that Jesus did when he inaugurated the reign of God. In other words, we become what Paul calls the "body of Christ" on earth. We become the eyes, feet, hands, and mouth of Jesus by doing what he did.

If we want to prepare for the coming reign/kingdom, we seek to *heal*. We may not be called to perform physical healings as Jesus did, but we are certainly called to prepare for the kingdom by working toward a transformation of the social conditions that cause physical illness. And we work toward the kingdom when we seek to implement programs whereby health and healing can take place, whether that be physical healing or the healing of broken relationships, mental illness, or spiritual sickness.

If we are to do the work of the kingdom, we must *overcome hatred, injustice, and violence* by siding with the outcast, the powerless, and the unpopular. We learn to love not just our friends and relatives but the stranger and the enemy. We should prepare for and work as hard for peace as we inevitably do for war, since the kingdom of God is a "peaceable kingdom" where "the wolf shall live with the lamb, . . . the nursing child shall play over the hole of the asp, and the weaned child shall put its hand on the adder's den" (Isa. 11:6, 8).

We keep awake for the kingdom when we fight against evil and sin. We stand in opposition to all of those social, political, and economic powers and principalities that seek to destroy people by disrupting relationships. We prepare for the reign of God by preaching the good news that in Jesus Christ love has overcome evil.

The coming and present kingdom is one of reconciliation and love. While there are periodic references to violence and upheaval in relation to the transition to the reign or kingdom of God (see Luke 21:5–28), these are overshadowed by the image of the reign of God as one of harmony and love. Jesus' entire ministry can be characterized as one of healing broken relationships: between human beings and between human beings and God. No longer are we estranged from God and neighbor. With the inbreaking reign of God that Jesus initiates, we have moved beyond the state of affairs described in Genesis 3 that resulted from the disobedience of the first humans. Jesus brings peace and reconciliation where there was once animosity and division. The relationship between God and humans has been mended, and human beings are being reconciled with one another.

Finally, we prepare for the kingdom by proclaiming the good news of this kingdom and the good news of Jesus Christ to the world. Evangelism is part of our ethical duty. We are to spread the good news of the kingdom of God in a world where bad news, evil, and despair threaten to overwhelm us. We are to tell the spiritually poor that in Jesus Christ the old ways are being destroyed and that they can become new creations if they believe in him and the Father who sent him. We are also called to evangelize to the world by living as a light in the darkness, as a city on the hill demonstrating to the world an alternative to the violence, hatred, and self-seeking that lead only to death. As the great Mennonite writer John Howard Yoder puts it, the proclamation of the kingdom of God calls us to a

> visible, socio-political, economic restructuring of relations among the people of God, achieved by divine intervention in the person of Jesus as the one Anointed and endued with the Spirit . . . a movement, extending his personality in both time and space, presenting an alternative to the structures that were there before, challeng[ing] the system as no mere words ever could.[12]

The kingdom of God involves the defeat of hatred, sickness, violence, the forces of demons, despair, and death. It is not just coincidence that when Jesus sends out his disciples, he connects all these actions with the kingdom of God: "As you go, proclaim the good news, 'The kingdom of heaven has come near.' Cure the sick, raise the dead, cleanse the lepers, cast out demons" (Matt. 10:7–8). All of the actions are manifestations of the reign of God and foreshadow the time when the kingdom or reign of God will be here in all its glorious fullness. All of these ministries that Jesus commands his disciples to perform represent the will of God overcoming the forces that act to hinder God's purpose for creation, namely, fellowship. God wills that we live lives of self-giving, mutual love with God and with one another. This is the "will" that shall be "done on earth as it is in heaven." Just like those disciples that Jesus sends out, Christians prepare for the kingdom by acting in opposition to those forces that function to destroy the purposes of God. At the very heart of Christian ethics is our obligation to work toward the kingdom of God. We do so by engaging in those ministries that occupied our Lord, but we also must develop those virtues that he embodied, virtues that correspond to a time when humans will no longer experience separation from God and one another as the result of sin. Clearly, the predominant virtue of the kingdom is love, which we shall explore in more detail in chapter 9.

Beyond these more general teachings about repentance, discipleship, and love, Jesus also taught about specific aspects of life in a world where the kingdom of God is breaking in. Let us now turn to Jesus' teaching on wealth, sexuality, and the law.

Jesus on Property and Wealth

Contrary to the popular depiction of Jesus as being concerned only with "spiritual" things, Jesus has a great deal to say about issues involving money, wealth, poverty, and greed. The proper use of our financial resources and the development of a proper attitude toward them are important ways of living out and preparing for God's kingdom on earth. We must be careful about falling into extremes when dealing with Jesus' attitude toward money. On the one hand, Jesus is not an ascetic. On the other hand, he is very suspicious of the dangers that almost inevitably attend the acquisition of money and possessions.

Jesus Was not an Ascetic

An ascetic is someone who consistently denies bodily pleasures such as good food, expensive clothing, entertainment, and other comforts associated with enjoying life. During the time of Jesus there were some Jews who sought to live a life of total self-denial. The community of Jews who wrote the Dead Sea Scrolls in the years before and after Jesus appear to have led a very ascetic lifestyle in the desert cliff-tops surrounding the Dead Sea.

Many Christians also have taken the ascetic route. After Christianity became the official religion of the Roman Empire in 313 CE, many Christians saw asceticism as a kind of self-sacrifice analogous to the martyrdom of the previous centuries. This "putting to death" of the desires of the self is nicely described in the following passage:

> They stretched out on the bare earth, rather than on beds,
> and they rest their heads on rocks, rather than on soft cushions.
> They put the herbs they eat for food
> on their knees, instead of on tables at meal-time.
> Instead of wine, they drink water;
> instead of ointments and creams on their body, there is squalor.
> Their bodies become dark for the love of Christ.[13]

While Jesus' journey into the desert for forty days and forty nights may represent a period of temporary self-denial, it is clear that Jesus was not an ascetic. In fact, in Luke 7:34, Jesus is accused of being a "glutton and a drunkard," a charge that while inaccurate, would have been completely absurd if Jesus had lived a life of total self-denial.

Moreover, on a number of occasions we find Jesus drinking wine and feasting in the houses of followers and the merely curious. Jesus sometimes accepted the hospitality of wealthy patrons, eating in their homes (Luke 7:36; 14:1), and the Gospel of John depicts Jesus celebrating at a wedding feast in

Cana, where he changes water into wine for the guests, certainly a strange miracle if he were an ascetic (John 2:1–11). Finally, in John 12:1–11, Jesus defends a woman who places expensive perfume on his head and feet. While this is certainly a symbolic representation of Jesus' preparation for his own death (since dead bodies were anointed with oil and spices before burial), it is also an indication that Jesus did not condemn all pleasures.

The Danger of Wealth: Poverty and Generosity as Ideals

On the other hand, Jesus repeatedly warns against the dangers and pitfalls of money. It is not too much to say that for Jesus, wealth represents one of the greatest hindrances to accepting him and his message of the kingdom of God. In the Sermon on the Plain, Jesus says:

> Blessed are you who are poor,
>   for yours is the kingdom of God.
> Blessed are you who are hungry now,
>   for you will be filled.
> . . . .
> But woe to you who are rich,
>   for you have received your consolation.
> Woe to you who are full now,
>   for you will be hungry.
>   (Luke 6:20–21, 24–25)

To a rich man who wishes to inherit eternal life and who has followed all the other commandments, Jesus gives a new command: "There is still one thing lacking. Sell all that you own and distribute the money to the poor, and you will have treasure in heaven; then come, follow me." When the man goes away sad, Jesus makes a remarkable statement: "How hard it is for those who have wealth to enter the kingdom of God! Indeed, it is easier for a camel to go through the eye of a needle than for someone who is rich to enter the kingdom of God" (Luke 18:18–25). And in one of the few places where Jesus talks about hell/damnation, he does so in the context of a discussion about wealth and poverty (Luke 16:19–31).

What can we draw from Jesus' repeated warnings about wealth in light of the fact that he rejects asceticism? As Clement of Alexandria observed as early as the second century:

> It is not what some hastily take it to be, a command to fling away the substance that belongs to him and to part with his riches, but to banish from the soul its opinions about riches, its attachment to them, its excessive desire,

its morbid excitement over them, its anxious cares, the thorns of our earthly existence which choke the seed of the true life.[14]

The danger of money lies in the attitude that almost always attends its acquisition. It is not wealth per se that makes it difficult for a person to enter the kingdom of God. Rather, it is the grasping after riches and the sense of self-sufficiency that accompany the accumulation of money. This is why the poor are often able to hear the message of Jesus and the ears of the rich remain closed. Poor persons can be just as immoral and greedy as rich persons. However, the poor are often in a better position to acknowledge their dependence upon God. Wealth and comfort can easily lead to both pride and self-righteousness.

Why are wealth and comfort such temptations and dangers in the Christian life? The answer lies in the fact that they can so easily hinder us from being the persons God intended. From the very beginning God has created human beings for covenant life. We are created for the dual ends of loving God and being in relationships of self-giving love with our neighbors. Wealth can easily hinder both of these sets of relationships, and thus work against the establishment of the reign of God. Money and its acquisition easily lend themselves to violations of both pillars of covenant faith—namely, the exclusive (and right) worship of God, and the practice of justice, mercy, and love toward neighbor.

Money and relationship with God: A focus on material riches at the expense of a focus on God   One danger of money is that the pursuit of wealth distracts us from worshiping, serving, and trusting God. Jesus tells us, "You cannot serve God and wealth" (Luke 16:13). He tells some of his followers, "Sell your possessions, and give alms. Make purses for yourselves that do not wear out, an unfailing treasure in heaven, where no thief comes near and no moth destroys. For where your treasure is, there your heart will be also" (Luke 12:33–34). Jesus sees money as such a danger because our energy and time are spent chasing after wealth under the delusion that it will provide happiness and a sense of security. We begin to place our ultimate trust in wealth and material possessions. But Jesus stresses that "one's life does not consist in the abundance of possessions" (Luke 12:15). To illustrate the dangers of greed, Jesus tells a parable that stresses the importance of building our relationship with God, rather than building up our bank accounts:

> The land of a rich man produced abundantly. And he thought to himself, "What should I do, for I have no place to store my crops?" Then he said, "I will do this: I will pull down my barns and build larger ones, and there I will store all my grain and my goods. And I will say to my soul, 'Soul, you

have ample goods laid up for many years; relax, eat, drink, be merry.'" But God said to him, "You fool! This very night your life is being demanded of you. And the things you have prepared, whose will they be?" So it is with those who store up treasures for themselves but are not rich toward God. (Luke 12:16–21)

Recall that every seventh year, Israelites were required to demonstrate their trust in God by not planting any crops. In contrast, the foolish man places his trust and security in his possessions. He spends his life worrying about his future financial security at the expense of his relationship with God. He is never satisfied. He wants to build bigger and bigger barns as security for himself. When his life is demanded of him that "very night," he has nothing to fall back on. His grain and his goods and his bigger barns do not make him "rich toward God."

Money and relationship with our fellow creatures
Covetousness and greed—   In the kingdom of God, there is no "rich and poor." Think back to Isaiah's vision of the kingdom, where people "shall build houses and inhabit them. . . . They shall not build and another inhabit" (Isa. 65:21–22). Money and greed not only represent a danger to our relationship with God but also can be the source of great hatred and division between human beings. Think to yourself how many of the world's problems are due to money. On the personal level, money is often the cause of the breakup of friendships and families. A husband and wife fight over and even divorce because of financial issues. Mothers or fathers spend so much time at work that they never see their children grow up. Friendships dissolve because one friend is too stingy or the other is too covetous. And on the social level, many, if not most, of the problems within nations and between nations have to do with wealth and the injustice and violence that so often surround it.

The Decalogue ends with a command against coveting, and Jesus himself warns against the dangers of greed: "Take care! Be on your guard against all kinds of greed" (Luke 12:15). Enough never seems to be enough, particularly for Americans and Europeans. We live in a culture that bombards us with advertisements implying that happiness is just one purchase away. The goal of corporations and their advertisers is to make people dissatisfied, so that they can sell them products which will alleviate their discontent. In a society driven by consumerism and materialism, greed has taken on the character of a virtue. We are encouraged to be dissatisfied with what we have been given and are manipulated into believing that we "need" more and more. This greed leads us to all kinds of actions and inactions that separate us from our friends and neighbors. Rather than creating a world that resembles God's coming reign, one in which we seek to be reconciled with God and neighbor, by our greed and covetousness we focus on self. Rather than furthering the kingdom, we hinder it by our constant acquisitiveness.

Wealth is often attained at the expense of justice— America has often been a land of opportunity for the dispossessed and a beacon of equality and freedom for the oppressed of the world. But we should be careful about assuming that our high standard of living is free of guilt. The hamburger we ate for lunch may have come at the expense of South American rain forests that are cleared to satisfy the ravenous American appetite for beef. The diamond and gold engagement ring we gave our loved one may have been made from products sold to support civil wars in Sudan, Liberia, and other African nations. The shirts we wear and the shoes we play in are often produced by sweatshop workers, child laborers, or underpaid immigrants. And with less than 5 percent of the world's population, Americans use 25 percent of the world's natural resources. Moreover, tragically, a great deal of American prosperity is at the expense of a history of slave labor and the genocide of the original inhabitants of the land. Surely the ancient Israelites said to Amos, Jeremiah, and Isaiah that they had worked hard for their wealth, that they had not "trampled on the heads of the poor," just as we Americans are quick to do. But as Ronald Sider observes, "Are we not guilty of greed when we demand an ever-higher standard of living while neglecting millions of children who are starving to death each year?"[15]

We are to work toward God's kingdom on earth. That kingdom is one of justice and peace. It is also one where infants do not die from malnutrition, where women are not forced to sell their bodies to feed their families, where third-world farmers can get a fair price for their crops, and where more than a billion people do not have to live on less than a single dollar a day. Christian wealth should not be an obstacle to our relationships with others; it should be an instrument for creating a world that reflects God's coming reign on earth. Nowhere does Jesus call for the abolishment of private property and money, as he himself depended upon wealthy patrons to support his ministry (Luke 8:1–3). However, wealth and an abundance of material goods represent one of the greatest dangers and temptations in the Christian life. How do we avoid such dangers and use our money to further, rather than hinder, God's kingdom?

How should Christians respond? If wealth is such a danger, then generosity is the ideal. In order to express the fact that they do not worship money, the followers of Christ should demonstrate generosity and economic charity as outward manifestations of their inward attitude.

Clement of Alexandria was right in saying that it is not the having of money which is immoral, but one's attitude toward it, for even poor people can be greedy and covetous. However, we should be careful about moving too quickly to this interpretation without feeling the full impact of Jesus' condemnation of wealth. Jesus intentionally chose a metaphor that makes it seem nearly impossible to have wealth and still be saved. He says that it is as impossible as a camel going through the eye of a needle. It *is* possible to enter into God's kingdom as a wealthy person, but it is extremely difficult. And the only way that it is possible is with God's help.

Too often, middle-class Christians assume that Jesus' warnings are directed only at the "mega-rich," such as Bill Gates and Donald Trump. But in the larger scheme of things, practically everyone who is reading this book is rich by the standards of the world. For example, the per capita Gross National Product in 1993 for Americans was $24,750, while in India (with approximately one billion people) the GNP was $300. While a dollar can buy more in India than America, as Sider notes, "That would be like trying to live in the U.S. on less than $110 a month!"[16]

We should be clear then that when Jesus warns against the dangers of wealth, it is not directed merely at those living in Beverly Hills or on Park Avenue. It is directed at all of us, who by comparison to the vast majority of the world, are rich and well fed. Few of us have ever known real hunger; even fewer of us could imagine the life of the Alarin family. Mr. Alarin works as an ice vendor in the Philippines, making about 70 cents a day. Mrs. Alarin supplements their income by staying up at night making coconut candy, which she sells for about 40 cents a day. When the president of World Vision visited their one-room hut, Mrs. Alarin told him, "I feel so sad when my children cry at night because they have no food. I know my life will never change. What can I do to solve my problems? I want my children to go to school, but how can we afford it? I am sick most of the time, but I can't go to the doctor because each visit costs two pesos."[17] (Two pesos is equal to about 40 cents.)

Generosity is the key to the economic life of Christians. Our wealth can be an instrument for the furtherance of God's kingdom. We can use it to do those things that Jesus did in bringing about the kingdom: healing the sick, feeding the hungry, evangelizing (spreading the good news), and so forth. Making money and having private property are not evil if they are used to further God's kingdom. If we can live more simply so that others may simply live, we are showing where our hearts lie.

Furthermore, it is important that generosity not be confined to giving to charities. To be generous is to work toward changing social systems that cause poverty and injustice in the first place. It means standing in solidarity with the poor and oppressed against self-serving politicians, against multinational corporations when they focus solely on profit, against international policies that seek to perpetuate a system in which the rich get ever richer at the expense of the poor. Such solidarity may be difficult when push comes to shove. Ask yourself if you would be willing to vote for a policy, plan, or tax that was economically detrimental to you but helpful for the community. Would you be willing to support a shelter for battered women in your neighborhood even if it might lower your property value? Would you be willing to vote for raising the minimum wage even if it might make some items more expensive for you? Would you be ready to vote for a system that guaranteed universal health care if it required additional taxes?

Obviously, the details of such hypothetical propositions would need to be illuminated. Yet it is important to at least think about what a more generous social attitude might look like. To begin to develop a sense of economic and social generosity is the beginning of a life where, like Jesus, we associate with the poor, the outcast, and the sinner. We must work toward the vision of God's kingdom on earth, where injustice, hunger, and dehumanizing poverty are replaced with compassionate love and justice.

Jesus on Sexual Ethics

If you were to listen to many preachers and religious commentators today, you would think that sexual issues were at the heart of Jesus' moral message. In fact, Jesus had remarkably little to say about matters pertaining to sexuality. And the few passages where he does discuss issues of marriage and sexual relations are usually the result of being asked a question by someone else. Otherwise, the record of Jesus on most of the issues surrounding marriage, family, and sexual conduct is surprisingly sparse.

It is difficult to know how to interpret Jesus' relative silence. Arguments from silence are notoriously unreliable. Take the hotly debated issue of homosexuality, for example. There is no reported saying of Jesus on this issue. How are we to interpret his apparent silence? Those who favor a more sympathetic stance toward homosexuality argue that the harsh condemnation of homosexuality in some conservative churches is misplaced, given the fact that Jesus is silent on the issue. On the other side, those who condemn homosexuality interpret Jesus' silence differently. They argue that Jesus is tacitly agreeing with the prevailing cultural and religious stance toward homosexuality among his contemporaries. Appealing to the more explicit condemnations in other parts of the New Testament, they argue that there was no need for Jesus to teach about something that was universally condemned by Jewish teachers.

The fact that Jesus has relatively little to say regarding sexual ethics may be interpreted similarly. Some conclude that sexual ethics was not central to Jesus' message, while others conclude that Jesus' silence represents a tacit approval of the sexual norms of his first-century Jewish context.

However, on two issues of sexual ethics—namely, adultery and divorce—we have more concrete evidence of Jesus' attitude. Jesus clearly condemns and forbids divorce. According to Jewish teaching, a man may divorce his wife if he presents her with a bill of divorce that would allow her to remarry (Deut. 24:1–2). During Jesus' day, some Jews, such as Rabbi Shimmei, prohibited divorce except in the case of adultery. However, a great many Jews believed that it was acceptable for a man to divorce his wife for almost any reason. Rabbi Hillel held that a burnt dinner was legitimate grounds for divorce and Rabbi Akiva said that a man could divorce his wife if he found another woman who is more beautiful. In the context of such views Jesus says:

> It was also said, "Whoever divorces his wife, let him give her a certificate of divorce." But I say to you that anyone who divorces his wife, except on the ground of unchastity, causes her to commit adultery; and whoever marries a divorced woman commits adultery. (Matt. 5:31–32)

This is a very stringent stance on the part of Jesus. In fact, in the Markan and Lukan version of this saying, divorce is forbidden even in the case of adultery (see Mark 10:11–12; Luke 16:18).

At first glance this seems extremely strict. But many scholars, such as the author of this book, believe that this prohibition must be read in its cultural context. During Jesus' time, divorce was a devastating event for a woman. Very few men would marry a divorced woman. And since there was little possibility for women to gain employment, divorce left many women destitute and helpless. With this in mind, what appears to be a harsh and unfeeling statement on the part of Jesus is actually a way of protecting women. No longer can men discard women at will, rendering them social outcasts. As is so often the case, Jesus is here displaying his unrelenting concern for the less powerful. This prohibition against divorce, therefore, represents Jesus' effort to protect the weaker members of society against the whims of the more powerful ones. This interpretation is supported by another saying of Jesus in which he declares that "in the resurrection they neither marry nor are given in marriage" (Matt. 22:30). Because ancient marriages were hierarchical power arrangements in which men were dominant over women and children, there will be no such relationships in the kingdom of God (or at the resurrection).

If this reading is correct, then Jesus' prohibition may not apply directly to the contemporary situation. Rather than appealing to the law itself, we must try to get behind the law to its larger principle (see the discussion of the uses of Scripture in chapter 4). The principle behind Jesus' prohibition is the protection of people's dignity. Therefore, it is hard to imagine that Jesus would counsel a woman to stay in a marriage in which she or her children were being abused, especially if all other avenues had been sought to change the behavior of her husband.

Other than divorce, the only thing that Jesus says directly concerning sexuality is his condemnation of adultery. We saw an implicit condemnation in his discussion of divorce, and we see it also in the story of the woman caught in adultery. Jesus tells the crowd that wants to stone her that the person without sin can cast the first stone. When everyone leaves, Jesus tells the woman, "Go your way, and from now on do not sin again" (John 8:11).

What contemporary ethical implications can we draw from this story? We find that while adultery is not an unpardonable sin, it is a sin. It is not to be winked at or condoned, despite the way our culture so often treats it in film and other media. Jesus takes seriously the vow of marriage, and therefore divorce and adultery are extremely serious actions. Frivolous divorce and any kind of adultery are sins. Jesus holds marriage as a God-ordained and holy relationship. He says that

> from the beginning of creation, "God made them male and female." "For this reason a man shall leave his father and mother and be joined to his wife, and the two shall become one flesh." So they are no longer two, but one flesh. Therefore what God has joined together, let no one separate. (Mark 10:6–9)

As with any sin, we must not forget that the final word is one of forgiveness on the part of God. Adultery and divorce are the cause of devastating pain and confusion. Therefore, it is particularly important that our Christian churches live out the call to proclaim God's loving forgiveness and that they provide a place for the healing caused by the breakdown of that most intimate of relationships, the family.

Jesus on Family

This brings us to the related issue of Jesus' attitude toward the family. Throughout the 1980s and 1990s, a movement calling itself the "family values" movement gained much support. The Center for Traditional American Family Values and James Dobson's Focus on the Family are just two well-known examples. Such groups seek to create a type of family-centered ethics.

These groups have done some valuable work. Yet it is a bit startling when we look at Jesus' actual sayings in regard to the family. This is to say that Jesus was a rather strange "family man." First, he did not marry, a very unusual life choice for a Jewish male in the first century. To marry and have children was not optional in traditional Jewish culture; it was a commandment (*mitzvot*) derived from the very first commandment in the Torah: "Be fruitful and multiply" (Gen. 1:22). Jewish ethicist Eugene Borowitz notes that "for Judaism, marriage is an overwhelmingly important human *duty* and spousal intercourse is intimately bound up with its fulfillment."[18]

Not only was Jesus not married, but he sometimes appears to downplay the importance of family ties. In Luke 8:19–21, Jesus replies to someone who tells him that his mother and brothers have come to see him, "My mother and my brothers are those who hear the word of God and do it." In another instance, Jesus tells the crowds, "Whoever comes to me and does not hate father and mother, wife and children, brothers and sisters, yes, and even life itself, cannot be my disciple" (Luke 14:26). Another passage reports Jesus saying, "Do you think that I have come to bring peace to the earth? No, I tell you, but rather division! From now on five in one household will be divided, . . . father against son, . . . mother against daughter" (Luke 12:51–54). Jesus even causes division within his own family (Mark 3:21) and in the family of James and John, who upon hearing the call of Jesus, "left their father Zebedee in the boat with the hired men, and followed him" (Mark 1:20).

On the other hand, as we have seen, Jesus directs some of his most ardent injunctions against divorce and adultery. For Jesus, the bringing together of male and female as "one flesh" is a bond established by God. In addition, Jesus displays an unconventional attitude toward the value of children. Rather than treating children as pieces of property to be seen and not heard, as was common in first-century Judaism, Jesus (rather scandalously) allows them to come to him and touch him (Luke 18:15–17).

If Jesus indeed held marriage and children in high esteem, how do we reconcile this with Jesus' other statements about leaving family for his sake and his coming to bring division rather than peace among family members? Jesus' strange pronouncements on family must be read in light of his call to radical discipleship. For Jesus, *all* values, *all* commitments, *all* goals, and *all* relationships are relative to the absolute commitment to God. Jesus demands absolute loyalty and devotion to himself and his message concerning the present and future reign of God. Such commitment to God and God's activity on earth places other commitments in a subservient role. In some cases, this may even mean departing from familial relationships that prevent one from a wholehearted dedication to God and preparation for the kingdom. In fact, this is why Jesus himself did not marry, so that he could devote his whole life to the preaching and establishment of the kingdom of God.

Followers of Jesus should treat the family as a God-established institution and blessing; they should not treat it as God. The emphasis on family can become an idol when love for family becomes so important that love of stranger and love of God are subordinated to it. But at its best, the family can be a close representation of the kingdom of God. Family life can be a "haven in a heartless world," where love, peace, and justice are expressed and where children are schooled in the Christian virtues.[19] Faithful family life approximates the kingdom of God, where we love others for who they are and not for what they can do or contribute. Family life teaches us to sacrifice for the good of others and to care for the needy without expectation of reciprocation. The early Christians called one another "brother" and "sister" because familial relationships were a foreshadowing of the kingdom of God.

Ultimately, Jesus recenters the moral life and redefines the family: "Whoever does the will of my Father in heaven is my brother and sister and mother" (Matt. 12:50). Family life, while valuable, is no longer the *ultimate* concern. Rather, God and God's representative on earth in Jesus Christ are the central focus of the moral and spiritual life. Jesus calls on us to expand the kind of love we show to family members so that it includes the stranger and even the enemy. To do so is to begin to model the kingdom of God on earth.

Jesus on Jewish Law

In our exploration of the ethics of the Old Testament, we discovered the centrality of the teachings called the Torah. At the end of that exploration we encountered some difficult questions about how Christians should understand and implement Jewish law. Those questions can now be better addressed in light of Jesus' view of Jewish law.

Jesus Accused of Violating Sabbath Law

On the one hand, Jesus is often portrayed violating Jewish law. One of the main accusations against Jesus is that he fails to keep the Sabbath. "This man is not from God, for he does not observe the sabbath" (John 9:16). Indeed, we have a number of written accounts where Jesus appears to be in clear violation of traditional Sabbath observance. In Luke 6:1–5, Jesus and his disciples are shown picking grain to eat as they walk along, a clear violation of Sabbath law. When some of the Pharisees accuse Jesus of "doing what is not lawful on the sabbath," Jesus tells them, "The Son of Man is lord of the sabbath." Here Jesus seems to be saying not only that he is in a position to interpret the law of Moses but that his authority is greater than the law. In the Markan version of this same story, Jesus says, "The sabbath was made for humankind, and not humankind for the sabbath" (Mark 2:27). Jesus is explaining that the Sabbath is a gift from God for the good of human beings, a time of rest, a time of worship, and a time of equality. *Jesus consistently violates any law concerning Sabbath observation that he feels gets in the way of human well-being and the advancement of the kingdom of God.*

We see this principle even more clearly in the several instances where Jesus heals on the Sabbath. Immediately following the story of picking grain on the Sabbath, we encounter a second apparent violation of Sabbath law when Jesus heals a man with a withered hand on the Sabbath (see also Luke 13:10–17). Jesus heals the man based on the following argument: "I ask you, is it lawful to do good or to do harm on the Sabbath, to save life or to destroy it?" (Luke 6:9). Jesus is not worried about following the letter of the law. Instead, he is focused on respecting the *purpose* of Sabbath law. For Jesus the Sabbath is an anticipation of the reign of God, when toil, competition, and hierarchy are put aside. God's rest on the Sabbath is a sign of the *shalom* of the world—peace and harmony and fullness at rest, a state of existence that also characterizes the kingdom of God. If this is the case, then making the sick man "whole" is perfectly appropriate on the Sabbath.

We see the same principle at work when Jesus heals a woman with a flow of blood:

Does not each of you on the sabbath untie his ox or his donkey from the manger, and lead it away to give it water? And ought not this woman, a daughter of Abraham whom Satan bound for eighteen long years, be set free from this bondage on the sabbath day? (Luke 13:15–16)

Recall that the Sabbath represents a setting free from toil. This notion of liberation is especially apparent in the Sabbath year and the jubilee year, when debts are forgiven and slaves set free. So Jesus reasons that the Sabbath is the perfect time for this woman to be set free from her illness, thus enabling her to be a more active and participatory member of the covenant community. He makes the community whole, healing not only the woman but the community as well. Moreover, he connects this Sabbath healing with the defeat of Satan, since the Sabbath is a foreshadowing of the kingdom of God, in which the powers of evil will be completely destroyed.

Besides the violation of Sabbath, Jesus and his followers are often portrayed as failing to keep fasts (Luke 5:33–39; 7:31–34) and of failing to perform ceremonial washing rituals before meals (Matt. 15:1–20). Jesus' response in this last episode is particularly indicative of his attitude toward the law. He says that it is not outward cleanliness that matters but inward purity of the heart. Expanding his response to cover both ceremonial washing and the kosher laws (clean and unclean foods) in general, he says:

> It is not what goes into the mouth that defiles a person, but it is what comes out of the mouth that defiles. . . . What comes out of the mouth proceeds from the heart, and this is what defiles. For out of the heart come evil intentions, murder, adultery, fornication, theft, false witness, slander. These are what defile a person, but to eat with unwashed hands does not defile. (Matt. 15:11, 18–20)

Finally, the Gospel writers also reveal that Jesus breaks other purity laws by touching or associating with unclean people such as lepers, Samaritans (John 4:1–13), or the woman who bathes his feet with her tears in the house of the indignant Pharisee (Luke 7:38).

Jesus Sometimes Supports the Law

From our discussion thus far, it might appear as if Jesus totally disregarded the Torah and that he encouraged his followers to do the same. But this is certainly not the case. In some places Jesus proclaims the legitimacy of the law. In Luke 16:17, Jesus says, "It is easier for heaven and earth to pass away, than for one stroke of a letter in the law to be dropped." Jesus is portrayed as customarily going to synagogue (Luke 4:16; 5:6) and keeping Passover, both activities that would have put him in the good graces of the keepers of the law. Moreover, Jesus often appeals to the Torah and upholds teachings from the Torah. When a man comes to Jesus and asks, "What must I do to inherit eternal life?" Jesus responds, "You know the commandments: 'You shall not commit adultery; You shall not murder; You shall not steal; You shall not bear false witness; Honor your father and mother'" (Luke 18:18–20). Although Jesus goes on to make an even greater demand upon the man, Jesus is clearly upholding the validity of the Torah.

Not only does Jesus reinforce such moral commandments as those found in the Decalogue, but in some instances Jesus is depicted as reinforcing some commandments that we might place in the category of ceremonial laws. After healing a man with leprosy, Jesus tells him to "go and show yourself to the priest, and, as Moses commanded, make an offering for your cleansing" (Luke 5:14).

Conclusions about Jesus and the Law

What should we take from this complex relationship between Jesus and the law? In some places he appears to disregard the law, while in others he explicitly states that he has *not* come to abolish the law and is depicted as having a favorable attitude toward torah. How should Christians approach the law in light of Jesus' attitude toward it?[20]

It helps to remember the purpose or goal of torah. The goal of the law was to put people into right relationship with God and with one another. Torah was the instrument for the mending of God-human relations and human-human relations. In light of this purpose we can better understand Jesus' attitude toward the law.

The law remains a gift from God in that it tells human beings what God wills   The law is an instrument by which God reveals God's will. Jesus critiques any notion that mere outward observance of the law is sufficient to enter the kingdom of God. Nevertheless, Jesus' favorable attitude toward the Decalogue indicates that for Christians the law can still act to guide us in our relationship with God and neighbor. To do so, it may be necessary to get beyond the surface of particular laws to the principles that are reflected in them, but this does not entail their complete abolition.

The law must be properly understood   The law needs to be interpreted in light of the two great commandments to love God and love our neighbor. When a man asks Jesus what he must do to inherit eternal life, Jesus asks him:

> "What is written in the law? What do you read there?" He answered, "You shall love the Lord your God with all your heart, and with all your soul, and with all your strength, and with all your mind; and your neighbor as yourself." And he said to him, "You have given the right answer; do this, and you will live." (Luke 10:26–28)

In this passage, Jesus agrees that the essence of the law is love for God and neighbor. Therefore, when the law begins to function in such a way as to hinder these primary relationships, we may need to question its applicability. We see this interpretive principle most clearly exemplified in Jesus' healing on the Sabbath. The law should guide us and assist us in loving God with our whole being and loving our neighbor as ourselves. And so Jesus criticizes the teachers of the law who "tie up heavy burdens, hard to bear, and lay them on the shoulders of others" (Matt. 23:4). These teachers have taken the good gift of the law and turned it into an unbearable burden. Moreover, they follow the letter of the law by giving a tenth of their goods, but they "have neglected the weightier matters of the law: justice and mercy and faith" (Matt. 23:23). Sabbath and law were made for people, but people were not made for the Sabbath and the law. When the law ceases to function as an instrument for aiding humans to love God and neighbor and instead becomes a hindrance, then it ceases to fulfill its primary function.

Jesus is the "end" of the law   Christians are set free from meticulous adherence to the law because of the life, death, and resurrection of Jesus. As we shall see more clearly when we come to Paul, Jesus acts as the atonement for the sins of humanity.[21] Sacrifices, ritual purity, and fasting were ways of trying to enter into right relationship with God. But with Jesus, the relationship between God and humans has been mended. Jesus is the end of the law in that he has fulfilled the very function of the law; he has reconciled humans to their Creator and Lord.

The kingdom and the law   Finally, with the consummation of the kingdom of God, Christians will do naturally that which the law demands. It will no longer be a burden but a great joy to do the will of God. This is how best to understand the eschatological vision we see in Ezekiel: "A new heart I will give you, and a new spirit I will put within you; and I will remove from your body the heart of stone and give you a heart of flesh. I will put my spirit within you, and make you follow my statutes and be careful to observe my ordinances" (Ezek. 36:26–27). The people will have a heart that burns to please God by doing God's will on earth as it is in heaven. We see the same notion in Jeremiah's description of the new covenant:

> This is the covenant that I will make with the house of Israel after those days, says the LORD: I will put my law within them, and I will write it on their hearts; and I will be their God, and they shall be my people. No longer shall they teach one another, or say to each other, "Know the LORD," for they shall all know me, from the least of them to the greatest. (Jer. 31:33–34)

When the kingdom of God is established, there will be no need for the law. Love of God and love of neighbor will be written on the very hearts of men and women. Although this is fulfilled ultimately in the future, it can be realized now as well, for those who are "raised with Christ" (see chapter 10 on the ethics of Paul).

The Sermon on the Mount: An Ethic for the Kingdom

We cannot end our treatment of the ethical teachings of Jesus without a discussion of the Sermon on the Mount. The Sermon on the Mount is a collection of teachings and sayings of Jesus that, according to Matthew, was delivered by Jesus on a mountain. Many scholars feel that this was probably not one continuous sermon but constitutes various sayings of Jesus that were gathered together in one place. The shorter Lukan version, found in Luke 6:17–49, is often referred to as the Sermon on the Plain.

Regardless of the original setting, the Sermon on the Mount is a rich source for Jesus' ethical teachings. In this "sermon," Jesus calls the people to a higher righteousness. Instead of telling the people that, in light of the kingdom, they are not expected to do anything, he tells them that "unless your righteousness exceeds that of the scribes and Pharisees, you will never enter the kingdom of heaven" (Matt. 5:20). On the one hand, Jesus has come to free his followers from a law code that is so unyielding, minute, and complex that it acts to divide people from one another and from God. On the other hand, Jesus is actually calling for a higher kind of righteousness, one that encompasses not simply the acts of the hands but the thoughts and feelings of the mind and heart.

This is evident in what are often referred to as the "antitheses." These are the sayings of Jesus in which he quotes an Old Testament law and then reinterprets it by saying, "But I say . . .":

> You have heard that it was said to those of ancient times, "You shall not murder"; and "whoever murders shall be liable to judgment." But I say to you that if you are angry with a brother or sister, you will be liable to judgment. (Matt. 5:21–22)

> You have heard that it was said, "You shall not commit adultery." But I say to you that everyone who looks at a woman with lust has already committed adultery with her in his heart. (Matt. 5:27)

Calling these "antitheses" is a little misleading, since an antithesis is analogous to an opposite, and Jesus is certainly not proclaiming the opposite of the original law. Rather than contradicting the original Torah commandment, Jesus is intensifying it. He is proclaiming an ethical standard even higher than that of the Pharisees (who tried to follow all 613 Torah commands exactly).

Christians know that with the life, death, and resurrection of Jesus Christ, the kingdom of God has been inaugurated. In the Sermon on the Mount, Jesus calls his followers to exhibit a mode of living and loving that reflects this new situation. Envy, lust, narrow self-interest, and hurtful anger are not acceptable for those who know of the new reign of God's righteous rule on earth. Jesus calls believers to a revolutionary kind of existence that mirrors the revolutionary character of God's kingdom. As Daniel Harrington and James Keenan summarize, "The sermon is best understood today as part of an ethics of Christian character or Christian virtue ethics. The kingdom of God is the horizon and goal. The sermon tells us how to prepare to enjoy its fullness and to act appropriately in the present."[22]

The idea that the Sermon on the Mount represents a portrait of the virtues of the kingdom of God can be seen most clearly in a set of Jesus' sayings called the Beatitudes (from the Latin for "blessed"), in which Jesus identifies a number of people that God has blessed.

> Blessed are the poor in spirit, for theirs is the kingdom of heaven.
> Blessed are those who mourn, for they will be comforted. . . .
> Blessed are those who hunger and thirst for righteousness, for they will be filled. . . .
> Blessed are the peacemakers, for they will be called children of God.
> Blessed are those who are persecuted for righteousness' sake, for theirs is the kingdom of heaven. (Matt. 5:3–4, 6, 9–10)

Once again, we can see how Jesus is defining a "kingdom ethic." In the kingdom of God, it is not the rich, satisfied, laughing, and admired that are the focus of God's blessing. In a world where God's values override human values and expectations, it is the poor, the hungry, the hated, and the excluded that are blessed by God. It is those who "bear the cross" that God lifts up, while, just as Mary foretold, God "has scattered the proud in the thoughts of their hearts . . . and lifted up the lowly; he has filled the hungry with good things, and sent the rich away empty" (Luke 1:51–53).

We saw above that Jesus' actions represent an inbreaking of the kingdom. But the same is also true of Jesus' virtues. The characteristics described in the Beatitudes correspond precisely to the character of Jesus himself. Jesus is meek, merciful, and pure in heart, and in Jesus we find the true peacemaker (see Col. 1:20). Jesus also hungers and thirsts for righteousness. David Scaer rightly observes that the background for this saying "is Israel's sojourning in the wilderness where for both food and water they were completely dependent upon God. The hungering and thirsting suggest that a person's total existence is dependent for life upon something outside of himself." [23] Moreover, those early Jews were on their way to the promised land, just as Christians are now.[24] Those who hunger and thirst for righteousness are the ones who long for the final coming of God's kingdom. They are the ones heeding Jesus' call to "repent, for the kingdom of God is at hand." They long for, ache for, hunger for the time and place when righteousness will prevail, when the bonds of hatred, evil, disease, and sin will be completely broken.

Jesus' Sermon on the Mount describes what life in preparation for the kingdom of God looks like. It is a portrait of a higher righteousness in both our actions and our virtues. In fact, Jesus' Sermon on the Mount sets such high expectations that some scholars have argued that his commands in the Sermon on the Mount are incapable of being fulfilled. According to this line of interpretation, Jesus' intention was not to establish a new set of laws by which we might actually live. His intention, rather, was to show how sinful human beings are, since they are incapable of living up to this extremely elevated ethical standard.

Such interpreters point to other sections of the Sermon on the Mount as evidence that Jesus' ethics are impractical and impossible in a world where sin still prevails:

> You have heard that it was said, "An eye for an eye and a tooth for a tooth." But I say to you, Do not resist an evildoer. But if anyone strikes you on the right cheek, turn the other also. (Matt. 5:38–39)

> You have heard that it was said, "You shall love your neighbor and hate your enemy." But I say to you, Love your enemies and pray for those who persecute you. (Matt. 5:43–44)

> Therefore I tell you, do not worry about your life, what you will eat or what you will drink, or about your body, what you will wear. (Matt. 6:25)

> Do not judge, so that you may not be judged. (Matt. 7:1)

Thinkers such as the highly influential American ethicist Reinhold Niebuhr believe that these commands represent an "impossible ethical ideal."[25] In a world full of sin, greed, and violence, it may be impossible to apply these commands of Jesus directly as a social ethic. Rather, these commands represent a kind of "kingdom ethic," a portrait of what ethics in the (future) kingdom of God will resemble. Niebuhr says:

> The ultimate moral demands upon man can never be affirmed in terms of the actual facts of human existence. They can be affirmed only in terms of a unity and a possibility, a divine reality which transcends human existence. The order of human existence is too imperiled by chaos, the goodness of man too corrupted by sin.[26]

Too often, Christians use some variety of Niebuhr's interpretation of the Sermon on the Mount—as an impossible perfectionist ideal—in order simply to avoid the hard work of trying to transform their lives and conform to the pattern of Christ. Glen Stassen has provided an excellent alternative to viewing these hard sayings as impossible ideals. He points out that in the Sermon on the Mount and elsewhere, Jesus provides practical guidelines for transforming our lives and breaking the vicious cycles of greed, judgment, lust, hatred, and violence: "Jesus taught *practice norms*. They are not mere inner attitudes, vague intentions, or moral convictions only, but regular practices to be engaged."[27] For example, Jesus is not simply saying, "Do not be angry." He provides a "practice norm" whereby we can transform our anger: "So when you are offering your gift at the altar, if you remember that your brother or sister has something against you, leave your gift there before the altar and go; first be reconciled to your brother or sister, and then come and offer your gift. Come to terms quickly with your accuser while you are on the way to court with him"(Matt. 5:23–25). These are practical guidelines for transforming ourselves and our relationships. To take another example, Jesus tells us to love our enemies but also provides a practice norm or "transforming initiative" by which we might do so: "Pray for those who persecute you" (Matt. 5:44). We may not be able to achieve a complete victory over the greed, lust, hatred, and violence in the world and in our own lives, but by engaging in these kinds of activities, Christians begin to develop kingdom virtues and to participate in the kingdom of God, which is breaking in all around us. As Stassen and Gushee rightly note, we are called to a

> grace-based, active participation in eschatological deliverance that begins now. . . . Jesus is pointing to participation in the grace of deliverance that characterizes the inbreaking of the reign of God. Jesus is indeed the prophetic Messiah who proclaims the inbreaking reign of God and points to specific ways of participation in the kingdom.[28]

Chapter 9

Imitation and the Life of Jesus

Biblical Readings

Gospel of Luke
Matthew 5–7; 25:31–46

Reading Guide

See chapter 8 reading guide.

Introduction

Many of you may be familiar with a recent movement known as WWJD, which means "What would Jesus do?" The point of the movement is to get individuals to imagine what Jesus might do in a particular situation. As an ethicist, I have found this movement to be fascinating. On the one hand, as a Christian, I am always glad when people appeal to the life and teachings of Jesus when making ethical decisions, both big and small. On the other hand, I struggle with a number of questions about this ethical methodology.

First, do we try to imitate what Jesus actually did, or do we speculate on what Jesus might do in our current situation? These might be different things. For example, in the previous chapter I argued that Jesus' attitude toward divorce might be different now than it was in the context of first-century Palestine.

Second, how do we know what Jesus would do in many situations today? It is unclear what Jesus would do about gun control, global warming, terrorist bombings, stem cell research, and so forth. This is the difficulty of using the *circumstantial* method described in chapter 4 of finding situations or circumstances in Scripture that are similar to our own. Because Jesus did not face such situations, we must go to the broader principles revealed in his teachings and life. But to do so is to move beyond the realm of "What would Jesus do?" to the question, "What should *I* do as a follower of Jesus?"

A third question is whether WWJD is sufficient. First, the ethical method presupposed by this question is one that focuses on actions and decisions. As we have seen, virtue ethicists argue that the moral life is more about the kinds of people we should *be* rather than what we should *do*. Second, is WWJD too narrow? Certainly, Jesus is the foundation of all Christian ethics. But that does not mean that we should ignore other teachings in the Bible, such as the Torah and prophets. Finally, are there things that Jesus did and "would do" that we are not called to do? Jesus was a human, but he was also divine. We are not called to walk on water and raise the dead.

Despite these questions, "What would Jesus do?" taps into a long tradition in Christianity that focuses on the "imitation of Christ" (*imitatio Christi*). In the fifth century the Council of Chalcedon described Jesus as "fully human and fully divine." Most Christians interpret this to mean that when it comes to Jesus' human nature, he was like us in every way. He needed to eat and drink. As a baby, his diapers had to be changed. He felt sadness and joy, pain and love. As important as this is, it is only a part of the significance of the claim that Jesus is fully human. The Chalcedonian formula also implies that Jesus is not just *a* human being; he is *the* human being. He is the epitome of what a human being should be. He is *fully* human, whereas we fail to live up to our full humanity. Because Jesus is the one truly human being, he should be the model for our lives as human beings. The way he lived, felt, thought, acted, and responded to others should be a model for those of us who strive to be the human creatures that God created. If we want to know what human beings are supposed to look like, we look not to one another, or even to Adam, but to Jesus of Nazareth. As Karl Barth notes, Jesus "is the source of our knowledge of the nature of man as created by God."[1]

Imitation, Repetition, and Following Jesus

Imitation does not mean rote repetition. We are not called to travel around Israel, preaching, healing, and casting out demons. A simplistic repetition of the life of Jesus would mean that we are not to get married, have children, or even plan for our financial future. It would mean that we could not defend ourselves against false charges or resist violent attacks.

As the biblical writers demonstrate, we are to be *like* Jesus; we are not called to *be* Jesus. In the Gospel of Luke, Jesus says, "A disciple is not above the teacher, but everyone who is fully qualified will be like the teacher" (Luke 6:40). In the book of Acts we see the students acting like the teacher. Peter, Philip, Stephen, and the other apostles preach, heal, perform exorcisms, and even perform a resurrection (Acts 9:36–41). Like Jesus they are persecuted for their actions; they are ridiculed, taken before Jewish and Roman authorities, and imprisoned. When we read how Stephen becomes the first Christian martyr, we cannot help but be reminded of the death of Jesus, especially in light of Stephen's final words: "Lord Jesus, receive my spirit" and "Lord, do not hold this sin against them" (Acts 7:59–60).

These parallels between the life of Christ and the lives of disciples should not be understood as rote imitations, as if Peter and Stephen *intended* to be ridiculed, stoned, and martyred. Rather, they are filled with the spirit of Christ and therefore naturally continue the kingdom work that he began. In so doing, they inevitably run into the same resistance and misunderstanding that Jesus faced. E. Earle Ellis is exactly right when he says, "These parallels are not to be understood merely as an existential imitation of Jesus, but as the working out of a corporate relation to Jesus. Jesus' disciples have his Spirit, proclaim his message, bear his cross and share his glory because they are, in Paul's idiom 'the body of Christ.'"[2] To be a Christian is to be guided by the spirit of Christ. This is what Jesus means when he appears to his disciples after his resurrection and tells them, "You will receive power when the Holy Spirit has come upon you; and you will be my witnesses in Jerusalem, in all Judea and Samaria, and to the ends of the earth" (Acts 1:8). If we have the spirit of Christ, we will follow the same path that he followed. It is not because we are merely going through the same motions as Jesus, but because we have been united with him (see chapter 10). His mission has become our mission, and his vision has become our vision. If we seek to have the same values and attitudes of Jesus, we will inevitably experience many of the same things that Jesus did, not because we are intentionally trying to relive his life, but because the world will treat us the same way it treated him. In a world full of self-centeredness, greed, cynicism, and violence, having the mind of Christ means that the world will treat "little Christs" the way it treated Jesus.

This is why the most common command of Jesus is not "Imitate me," but "Follow me." Jesus is not asking his disciples to relive his life, but to walk in the world with the same attitudes, virtues, and priorities that he displayed during his pilgrimage on earth. *Imitatio Christi* is more about imitation of virtues and emotions than imitation of actions. If we can learn to feel what Christ felt and if we can develop the virtues that Christ developed, then we will naturally do many of the things that he did: care for the poor, preach the good news, stand against injustice, teach, preach, heal, and, in the end, willingly suffer for the sake of the kingdom. Imitation of Christ involves learning to see the world the way Jesus did.

Jesus shows us what a truly human life looks like. He demonstrates what a Spirit-filled, God-centered life is like. But each of us is unique. We are not called to simply parrot the actions of Jesus. Jesus should act as a model, not as a blueprint, for our lives.

An example might help. Often I will make available to my students a "model" paper so that they can understand what a good piece of biblical exegesis or theological ethics looks like. The goal is not for students simply to restate the argument of the model paper but rather to draw from the paper the key features that make for an effective argument: clarity of presentation, precision of thesis, organization, and so forth. They then take these broad themes and seek to apply them to their own unique papers. The same is true for the life of Jesus. For Jesus demonstrated that a Spirit-filled and fully human life is so centered around God that, *for him*, it meant leaving parents and siblings. We should take this as an example of what such a life might entail, but not as an exact blueprint for our own lives. We see from Jesus' example that all the things that we normally hold as valuable must be put in their proper relationship with God. However, just because Jesus left his mother and brothers and at times refused to even see them does not mean that we must turn our backs on family life to become disciples of Christ. It does mean that if we have the same mind and priorities as Christ, then all things, including family relationships, are subordinate to the primary relationship we have with God.

Jesus Models the Christian Life

So if we are going to use Jesus' life as a model, what are the key features of that life which function as paradigms for a truly human life? I would suggest three key elements of Jesus' life: (1) love, (2) bearing the cross, and (3) liberating servanthood. These three aspects have quite a bit of overlap. This should not surprise us since they all reflect Jesus' initiation and anticipation of God's final reign on earth.

Love

Just then a lawyer stood up to test Jesus. "Teacher," he said, "what must I do to inherit eternal life?" He said to him, "What is written in the law? What do you read there?" He answered, "You shall love the Lord your God with all your heart, and with all your soul, and with all your strength, and with all your mind; and your neighbor as yourself." And he said to him, "You have given the right answer; do this, and you will live." (Luke 10:25–28)

The idea that love of God and neighbor is central to the good life was not new with Jesus; the expert in the law correctly identified its centrality. However, Jesus did give love a powerful, new content by identifying it with his own actions. In fact, in one of the few places where Jesus appeals directly to imitation, he does so in regard to love.

> I give you a new commandment, that you love one another. Just as I have loved you, you also should love one another. By this everyone will know that you are my disciples, if you have love for one another. (John 13:34–35)

> This is my commandment, that you love one another as I have loved you. (John 15:12)

Love is one of the most overused and least precise words in the English language; we use the same word to describe our relationship with a mind-boggling variety of people and things: "I love my country. I love my wife. I love my friend Dave. I love my dog. I love my new bike. I love my brother. I love God." Clearly, love means different things in each of these sentences and yet we use the same word to describe each type of relationship. This kind of vagueness leads Richard B. Hays to reject love as a "focal image" for New Testament ethics. "The term has become debased in popular discourse; it has lost its power of discrimination, having become a cover for all manner of vapid self-indulgence."[3] Hays is correct when he claims that the overuse of the term has diluted and obscured its biblical meaning. That said, the answer is not to jettison the word but to seek to define it biblically and to distinguish its biblical usage from other uses.

Toward this end, when discussing the type of love that Jesus commands and that he embodies in his life I will often use the Greek word *agape*. There are four words for love in Greek. *Philia* is the love that friends feel for one another. *Storge* describes familial love, as between brothers and sisters. *Eros* describes the affection and desire that characterizes the love between husband and wife or lovers in general.

Agape has characteristics of each of these types of love but is different in some ways from all of them, just as the love one feels for friends is different from the love one feels for one's lover. Let us try to get a sense of what this love looks like by exploring how Jesus expresses his love for others. We will examine three characteristics of *agape* that are revealed in Jesus' life and ministry:

1. *Agape* is not the same as liking, but it does have an emotional component.

2. *Agape* is inclusive.
3. *Agape* seeks *shalom.*

Agape *Is Not the Same Thing as "Liking" Someone*

In contrast to *philia* or *eros, agape* love is not a command to feel affection for everyone. While it is only speculation, I suspect that Jesus did not particularly like some of the self-righteous and hard-hearted Pharisees that he met, whom he calls "fools" and "serpents" (Luke 11:40; Matt. 23:33). Personally, I doubt that I will ever like Saddam Hussein or the leader of the KKK. But that does not mean that I should not feel compassion for them, help them in need, and pray for their ultimate salvation. Rather than a kind of affection, *agape* is an active concern for others. It is the desire to see them flourish as God intended them to. It is to treat them as precious in God's sight and therefore to be as concerned about their well-being as our own.

"Love your neighbor as yourself," Jesus says. Paul Ramsey asks us to think about how we love ourselves as a model of *agape:*

> Answer this question and you will know how a Christian should love his neighbor. You naturally love yourself for your own sake. You wish your own good, and you do so even when you may have a certain distaste for the kind of person you are. Liking yourself or thinking yourself very nice, or not, has fundamentally nothing to do with the matter. . . . You love yourself more than you love any good qualities or worth you may possess. . . . Christian love means such love for self inverted. . . . The commandment requires the Christian to aim at his neighbor's good just as unswervingly as man by nature wishes his own.[4]

Ramsey says that even if we don't necessarily like who we are, we still wish our own good. The same is often the case with family members. You may not be friends with your brothers or sisters, but you probably still care what happens to them and would lend them aid in times of trouble. You want the best for them. This is how we should love all people.

Ramsey is correct that *agape* is not the same as liking someone, wanting to spend time with him and desiring his presence. Yet some Christian ethicists have gone too far in emptying *agape* of any emotional content, transforming it into a kind of general Kant-like attitude of respect or concern.

If Jesus is our guide, *agape* is not reducible to a general attitude of respect. One of the most striking features of Jesus' life and ministry was his *compassion* toward other people. Jesus did more than respect the many downtrodden and outcast peasants among whom he spent most of his life; he felt compassion for them. To be compassionate is to "feel with" (*co + passio*). It is to feel the sufferings of others as if they were your own. Jesus becomes so identified with people that their suffering becomes his suffering. It is not simply on the cross that Jesus takes on the sufferings of humanity, but throughout his entire life. When Jesus meets a widow whose only son had died, Luke tells us that the reason he resurrects the man is because "he [Jesus] had compassion on her" (Luke 7:13). Another time, Jesus encounters a begging leper and "filled with compassion, Jesus reached out his hand and touched the man" (Mark 1:41 NIV). Jesus' compassion is never condescending or patronizing. Rather, his compassion involves solidarity with other people toward the goal of transforming them by his love. Jesus sees in the least and the lowest members of society children of God, made in the image of his Father.

Agape is learning to feel with and for others. In his capacity to join in the suffering of others, Jesus is the true "image of God." He clearly reflects the God whom we have met throughout the Old Testament, a God who demonstrates *hesed* (steadfast love), a God who often chooses the underdogs of society and becomes identified with them. "I know (Hebrew, *yada*) their sufferings," Yahweh tells Moses, referring to the hardships of the Israelite slaves in Egypt (Exod. 3:7). *Yada* means more than to intellectually know; it means "to experience." This is what true love means, to become so identified with the needs, desires, and experiences of another that they become one's own. This is why the model of compassionate love so often invoked in Scripture is that of mother or father. Mothers and fathers are often so in tune with the needs and desires of their children that they not only feel "for" their children, but they actually feel the pain and joys of their children. The joy of the child is the joy of the mother and the heartache and pain of the child are the heartache and pain of the father. It may be difficult to feel compassion for strangers and enemies, but as we saw in our earlier discussion of the emotions, it is possible to transform one's emotions through Bible reading, prayer, and service. Just as we learn indifference and hate, we can learn to feel compassion for people outside our small circle of friends and family, especially if we have put to death the old self and been raised anew with Christ (see chapter 10).

Christians believe that on the cross Jesus "takes on the sins" of humanity. Through his crucifixion he takes on the suffering and death that we sinful, disobedient creatures deserve. But his death is simply a culmination of his life. Not merely in his dying but throughout his entire life, he enters into the suffering and pain of his fellow human beings through his unreserved love.

Agape *Is Inclusive*

We have seen how *agape* is similar to family love (*storge*) in that we feel compassionate concern for family members even if we would not otherwise be friends with them. But *agape* differs from *storge* in one very important respect: It is universal. It is not just compassion that characterizes the life of Jesus, but a universal compassion, what Edward LeRoy Long refers to as "compassionate inclusivity."[5] Jesus demonstrates love not just for his family and friends, and not just for the powerful, beautiful, or righteous, but for the sinner, the outcast, and the stranger. Jesus' love knows no borders, and like the Father who sent him, Jesus has a special concern for those people who too often fall outside of the scope of most people's love and concern.

In Jesus' day (not unlike our own), good, "upstanding" people were extremely careful about whom they associated with, lest they become identified with the wrong kind of people, such as tax collectors, Gentiles, and sinners. Many of these people were considered "unclean" by the leaders of Jewish society. We saw in the last chapter how Jesus often offended these so-called "righteous people" by touching and interacting with unclean people, thus breaking certain commandments of the Torah. Lepers were both spiritually and physically ostracized from the community of faith, and Jesus touched them throughout his ministry. But this is just one example of the scandalously wide scope of his love. Throughout Jesus' life and short ministry, he displayed the same kind of love and solidarity with other types of people who were often overlooked or downtrodden. For example, Jesus broke with the social norm by dealing with children. First-century Palestinian Jewish men would normally not interact with children, even their own. Children were generally viewed simply as property, with few if any rights. While popular Christian art often oversentimentalizes Jesus' treatment of children, it is nonetheless true that when his disciples rebuke some children for coming to Jesus and touching him, Jesus breaks with social custom by calling the children to him, saying, "Let the little children come to me; do not stop them; for it is to such as these the kingdom of God belongs" (Mark 10:14). Jesus' actions, far from being sweet and sentimental, are actually rather scandalous, because he refuses to view children as other adult males do, namely, as nuisances or even merely property. Instead, he demonstrates as much love and concern for them as he does for adult Jewish men.

Jesus displayed the same kind of scandalously inclusive love for women. Jesus' attitude and treatment of women bordered on revolutionary. Jesus often violated strict social norms by talking with strange women, eating with women, and generally befriending women, such as Mary and Martha. John tells us that the disciples were "astonished that he was speaking with a woman" because for the most part, women were treated as nonpersons (John 4:27). As Wolfgang Schrage observes:

Jewish women at the time of Jesus ranked in many ways with slaves and children. Their status was inferior both socially and religiously. They could not read from the Torah, were not counted in determining whether the minimum congregation for synagogue worship was present, were not required to fulfill certain commandments and recite certain prayers, and so forth. They were segregated in worship.[6]

Certainly, Jesus did not overturn all of the religious and social customs concerning women. But what he did do was love them as fellow human beings and children of God who were loved by their Father. Jesus saw no moral distinction between the sexes in the kingdom of God. In his own ministry he seemed oblivious to such distinctions, calling both men and women to repentance and discipleship. Luke 8:1–3 describes a number of women who were disciples of Jesus, including "Mary, Joanna, Susanna and many others . . . [who] were helping to support them out of their own means" (see also Mark 15:41). In fact, one of the very first Christian evangelists to non-Jews was a Samaritan woman (John 4:1–29). And one point on which all four Gospels agree is that the most faithful of Jesus' disciples were women. It is almost exclusively women who remain loyal to Jesus after his arrest, and they are specifically mentioned as being found at the foot of the cross when practically all the other disciples had fled. And it is to women that Jesus first appears after his resurrection, certainly a sign of his respect and love for women.

While Jesus can occasionally be seen eating at the houses of the rich and powerful, he also expresses his love for the outcast and the sinner by eating with them. He identifies with them to such a degree that eventually their lot (being outcast, ridiculed, and abused) becomes his lot. He is called a "friend of tax collectors and sinners" and dies the death of the outcast (Matt. 11:19).

What would it mean in our own time to imitate such inclusive love? It seems that many of our religious leaders are as eager as the Pharisees and Sadducees to determine who is "in" and who is "out," who is saved and who is not, who is a "good Christian" and who is not. But as Christians, we must act in solidarity not only with the actual poor and outcast but also with the morally and spiritually poor and outcast. When it comes to love, we should always err on the side of inclusion. When, as individuals or as a church, we begin to exclude people as unworthy and unrighteous we are failing to live up to the model of Christ's love. Christ is simply modeling the attitude of the God we have seen all throughout Scripture, a God of steadfast love (*hesed*), especially for the "widows and orphans." When Jesus says that he has come to save sinners he is simply continuing the work of a God who consistently sides with the powerless and downtrodden.

That we should always seek to make the circle of our love wider and not smaller is one of the key points Jesus makes in the parable of the Good Samaritan, which he tells to the lawyer who correctly identifies that love of God and neighbor are central to eternal life. The lawyer asks Jesus a second question: "Who is my neighbor?" It seems that what the lawyer really wants to know is "Whom don't I have to love? Who falls outside of the circle of friends, family, and countrymen that I have to love?"

Jesus refuses to get caught up in deciding who is and who is not an object of our love and concern. Instead, he tells a story that turns the question back upon the questioner. At the end of the story Jesus answers a different question than the one the lawyer asked: "Which of these three, do you think, was a neighbor to the man who fell into the hands of the robbers?" (Luke 10:36). Instead of looking for something to love in our neighbors, some quality that allows them to fall within the realm of our compassionate concern, Jesus challenges us to look at ourselves and ask what it would look like for us to *show* neighbor love.

Even though Jesus does not answer the lawyer's question directly, he does imply an answer. The lawyer wants to know whom he can safely *not* love. By showing what neighbor love looks like through the Samaritan's actions, Jesus implies that there is no way to limit the scope of *agape*. The neighbor is everyone. "There is in the whole world not a single person who can be recognized with such ease and certainty as one's neighbor," says Søren Kierkegaard. "You can never confuse him with anyone else, for indeed all men are your neighbor. . . . When you open the door which you shut in order to pray to God, the first person you meet as you go out is your neighbor whom you shall love. Wonderful!"[7]

This means that we are called not just to love those who love us, for "even sinners love those who love them" (Luke 6:32). We must love our enemies. The man rescued by the Samaritan, if Jewish, would have been a sworn enemy of the Samaritan and probably contemptuous, even hostile, to him. Jesus calls us to love our enemies and to pray for those who abuse us (Luke 6:27–32). This is precisely the kind of love shown by Jesus himself. He does not love only those persons he deems "worthy." He does not love only those persons who love him. His love is universal, extending even to those who seek to destroy him. The ultimate display of this kind of love is Jesus' willingness to go to the cross and to love even those people who instigated and carried out his crucifixion.

Agape *Seeks* Shalom: *Forgiving and Peacemaking*

This leads us to a third characteristic of *agape*. The kind of love modeled by Jesus is no mushy greeting-card sentimentality. It is radical and world-transforming. When Jesus gives the disciples the "new command" to love as he has loved them, he is calling them to a new way of being in the world, the way of peace and harmony that rejects the violence characterizing so many human relationships. The *agape* that Jesus demonstrates is characterized by nonviolent reconciliation between people, that is to say, forgiveness and peacemaking. In Hebrew, the word *shalom* is often appropriately translated as "peace." But it also connotes completeness, wholeness, and harmony. *Agape* seeks *shalom*; it seeks harmony and peace.

Agape breaks down barriers by refusing to treat the other as the enemy. It is a reconciling love. It is an expression of the coming kingdom in which the sin and hatred that divide us from one another are replaced by harmony and peace. We saw in chapter 8 that Jesus' forgiveness of sins foreshadows the coming kingdom. Love and forgiveness go hand in hand. Thomas Hobbes famously argued that the natural state of humanity is "war of all against all." Not according to Scripture. For Christians, love is the natural state that God intends for all humans, and love goes hand in hand with forgiveness, as Jesus notes: "The one to whom little is forgiven, loves little" (Luke 7:47). Forgiveness overcomes the sin that violates the harmony for which God created us. Forgiveness foreshadows the reconciliation that will be consummated at the end of this heaven and earth and the creation of the new heaven and earth. This is to say that there will be peace between humans and between humans and God; there will be *shalom*.

When we love others, we refuse to simply impose our wills upon them by force, to use violence to advance our *own* desires. Love seeks *shalom*. Throughout his ministry, Jesus consistently advocated peacemaking. In this sense, it is proper to describe Jesus as a pacifist. Whether or not he advocated the complete rejection of all violence, even in the defense of life, liberty, and justice, is a controversial point among Christians. But the word "pacifist" comes from the Latin *pacem facere*, "to make peace." Jesus consistently seeks to make peace between people and groups of people. The love that Jesus displays breaks down barriers between men and women, Jews and Gentiles, slaves and masters. In other words, by loving even his enemies, he seeks *shalom* as an anticipation of God's kingdom, where "they shall not hurt or destroy on all my holy mountain" (Isa. 65:25).

If violence is ever a possibility for Christians, it must always be a very last resort and done with incredible seriousness and regret. We must prepare and work for peace as hard as we seem to prepare for war. If we really love everyone as we love ourselves, if we love other people's children as much as we love our own, we must reject violence except under the most extreme circumstances and only as a means of protecting innocent neighbors against harm. Love demands that we work toward forgiveness and peace, because revenge, hatred, and retaliation have no place in the kingdom of God.

Bearing the Cross

Jesus led a life of joyful celebration. He was aware, more than anyone before him or after him, of the abounding love of God the Father. And so his life was a Spirit-filled celebration and praise of God's goodness. Nevertheless, his life was also characterized by profound self-denial and suffering. He calls this "bearing the cross." Jesus did not bear the cross only at his crucifixion; cross bearing characterized his entire life. He tells his disciples that if they are to follow him, they must do the same: "If any want to become my followers, let them deny themselves and take up their cross daily and follow me. For those who want to save their life will lose it, and those who lose their life for my sake will save it" (Luke 9:23–24). To take up the cross involves self-denial in the service of God and a willingness to suffer for God's kingdom.

Self-Denial

We have already seen that the Christian life is not one of absolute asceticism. Genesis 1 tells us that creation and bodily existence are "good," and Jesus himself took joy in earthly life. Following the example of Christ, we know that self-denial does not mean a complete rejection of all things pleasurable. What it does mean is an ever vigilant effort to submit one's own will to the will of God. To take up one's cross is to put aside self-interest and self-centeredness and place oneself under the sovereign rule of the creator and sustainer of the universe. Jesus did this throughout his entire life. In one of the few stories from his childhood, we hear Jesus say to his befuddled parents when they find him in the Jerusalem temple, "Why were you searching for me? Did you not know that I must be in my Father's house?" (Luke 2:49). While Jesus certainly grew and developed in his understanding of God's will for his life, from his early childhood he knew that he had to be focused not on his own plans but on the will of the Father. We see this most clearly at the end of his life in the garden of Gethsemane on the night of his arrest. In one of the most powerful scenes in all of Scripture, Jesus prays to his Father, "Father, if you are willing, remove this cup from me; yet, not my will but yours be done" (Luke 22:42). Jesus is not a masochist. He does not desire the excruciating pain and humiliation of a Roman crucifixion. But he submits his will to that of the Father. He wants what all people want who recognize the goodness of God's gift of life—to live. But what he wants even more is to do the will of the one who sent him. He denies his natural human fear of death and suffering and his normal human desire to live in order to be "obedient to the point of death—even death on a cross" (Phil. 2:8).

If we want to follow the example of Christ we must take up our cross. Jesus does not tell us to take up *his* cross; we must take up *our own*. His road of self-denial and submission to the Father is not the exact same road that we must travel. Each cross is unique because the will of each individual is unique. For some people, self-denial may mean taking on a task that is burdensome and difficult, for example, a son who takes a lower paying job to be near his sick parents. For others, it may not so much involve taking on a burden as the self-denial of emotions or attitudes. It might involve what Calvin calls a "mortification" (putting to death) of anger, jealousy, or greed. But in all cases it involves a moving from a life centered on self to a life centered on God. As Calvin says, "This self-denial has far-reaching implications. We are to renounce our own point of view, turn away from all covetous desires of the flesh, become as nothing in order that God may live in us and control us."[8] If we are to take up our cross and deny ourselves we must undergo a "Copernican revolution" in which God and others become the center of our lives and not ourselves. As Dietrich Bonhoeffer writes, "Self denial is never just a series of isolated acts of mortification or asceticism. . . . To deny oneself is to be aware only of Christ and no more of self, to see only him who goes before and no more the road which is too hard for us."[9]

This is why Jesus teaches us to pray: "Thy will be done on earth as it is in heaven." In addition to invoking the coming kingdom of God on earth, this prayer expresses a desire that God's will might be done in our individual lives. This is what St. Francis meant when he prayed:

> O Divine Master, grant that I may not so much seek
> To be consoled as to console.
> To be understood as to understand.
> To be loved as to love.

Of course, the great paradox is that by denying self and living for others under the will of God, we become what we were intended by God to be. This is what Jesus means when he says that "those who lose their life for my sake will save it" (Luke 9:24). It is only by breaking out of a life of self-willing and self-centeredness that we can live up to the image of a God who *is* love and self-giving. We see this self-giving love in the life of the triune God as God the Father, God the Son, and God the Holy Spirit live in a community of self-giving and self-glorifying love. And we see it revealed in the life and obedient death of Jesus. It is when we deny our sinful self-centered desires that we gain the life that God intended and we become fully human. We save our lives both here on earth and for eternity. And so the above prayer of St. Francis ends by saying:

> For it is in giving that we receive.
> It is in pardoning that we are pardoned.
> It is in dying that we are born to eternal life.

Willingness to Suffer

I proposed in our exploration of virtue that one of the prevalent virtues of Christians is joy. This does not mean that Christian lives are free of suffering and mishap. All too often, new Christians go through a period of disillusionment after the initial rush and thrill of newly discovering God in Christ wears off and they realize that, in many ways, living the Christian life makes things *more* difficult. To bear the cross means more than self-denial; it implies a willingness to suffer for the sake of God in Christ. As Dietrich Bonhoeffer so eloquently puts it, "When Christ calls a man, he bids him come and die."[10] To bear the cross involves a willingness to put aside the comfortable, the popular, and the convenient and take the difficult and unpopular path.

Jesus was repeatedly being tempted to take the easy way—the way of power and control, a way that did not lead to the cross. Satan's last two temptations of Jesus in the wilderness both represent the enticement to choose the path of comfort, glory, and honor while avoiding the suffering and humiliation of the cross. The same temptation is laid before Jesus by Satan in the form of Peter. Jesus has just been discussing the fact that his destiny is to "undergo great suffering, and be rejected by the elders, the chief priests, and the scribes, and be killed, and after three days rise again" (Mark 8:31). Upon hearing this, Peter begins to rebuke him, because Peter expects the Messiah to be a glorious and mighty king in the mold of David, certainly not one who would suffer the most degrading and vile death known at that time. In his rebuke, Peter is tempting Jesus to act like the Messiah that everyone is expecting; he is tempting Jesus to destroy the Romans and seize control by force. But Jesus recognizes the same old temptation of Satan and says to Peter, "Get behind me, Satan! For you are setting your mind not on divine things but on human things" (Mark 8:33). Jesus then begins to teach his disciples and the crowd about bearing the cross and the necessity of suffering because of their identification with him and his words (Mark 8:37). To bear the cross means a willingness to suffer for the glory of God and God's kingdom.

Much of the suffering of this world is a result of human sin and the brokenness of creation as a result of that sin. God calls upon us to relieve that suffering, as Jesus did. However, to suffer because of our commitment to Christ is none other than to "take up our cross and follow" Jesus. This is the kind of suffering that both Peter and Paul extol:

> If any of you suffers as a Christian, do not consider it a disgrace, but glorify God because you bear this name. . . . Therefore, let those suffering in accordance with God's will entrust themselves to a faithful Creator, while continuing to do good. (1 Pet. 4:16, 19)

> For he [God] has graciously granted you the privilege not only of believing in Christ, but of suffering for him as well. (Phil. 1:29)

Liberation and Servanthood

Scripture is clear that some suffering can be beneficial and redemptive, especially if it is voluntary suffering for the sake of Christ. But not all suffering is good and redemptive. This is made absolutely clear by Jesus' example of liberating servanthood. Jesus says that he came to "not to be served but to serve," and his life clearly reflects that (Matt. 20:28). His entire adult ministry is one of serving the spiritual, emotional, and physical needs of the people he encounters. Paul tells us that although Jesus is God, he did not express his divinity and power by controlling, dominating, and placing himself above others. Rather, he emptied himself and "taking the form of a slave . . . he humbled himself and became obedient to the point of death—even death on a cross" (Phil. 2:7–8). His life as well as his death was an act of humble service. One of the distinguishing marks of Christians is the way in which we imitate Jesus' humble, liberating servanthood. In one of the few explicit references to "imitation," Jesus washes his disciples' feet, an act reserved for slaves and servants. He then tells his disciples, "So if I, your Lord and Teacher, have washed your feet, you also ought to wash one another's feet. For I have set you an example, that you also should do as I have done to you" (John 13:14–15).

The Gospels depict not the military king that so many Jews associated with the Messiah, but the "Suffering Servant" described by Isaiah. Jesus seeks neither wealth nor power. In fact, he expressly rejects the temptations of wealth (bread), power ("all authority"), and glory ("all splendor") when struggling with Satan in the wilderness (Luke 4:1–13). Instead, his life is characterized by self-giving love and service. Along with forgiving people their sins and calling them to repentance and spiritual renewal, Jesus also concerns himself with people's physical condition: whether they have enough to eat, whether they are clothed, whether they are physically whole. Jesus heals and casts out demons, brings good news to the poor, and stands squarely against all acts of injustice, especially toward the downtrodden and marginalized. In so doing,

Jesus opposes those social, political, or economic conditions that continue to fight against the coming kingdom of God in which such things as hunger and injustice and domination will be abolished. As Robert McAfee Brown writes:

> Jesus' mission is "a visible socio-political-economic restructuring of relations among the people of God" (Yoder, *The Politics of Jesus*, p. 39). The message is shatteringly direct: the good news is for the poor and oppressed; it is liberation from bondage, whether the bondage is political, economic, social, or all three.[11]

Jesus calls upon us to take up our cross and follow him. Jesus' ministry involves an active but nonviolent resistance to the powers of evil. Another way of saying this is that Jesus is about the task of bringing *justice*, liberating both the oppressed and the oppressors.

If we are to imitate Christ, we must humble ourselves and become servants. We must, in the words of St. Francis's prayer, "not so much seek to be served as to serve." Disciples of Christ need to be focused on liberating people from their bondage, both spiritual and physical. Like Christ, we must stand in the line of those Old Testament prophets who unswervingly criticize unjust and unmerciful economic practices. We must stand against the violation of everyone's rights—even when that might be seen as idealistic or even unpatriotic. Just as Jesus' servanthood (and love) brought him into conflict with the political and religious authorities, Christians must be willing to bear the cross and suffer in their role as servants.

We can do so, knowing that we are not fighting a losing cause. Christ has won the battle against the forces of injustice, cruelty, sin, and death. The reign of God is breaking in. But as disciples of the king of that kingdom, Christians must work diligently to live into the kingdom of God, a kingdom where the modern equivalent of "widows and orphans" are treated the same as CEOs, presidents, and star football players. If we wish to live up to the name *Christian* we must take up our cross, in imitation of Christ, and become servants of liberation for the kingdom of God.

Chapter 10

The Ethics of Paul

Grace and New Creation

Biblical Readings

Romans 1–8; 12–15
Galatians 1–3; 5

Reading Guide

We have seen that there are three areas where we might focus our attention when trying to understand the significance of Jesus for Christian ethics: his teachings, his life, and the importance of his death and resurrection.[1] In chapters 8 and 9, we examined the teachings and life of Jesus. We now turn our attention to the ethics of Paul, who focuses on what the death and resurrection of Jesus Christ mean for those who are "new creations" in Christ.

In approximately 30 CE, the Roman authorities executed Jesus of Nazareth after trials before Pilate and the Sanhedrin (Jewish high court). The Gospels, which formed the basis of our exploration in the previous two chapters, cover the life, death, and resurrection of Jesus. They were written from thirty-five to sixty-five years after his death. The most important Christian literature that was produced between the time of Jesus' death and the writing of the Gospels are the letters of Paul, which also deal with the events of that same period.

At the point of Jesus' death, the Jesus movement was extremely small, with probably no more than a few hundred dedicated members. Moreover, with a few exceptions, it was a strictly Jewish movement; few if any Gentiles (non-Jews) were part of the early church. All this changed with the ministry of Saul of Tarsus, whom we know as Paul. Paul is quite simply the most important figure in Christianity after Jesus. In addition to being the author of nearly a third of the New Testament, it was Paul and his coworkers who transformed

Christianity from a minor messianic brand of Judaism into a message with universal appeal.

Paul came from a strong Jewish background and was trained as a Pharisee (Phil. 3:4–6; Acts 22:3). He never knew Jesus in the flesh and was originally a persecutor of Christians (Acts 9:1–3). But after a dramatic, life-changing encounter with the risen Christ, he felt called by God to preach about the life-giving significance of Jesus' crucifixion and resurrection, especially among the Gentiles. Traveling from city to city, Paul would use the local synagogue (if there was one) as his base for evangelizing Jews and Gentiles alike. His travels took him thousands of miles throughout Greece, Asia Minor, Syria, and Palestine. With the help of men such as Silas and Barnabas, Paul would spend anywhere from a few months to a few years starting and nurturing a community of believers in a city or region such as Philippi, Galatia, or Corinth. He would then continue his missionary journey and might not see the churches he started for years on end. Between visits, Paul wrote letters, or "epistles," in order to instruct, correct, and encourage these newly formed Christian faith communities. He often wrote in response to reports or letters sent to him, identifying problems or questions facing these nascent Christian communities.

The letter to the Romans is the one exception. Paul was not the founder of the church in Rome. He is writing to the Christian believers in Rome in anticipation of his first visit to them, introducing himself and, more importantly, his theological position. Because Paul is not addressing particular questions or issues that have been addressed to him, Romans is Paul's most systematic letter and therefore the most important summary of Paul's thought.

After a brief introduction in which he touches on the major themes of the letter (Rom. 1:1–15), Paul begins describing Gentile society (1:18–32). Paul explains that God's power and nature were accessible to *all* human beings from the creation of the world (by simply looking around at the nature of things) but that Gentiles suppressed the truth about God and refused to honor God. As a result, their hearts were darkened and they began to worship the images of humans and animals. The resulting condition can aptly be described as a moral disintegration in which persons are enslaved to their passions and desires, incapable of rescuing themselves.

After this striking description of the sinfulness of Gentile society, Paul turns in Romans 2 to characterize persons from a Jewish background who claim to be successfully observing the law of Moses. Not only does Paul claim that the law cannot provide righteousness, he also rebukes those who would pass judgment on others (2:3–4). Even though the Jewish people have a remarkable advantage because of the law and the promises of God (3:1–2), they cannot claim any privilege before God. The point of Paul's long diatribe is clearly stated throughout the third chapter: "Both Jews and Greeks are under the power of sin" (3:9), and "all have sinned and fall short of the glory of God" (3:23).

After laying the foundation for his argument, that both Jews and Gentiles are enslaved by sin, Paul proceeds to the heart of his argument. In one of the most important passages in all of Scripture he says:

> But now, apart from law, the righteousness of God has been disclosed, and is attested by the law and the prophets, the righteouness of God through faith in [or "the faithfulness of"] Jesus Christ for all who believe. For there is no distinction, since all have sinned and fall short of the glory of God; they are now justified by his grace as a gift, through the redemption that is in Christ Jesus. (Rom. 3:21–24)

We will explore the significance of these verses more fully below, but as you read the first eight chapters of Romans, look for these key ideas: righteousness/justification, faith or belief, the nature and consequences of sin, the role and function of the law (given by Moses in the Torah), the nature of God's grace, and the transforming power of God's Holy Spirit. Then, when you come to the more specific ethical imperatives and examples beginning in chapter 12, consider how they are related to the concepts of justification, faith, and grace that Paul has developed in the first part of his letter. In Paul's letters, you will notice an important shift in the basis for making moral decisions in the context of a faithful life. Paul does *not* say to his readers, "Learn about the life and teachings of Jesus and then try to follow his example." Indeed, citations of Jesus' teachings and references to Jesus' life are relatively rare in Paul's letters. Paul focuses instead upon the significance of Jesus' death and resurrection (what he calls "the cross") and the transforming power of God's Spirit that enables persons to live in conformity to Christ.

Although Paul's style of argumentation in Romans may be difficult to follow at times, if you stay focused on these key ideas and related concepts, you will not miss its overall purpose and relevance for Christian ethics.

Introduction to the Ethics of Paul

The importance of the apostle Paul for Christian ethics cannot be overstated. Paul's writings are frequently quoted in support of any number of ethical issues, including sexual behavior, divorce and remarriage, social obligations, and submission to governmental authorities. Paul's letters include numerous exhortations about how to serve God and live as members of the Christian community. Why not go directly to these instructions, collect them together, and use them as a law for moral action?

Although it may seem tempting to approach Paul's letters in this way, there are some important reasons not to do so, reasons that echo many of our earlier concerns about using Scripture primarily as a book of laws. First, specific moral commands actually comprise a small part of Paul's overall writings. This was intentional on his part. As we shall discuss below, Paul was adamant about the fact that observance of the Jewish law, including the keeping of ethical mandates, should not form the basis for one's relationship with God. Many of Paul's opponents were arguing that Gentile Christians must keep the law of Moses in order to be fully accepted by God. Against this, Paul was careful not to develop a new law code that might be construed as an alternative means for achieving righteousness.

A second reason for not focusing primarily upon Paul's moral exhortations is closely related to the first. Paul's letters usually follow a similar pattern. In the first part, he conveys most of his information through the use of indicative verb forms, stating direct facts about the condition of humanity, the means of salvation in Christ, and the results of this salvation; in other words, he begins by "indicating" what God has done and is doing. Only after Paul has clearly explained the message of the gospel and God's purposes does he move into specific imperatives or commands about how people should live. For example, throughout Romans 1–11, Paul uses indicative verb forms to advance his arguments about justification by grace. We can see Paul's shift into the imperative mood quite clearly in Romans 12:1–2: "*Therefore*, I urge you, brothers, in view of God's mercy, to offer your bodies as living sacrifices" (NIV). This appeal only makes sense as an extension of his proclamation about God's mercy in chapters 9 through 11. Because of this, Paul's ethical imperatives should not be taken out of their theological context.

A third and final reason for not focusing primarily upon Paul's moral exhortations has to do with the problem of historical and cultural context, which we have encountered so often. Since Paul wrote to specific communities in the first-century Mediterranean world, many of his moral admonitions are conditioned by the social customs of his day. This problem is readily apparent, for example, when we try to discern Paul's teachings about the role of women and slaves. Should women "remain silent in the churches" as 1 Corinthians 14:34–35 suggests? Are slaves truly to "obey [their] earthly masters with fear and trembling" as indicated in Ephesians 6:5? Or are these guidelines about women's roles and slaves limited to particular historical problems and social conditions in Corinth and Ephesus? Our task will be to determine as much as possible the ways in which Paul's ethical teachings are grounded in larger theological themes and shaped by his overall understanding of the gospel.

Paul's Gospel of Justification by Grace

Have you ever asked yourself, "What must I do to make God love and accept me?" or "How can I be saved?" If you have, you are grappling with the same questions that occupy Paul. The central concern for this greatest of Christian writers is how persons can be declared righteous ("justified") before God and thereby live as righteous, morally virtuous persons. We can state this concern in the form of some key questions:

> What exactly does Paul mean when he says that persons are declared
> righteous ("justified") by God's grace (Rom. 3:24)?
> What is the role of faith?
> Do Christians have to begin living righteously before they can receive
> God's gift of righteousness?

Before we can deal with specific ethical issues, we must grapple with Paul's understanding of the human condition and justification by grace through faith.

Humans Are Slaves to Sin and Cannot Save Themselves

It should not surprise us that Paul's view of humankind draws directly upon the biblical worldview that we have seen throughout this book. Although humans were created in God's image, their relationship with God and others has been ruptured because of Adam and Eve's willful transgression against God. All persons, regardless of their religious background or personal worthiness as individuals, are affected by the disobedience of the first human beings and continue to reenact that disobedience in their own lives.

Paul describes the innate condition of humans as being enslaved to sin (Rom. 6:19–20), unable to control their sinful passions (Rom. 7:5, 23) and hostile to God (Rom. 8:6–8; see also Eph. 2:1–3). Indeed, Paul uses the language of "death" to describe the human condition, because the attempt to please God on one's own, apart from the Spirit, brings more and more separation from God (Rom. 7:5, 11). In Paul's view, human beings apart from God are in a seemingly impossible moral situation; even when they desire to do the right thing, they are unable to do so because of the sin that dwells within them. Those who live apart from God are controlled by their sinful nature ("the flesh"; 7:5) and enslaved to sin (7:25). Since nothing good resides in the sinful nature (7:18), Paul describes this condition as a form of death. Apart from the life-transforming presence of God's Spirit, human beings are unable to free themselves from their sinful desires. Since humans are dead in their sins and alienated from God, from one another, and even from themselves, they need to be given new life.

"Who Will Rescue Me from This Body of Death?" Justification by Grace

According to Paul, a radical solution is necessary to bring about any spiritual or moral change in a person's life. Since humans are enslaved to sin and controlled by their sinful nature, they need to be set free; they cannot do it on their own. At the height of his description of the struggle for control over sin, Paul cries out in Romans 7:24, "Wretched man that I am! Who will rescue me from this body of death?" The answer? Only God can do it, through the death and resurrection of Jesus Christ. Therefore, the only solution for the enslavement to sin is for persons to identify with Christ in his death on the cross, thereby dying to their sinful nature and experiencing freedom from sin's enslaving power. Let us explore Paul's description of how human beings are rescued from the body of death.

In Romans 1:16–17, Paul describes the gospel as the power of God for salvation because "the righteousness from God" has been revealed in it. For Paul, righteousness is not only an attribute *of* God but also a condition that comes *from* God, conferred upon those who believe.[2] In other words, righteousness is both a divine characteristic and a quality of existence bestowed upon believers by God. The same Greek word (*dikaiosyne*) can be translated either as "righteousness" or as "justification."

What does Paul mean when he says that we are justified? First, righteousness/justification involves the judicial idea of acquittal, in which the innocence of a guilty person is affirmed. It is as if you are standing before a judge who declares that your guilt has been removed because the penalty has been paid. In other words, Paul is stating that because of the death and resurrection of Christ, God has declared persons to be not guilty. But even more than this, righteousness/justification pertains to right standing before God. People who are justified have been *fully accepted by God*. God has forgiven us; we are once again placed back into right relationship with God. The sin that separated us from God no longer does so. Finally, righteousness/justification also includes a restoration of right relationships with others in the faith community. Because we have been justified and therefore reconciled to God, we are set free to forgive, love, and serve others.

Therefore, in a few brief verses, Paul suggestively points to a central idea that he will develop throughout this entire letter—indeed, throughout most of his writings: *God* initiates the saving power of the gospel. Although human faith and belief are necessary for persons to receive God's righteousness, persons can not initiate their own experience of righteousness. God's love was demonstrated for people *while they were still sinners* (Rom. 5:8). Because of this, there is no basis for persons to boast about their moral or spiritual superiority.

Paul returns to the theme of righteousness/justification more fully in Romans 3:21–26. Here we come to the heart of Paul's teaching about justification by grace. There are three important points about God's righteousness/justification that need to be considered. First, Paul states in verse 21 that the righteousness from God has been made known "apart from law." "The law and the prophets" (Paul's shorthand way of referring to the Hebrew Scriptures) testify to God's righteousness/justification, but they do not directly make it known and they cannot bring it about. Paul, who as a former Pharisee once put great trust in the law, now emphasizes that the keeping of torah does *not* enable persons to be considered righteous before God. When he refers to the "law" or, more precisely, "works of the law" (as in Rom. 3:20; Gal. 3:10, and elsewhere), Paul is particularly concerned about those observances that promote Jewish identity (especially circumcision, dietary restrictions, and the keeping of Sabbath and other holy days). But the principle extends beyond this particular definition of "law"; people cannot be made righteous by keeping religious observances or by following certain rules and regulations of morality.

Second, justification is not something that *we* achieve. We cannot be accepted and put back into harmony with God by our good deeds. Our reconciliation with God, according to Paul, is not something that we can earn or that we even deserve. It is a free gift, as Paul declares in Romans 3:24: "They are now justified by his grace as a gift." We do not earn gifts. If you and I earned justification, then it would be a payment, not a gift; it would be something that we deserved.

Third, the gift of justification is brought about through the faithfulness of Jesus Christ's obedience (Phil. 2:8). Paul states in verse 22 that righteousness from God comes "through faith in Jesus Christ for all who believe." Here the translation of the term "faith in Jesus" may be somewhat misleading. There is good evidence to suggest that, as in Romans 1:17 and Galatians 2:16, the phrase here is best understood as the faith(fulness) *of* Christ rather than faith *in* Christ.[3] What exactly does this mean? By referring to the faithfulness *of* Christ, Paul has in view the obedience and trust that Jesus displayed by accepting death on the cross. Therefore, the manifestation of God's righteousness and the basis for our salvation becomes Christ's faith/trust rather than human faith. We are saved not by our good works or by our faith but by God's grace, displayed in his offering of himself in the person of Christ. Paul explains this further in Romans 3:24 when he states that persons are "justified by his grace as a gift, through the redemption that is in Christ Jesus."

This raises an important issue: Does salvation by God's grace (exhibited in the "faithfulness of Christ") diminish the role of human faith? In other words, are we not also supposed to have faith in Christ as well? Paul anticipates these questions in Romans 3 by saying that God's righteousness comes to "all who believe." Indeed, active faith is essential. We must actively receive and trust in what God has done for us. We must accept the gift. Our acceptance of the gift makes it no less a gift. As Gregory A. Boyd notes, "A gift is not less of a gift because it is accepted. . . . One must choose to place one's trust (faith) in God's gracious provision. This choice is not in any sense the *cause* of their salvation, but it is a *condition* that must be met for the gift of salvation to be applied to their life."[4] This is why we use the language of describing salvation as justification *by* grace *through* faith. We must accept the gift, but our faith is not the cause of the gift. Our faith is not what saves us; God's free offer of forgiveness justifies us. However, we cannot be saved without our faith; we must accept the gift.

Why We Cannot Achieve Our Own Salvation by Good Deeds

So far we have seen that the heart of the good news, according to Paul, is that God loves us so much that he freely forgives us and justifies (as a gift) through the sacrifice of his son on the cross. Nothing that we can do will earn our righteousness before God. We must simply accept God's free offer of forgiveness and reconciliation.

In terms of ethics, the most important aspect of Paul's theological outlook is the inability of human beings to achieve salvation by good deeds. But why is it that we cannot achieve justification by our good behavior? If we lead a generally good life, don't we deserve salvation? To understand why we cannot justify ourselves before God, it is helpful to think of justification in terms of relationship. As we have seen throughout this book, the dominant characteristic of sin is that it results in disrupted relationships. In regard to sins against humans or against God, for the relationship to be healed the person that was sinned *against* must forgive. Imagine the following scenario: In a moment of sinful weakness, you cheat on your spouse and he or she discovers your infidelity. This causes pain and division between the two of you (and also between you and God). You have broken an incredibly important covenant. No matter how faithful you are afterward, healing and reconciliation cannot occur until your spouse forgives you. That forgiveness is not deserved or earned; it comes as a free gift. As we shall discuss below, you are now required to live up to that forgiveness, but it is not your actions that earn it. Moreover, it would not do much good to say to your spouse, "Honey, I know I was unfaithful last Tuesday, but I *was* faithful the other 364 days of the year." You are supposed to be faithful every day; any violation causes hurt and disrupts the harmony of the relationship.

A common image of heaven is of Saint Peter with a ledger book containing all of the deeds from your life. The image implies that you enter into heaven if your good deeds outweigh your evil ones. This is completely foreign to Paul's understanding. Like a husband or wife, we are supposed to be faithful and righteous *all* of the time. Any and every sin causes a disruption of our relationship with God. All it takes is a single violation to result in our breaking of covenant and therefore our deserved condemnation. This is why the law, according to Paul, cannot save us, since no one, Christ excepted, is capable of following all of the law all of the time, even in their hearts. *All* persons have missed the mark of God's holiness; *all* persons fall short of God's glory.[5] Once we have sinned and offended God, it is up to *God* to forgive *us*. It comes as a free gift that has been offered to all through the death and resurrection of Christ. To say that we can save ourselves through our good deeds is to say that the death of Christ was not necessary. And so in his letter to the Galatians, Paul reprimands his audience for accepting the idea that law-observance could add to their faith and make them more pleasing to God by saying that "if justification comes through the law, then Christ died for nothing" (Gal. 2:21).

The good news for Paul is that God does not hold our sins against us but freely forgives us. For Paul, the very heart of the good news is that "we know that a person is justified not by the works of the law but through faith in Jesus Christ. And we have come to believe in Christ Jesus, so that we might be justified by faith in Christ, and not by doing the works of the law, because no one will be justified by the works of the law" (Gal. 2:16). Because of God's great love for human beings, we are freely forgiven. God sends his son to effect that forgiveness through his obedient death on the cross, through the faithfulness of Christ.

The Experience of Justification: Uniting with Christ in Death and New Life

In proclaiming the good news of justification by grace, Paul ran into a great deal of resistance. For Jews, the Torah was the greatest of God's gifts and the way to salvation. Paul was apparently challenging the very heart of their belief system. But Paul believed that the law could no longer fulfill its intended function. Recall that the law was a way of trying to fix the broken relationships in the world. All of the Torah can be seen as a way to reconcile humans with one another or humans with God. But Paul believed that it can never achieve this purpose completely. In fact, Paul believed that the primary function of the law is that "through the law comes the knowledge of sin" (Rom. 4:20). Paul ran into stark opposition to his ideas by those who wished to hold on to the law as a means of salvation, by those who claimed that faith in Christ is necessary but not sufficient, that one is also saved by good works. Paul stood firm in rejecting such a compromised position.

Despite Paul's clear and consistent claim that we are saved not by *our* actions but by our trust in *God's* actions, many contemporary Christians continue to advance a kind of works righteousness (that we are made righteous by works). This is found in the common notion that good people go to heaven and bad people go to hell. For Paul, *all* people are bad. There is no one who is good and deserves salvation; all who believe are saved by the *grace* of God. So why does this misconception continue? One can easily understand why people continue to dilute Paul's radical claim that our justification is purely a free gift of God. The first reaction that we sinful creatures often have to such good news is "Great, then what I do doesn't matter. I can go on living the same sinful life I have always lived."

Paul recognized that this would be a common reaction. In fact, the Christian community in Corinth was using its freedom from the constraints of the law to justify such behaviors as prostitution (1 Cor. 6:15) and gluttony (6:13). So when Paul writes to the church in Rome, proclaiming the good news that through the cross of Christ our sins are freely forgiven, he anticipates the typical response by raising the rhetorical question, "What then are we to say? Should we continue in sin in order that grace may abound?" (Rom. 6:1). Paul's response to this question sheds light on his theological and moral vision:

> By no means! How can we who died to sin go on living in it? Do you not know that all of us who have been baptized into Christ Jesus were baptized into his death? Therefore we have been buried with him by baptism into death, so that, just as Christ was raised from the dead by the glory of the Father, so we too might walk in newness of life. . . . We know that our old self was crucified with him so that the body of sin might be destroyed, and we might no longer be enslaved to sin. . . . So you also must consider yourselves dead to sin and alive to God in Christ Jesus. (Rom. 6:2–4, 6, 11)

Initially, Paul's answer sounds like a non sequitur, like it does not quite answer the rhetorical question. Paul's answer invokes two images: baptism and crucifixion. But how does that answer the question?

Putting to Death the Old Self and Raising the New

What baptism and crucifixion have in common are the dual events of dying and rising. In baptism, persons are dunked under the water; they symbolically die. They are then raised up out of the water to new life. The image of crucifixion invokes the same ideas. We crucify the old self, with its sinful passions and self-centeredness, and we are resurrected as new persons. When persons become united with Christ by placing their complete trust in him, they identify with Christ's death and resurrection. Spiritually speaking, they have died to their sinful nature (which Paul calls *sarx*, "the flesh") and are now free from that which once enslaved them (Rom. 7:6). Here we see a clear echo of Jesus' command to "take up your cross and follow me," because those who want to gain life must lose it. If we want to become truly alive by living the life God envisioned for us, we must put to death the old self with its sins and self-centeredness.

According to Paul, if we have accepted the free gift of forgiveness and reconciliation made by God through Christ, we will be transformed. We will desire no longer to sin. Paul proclaims that no one who has died to a life of sin will want to live in it any longer, because they now experience the love, joy, and freedom of being united with Christ (Rom. 6:1–2). Therefore, those who have accepted God's gift of justification and have become identified with Christ can now experience a new quality of life. This does not mean that they will never sin again, but it does mean that they are now free both from the enslaving power of sin and from the condemnation and judgment associated with a life of sinfulness (Rom. 8:1–2).

Christ's death and resurrection form the basis for moral actions in this world. Paul exhorts his audience to consider themselves dead to sin and alive to God in Christ (Rom. 6:11). Because they now have been united with Christ, they are exhorted to offer themselves to God "as those who have been brought from death to life" (Rom. 6:13). In Galatians 2:20, Paul declares that "I have been crucified with Christ and I no longer live, but Christ lives in me. The life I live in the body, I live by faith in the Son of God, who loved me and gave himself for me" (NIV). Drawing on his own experience, Paul explains that he has become so identified with Christ that he has, in effect, died to the condition of sinfulness that kept him alienated from God and others. This is explained further in Galatians 5:24, where he states that "those who belong to Christ Jesus have crucified the sinful nature [*sarx*] with its passions and desires" (NIV). Whereas Paul had once been enslaved by his sinful nature, as a result of justification by grace, he now experiences new life and freedom. Believers are able to do this because, in Christ, they "serve in the new life of the Spirit" (Rom. 7:6). As Paul explains elsewhere, those who are in Christ experience a "new creation" in which they embody and demonstrate the "righteousness of God" in their lives (2 Cor. 5:17, 21).

If all we think about is how much sin we can get away with, we probably are not saved, because we are still thinking in the old way: focusing on self and trying to justify ourselves. Paul is saying that the old self is dead. We have been set free from the life of destructive sinfulness. How then could those who have put to death the old life continue to live in it? Instead, they will be raised up into a new kind of existence. As a result of their justification their lives will be transformed. The old ways of being, thinking, and acting are put to death, and new ways are raised up.

Paul's Copernican Revolution

What Paul is advocating is nothing less than a Copernican revolution in the way that justification and good works are related. The Mosaic covenant said that the way to become righteous in the sight of God was to do good works of the law. One can picture this as: *Old covenant: Good deeds>>>justification*. Being in right relationship with God follows upon good deeds and works of the law. Paul says that with the death and resurrection of Jesus Christ, God has established a new covenant, a new way of relating to human beings. In the new covenant, we are not made righteous by good deeds but by a free gift of God that we should accept through faith. As a result of our being forgiven and put back into right relationship with God, we will naturally bring forth good works: *New covenant: Justification>>>good deeds*. Salvation is not a result of good deeds; good deeds are a result of our justification by God's free grace.

This revolution is reflected in both the content and form of Paul's letters. Paul always begins his letters with *God's actions* in and through his Son Jesus Christ (the indicative). Paul then proceeds to discuss the significance of how human beings should live, think, and feel as a result of God's actions (the imperative). In many of Paul's letters, the shift from God's act of justification to the consequences of this justification in the lives of human beings is fairly evident. Romans 1–11 is one long treatise on human sin and justification by grace. Paul begins his ethical instruction (called *parenesis*) in chapter 12 with the key word "therefore." "I appeal to you, *therefore*, brothers and sisters, by the mercy of God, to present your bodies as a living sacrifice, holy and acceptable to God, which is your spiritual worship" (Rom. 12:1). As an act of gratitude for God's grace, believers are exhorted to offer their entire selves to God, reject the pattern of this world and be transformed by an ongoing renewal of their minds. The idea that the Christian life is a *response* to God's merciful actions is also found in the letter to the Galatians where, after emphasizing our freedom from the burdens of the law, Paul turns to his ethical instruction: "For freedom Christ has set us free. . . . Only do not use your freedom as an opportunity for self-indulgence" (Gal. 5:1, 13). By this Paul means that we have been set free from having to earn God's love or make ourselves righteous in God's eyes, but we should not use that freedom as an excuse to go on sinning. On the contrary, because we have been set free, we are now set free *to serve and love* without being constantly afraid that our efforts are unworthy. Freedom for Paul is not freedom to do anything at all, but freedom to serve, freedom to be the creatures God originally created us to be—the kind of freedom exercised by the one truly human being, Jesus Christ.

Paul is essentially saying: You have been saved, now go live like it. You have been forgiven and put back into right relationship with God. Now go live like it by expressing your peace with God in your relationships with others. Live out your salvation. Live out your reconciliation with God. Live as if you are a new being, the one God originally intended, one who loves God and neighbor. Reflect in your lives the good gift of justification that God has given you.

The Results of Justification:
Spirit-Guided Virtues Expressed in Community

We can now begin to see that just as the proclamation of the kingdom of God is the foundation for all of Jesus' ethical teachings, most of Paul's moral exhortations are held together by justification by grace. If we are put back into right relationship with God, it will transform our relationships with everything and everyone around us.

Paul says that what results from our acceptance of God's love and forgiveness is the "fruit of the Spirit." Contemporary readers of Paul's letters often inappropriately view the work of the Holy Spirit primarily in individualistic terms. That is, many of us tend to view the gift of God's Spirit as satisfying our individual needs or providing us with personal fulfillment. Although God's Spirit does empower and guide persons in their life of faith, Paul would strongly reject these individualistic interpretations. Paul repeatedly emphasizes that *God gave the Spirit primarily for the purpose of restoring broken relationships so that Christian community may be strengthened.* One of the places where this principle can be clearly seen is the contrast in Galatians 5:19–26 between the "works of the flesh" and the "fruit of the Spirit." The works of the flesh cause division and hatred; the fruit of the Spirit builds up community and strengthens human relationships.

Paul seems intentional about using the image of fruit because fruit is a natural by-product of a tree, bush, or other plant. Think of it this way: A tree does not struggle to produce its fruit. You don't see an apple tree furiously straining or forcing itself to generate its apples. Instead, if the tree is healthy and the conditions are right for growing, the fruit comes forth without special effort. Likewise, those who have accepted God's offer of forgiveness in Christ, identified with Christ, and been crucified and resurrected with him, are empowered by the Holy Spirit to produce these virtuous behaviors; they will come forth naturally. Paul's writings are too often used as a source of new laws for the Christian life. Paul himself would be wary about setting up a new law to replace the old law. In fact, after listing the fruits of the Spirit in Galatians, Paul says, "There is no law against such things" (Gal. 5:23). Rather than thinking in deontological or consequentialist terms, Paul seems to be much closer to a virtue ethicist. He is outlining what Spirit-filled people look like by discussing what virtues they display, virtues that reflect the fact that they *have been* reconciled to God and neighbor.

It would take an entire book to discuss all of the fruits of the Spirit and virtues listed by Paul that result from being justified and united with Christ. Nor shall I attempt to discuss the many specific moral teachings by Paul on such subjects as marriage, obedience to government, the role of women, and treatment of the poor. Instead, we will have to limit our exploration to four fruits of the Spirit that are borne from the tree of justification by grace: love, forgiveness, humility, and joy. These virtues are quite similar to the ones expressed by Jesus throughout his life.

Love

The virtues described by Paul as "fruits of the Spirit" are given by God, demonstrated in the life of Christ, and experienced in the life of believers because of the empowering presence of God's Spirit. Almost all of the virtues espoused by Paul involve reconciliation; they are life giving and life sustaining. Because we have been justified and put back into harmony with God, we should live out that reconciliation with others. Not surprisingly, the virtue of love (*agape*) is given priority of placement as the most important ethical concept for believers in Christ:

Let love be genuine; hate what is evil, hold fast to what is good; love one another with mutual affection. (Rom. 12:9)

Owe no one anything, except to love one another; for the one who loves another has fulfilled the law. (Rom. 13:8)

To the extent that Paul does offer commands for members of his community, the command to love almost always tops the list. For example, in Romans 12:9–21, Paul begins a long list of imperatives with "Let love be genuine." In Galatians 5:14, Paul claims that the entire Torah can be summarized by the command to "love your neighbor as yourself" (see also Rom. 13:8).

God has expressed his unqualified love for us by giving of his very self on the cross: "God proves his love for us in that while we still were sinners Christ died for us" (Rom. 5:8). Therefore, we should express that love for one another. We should live out the love God has shown us in our lives with others. The quality of love being described here is best characterized as *agape*, that other-centered, active caring that promotes human flourishing and community, which has its fullest expression in the self-giving sacrifice of Christ. Because God loves us, we should *therefore* love one another.

Forgiveness and Peace

In our exploration of *agape* in chapter 9, we saw the close connection in Jesus' life between love, peace, and forgiveness. We find a similar emphasis on seeking forgiveness and peace in Paul's writings:

Be kind to one another, tenderhearted, forgiving one another, as God in Christ has forgiven you. (Eph. 4:32)

Do not repay anyone evil for evil. . . . If it is possible, so far as it depends on you, live peaceably with all. Beloved, never avenge yourselves, but leave room for the wrath of God. . . . Do not be overcome by evil, but overcome evil with good. (Rom. 12:17–19, 21)

Once again, the imperative (what *we* should do) is a natural outgrowth of the indicative (what *God* has done). Paul has already established that "we are justified by faith, we have peace with God through our Lord Jesus Christ . . . [and] while we were enemies, we were reconciled to God through the death of his Son" (Rom. 5:1, 10). We have been forgiven. We have been put at peace with God. We should therefore express this state of affairs in our lives. We should manifest our forgiveness and peace with God through our relationships with others. We do not seek peace and extend forgiveness *in order to* be justified;

we do so *because* we are justified. Because God has forgiven us, we should *therefore* forgive others.

Humility

Another key virtue or fruit of the Spirit for Paul is humility. God loves and values each of us; we should love and value ourselves. Humility is not so much thinking less of yourself, but thinking of yourself less and focusing on the virtues and needs of others:

> Do not be haughty, but associate with the lowly; do not claim to be wiser than you are. (Rom. 12:16)

> Do nothing from selfish ambition or conceit, but in humility regard others as better than yourselves. Let each of you look not to your own interests, but to the interests of others. (Phil. 2:3–4)

There are two reasons that humility is a key virtue for Paul. First, we do not save ourselves. We have nothing to boast about. Immediately following the key passage on justification by grace in Romans 3:21–26, Paul writes, "Then what becomes of boasting? It is excluded" (3:27). Second, conceit and boasting are ways we try to put ourselves above others. Think of your own experience with people who are arrogant and boastful. They act this way to feel superior to others and in so doing place a barrier between themselves and those that are "beneath them." Humility reconciles; arrogance divides. Because we have been reconciled with God and neighbor through a free gift of God, we have nothing to boast about, either before God or our neighbor.

Joy

Finally, the life of justified believers is one of joy:

> Rejoice in the Lord always; again I will say, Rejoice. (Phil. 4:4)

> The fruit of the Spirit is love, *joy*, peace, patience, kindness, generosity, faithfulness, gentleness, and self-control. (Gal. 5:22–23)

For Paul, the fact that God loves us unconditionally and sacrificially is the best of news. There can be no better news than the proclamation that God does not hold our sins against us but is reconciling us to God's self through Jesus Christ. This is the gospel. In light of such a gift, the proper response is one of joy and thanksgiving.

Conclusion

From the very first pages of this book, we have seen the importance of faith claims for the ethical lives of believers. What Christians believe about the character and will of God shapes our character and actions. How we view ourselves, other human beings, and the created world determines the kinds of lives we will try to live. Ethics and faith are essentially indistinguishable.

Paul clearly embodies this understanding of the moral life. His entire ethical outlook is determined by what God has done through Jesus Christ. In both the content and the structure of his letters, he begins by indicating who human beings are, what their condition is, and how God is rescuing them in Christ Jesus. In other words, he begins with faith statements indicating what God has done. Only in light of the "new creations" that God has created can we rightly discern the outline of the moral life, a life lived in *response* to God's grace.

Epilogue

Looking Back and Looking Ahead

*I*n this book, we have been journeying together through the field of Christian ethics. But the reality is even grander. As a Christian believer you are part of the great cosmic pilgrimage that God has undertaken with humanity. It began at the creation of the universe when God entered into covenant with human beings and with all living creatures. It will continue until Christ consummates that covenant by coming again to establish God's kingdom on earth. Then a new stage will begin in which humans and God will live in eternal harmony on earth, as well as in heaven.

You are in the midst of this great journey of the human race with God; some of your fellow travelers have included Adam, Eve, Moses, Amos, and Paul. Who knows whether you are closer to the beginning or the end of this great journey of God with us? But what a privilege it is to be invited on the journey! There is no traveler in the eons of time or in the vast breadth of the universe who experiences the trip as you do, and no one who has the same relationship with God that you have.

With the privilege of the journey comes an awesome responsibility—to properly live out the role God intended for us. The purpose of this book is to help us better understand how to be the kinds of people that God has created and called us to be. It is probably unnecessary to retrace all of the steps of our exploration, but it might be useful to recall some of the highlights of our trip that shape Christian morality, to recall some of the key confessions of faith that guide Christians in their life with God. Recall that confessions are statements of belief about God, humans, and the created universe. These belief statements determine how we see the world we inhabit and therefore how we act, feel, and think. If you recall little else from your journey through this book, hold fast to the notion that statements of belief and morality go hand in hand. Being a Christian is a lifelong effort to learn to see the world rightly and then to manifest our beliefs in our actions, virtues, and emotions.

Looking Back

God created everything out of God's power and love. God is completely sovereign, so there is no other power in the world worthy of our ultimate allegiance or fear. And God created human beings for a purpose. God created us for love. God desires that we enter into covenant relationship with other human beings and with God. We are made in the image of a God of loving community (Father, Son, and Holy Spirit). We image that God when we enter into relationships of love and care with others. And because the physical world is good, caring for others involves caring for them spiritually *and* physically.

However, human beings failed to live up to the task of imaging God through love of God and neighbor. Failing to trust God and seeking to live autonomously, the first couple disobeyed God's commands. In so doing, they introduced brokenness and disruption into what were once harmonious relationships: between human beings, between God and human beings, and between humans and the natural world. This is sin. Sin is the beginning of death, as it introduces separation where there was once unity. Genesis 3 is less concerned about where sin comes from than with what sin looks like and produces. Genesis 3 depicts an archetype of all human behavior. Each of us relives that story, refusing to trust and obey God and therefore creating disruption in our relationships with God and others.

Despite human resistance and sin, God remained faithful. Through Noah and Abraham, God entered into specific covenants with human beings. Then, in the Mosaic covenant, God sought to establish a new kind of community, a treasured people out of all the people of the earth. God sought to mend the brokenness created by human sinfulness through the giving of the Torah, the charter document of this alternative community. God established two pillars for covenantal faithfulness: proper and exclusive worship of Yahweh, and justice and mercy between human beings. Nearly every instruction or commandment in the Torah falls under one of these two pillars and seeks to guide humans in their effort to live out their created purpose.

Because of the obstinate sinfulness of the human race, the laws that God provided in the Torah, however, did not fulfill their function. Therefore, God sent prophets to call the people back to the covenant promises made on Mount Sinai. As spokespeople for God, the prophets called the people to repent, to turn back to the exclusive worship of Yahweh. They pleaded with them to reestablish justice, mercy, and special care for the weak and powerless.

But the people still did not listen. So God sent his own son as the final prophet to proclaim the coming kingdom of God, where the destruction, violence, and hatred wrought by human sin and the powers of evil would be destroyed. Through the death and resurrection of his Son, we have been justified; we have been made right with God. We are now called to live in the light of this good news, to live as new creations, in anticipation of the re-creation of heaven and earth.

Looking Ahead

This is the great cosmic journey of God with human beings, the journey of which we are each a small but significant part. Your journey is not over. It has just begun. Your entire life is an amazing, absolutely unique task of molding yourself into the kind of being that is pleasing to God. All other projects will end. The project that is *you* goes on till your final breath. Even then, your pilgrimage with God does not end. Your entire life is one of "quiet social vocation of soulcraft"; it is one of preparing yourself for meeting Jesus Christ face to face.

Between now and that day, you must work on your vocation. You can become a good ethicist by reading ethics books and discussing ethics with others. However, you cannot become a good Christian only by reading books on Christian ethics. While reading what others have written about the moral life of Christians is important, your vocation is more than an intellectual one; it is an existential and experiential one. You can be a geography whiz by looking at maps. But you will never be an explorer until you make the journey your own. I leave you with four tools for your journey with God, four time-tested ways for you to mold yourself into a better disciple of Jesus Christ: Scripture reading, church participation, service, and prayer.

First, spend time reading Scripture. The word of God is the "lamp unto our feet" (Ps. 119:105). There is simply no substitute for consistent, ongoing Bible reading. Don't just go to the Bible when you need answers; let it create the questions. Allow it to transform you by learning to see the world through the lens of Scripture.

Second, enter into the corporate life of the Christian community. Surround yourself with fellow Christians. Americans, in particular, often view religion as a private, individualistic matter. But throughout Scripture, God calls communities and groups of people. Even Jesus surrounded himself with disciples. If we truly want to become better disciples of Jesus Christ, we must surround ourselves with fellow Christians who will guide us, nurture us, confront us, and encourage us. Our Christian characters are molded and shaped in community. And since the central act of our faith community is worship, we should regard regular corporate worship as a key part of our moral formation, as the time and place where we learn to see the world rightly, develop the Christian virtues, and thus behave as Christians.

Third, you must serve others. James warns his readers to be "doers of the word, and not merely hearers who deceive themselves" (Jas. 1:22). Being a good Christian ethicist and being a good Christian are not synonymous. You can know all of the theory and all of the biblical material, but unless and until you begin to live out your wisdom in the world, your knowledge is just a "clanging bell," to use Paul's metaphor. If we were created for lives of love, care, and service, then we must go forth and minister in Christ's name. If we are to live up to our calling, we must enter into a hostile and hurting world and work for God's kingdom. In so doing, we not only express our character, but we shape it. If we want to learn to be forgiving, we forgive. If we want to develop humility, we serve humbly. And if we want to learn to love more, we need to act more loving.

Finally, a key part of our journey of moral formation is prayer. Through praise, thanksgiving, confession, intercession, and simply meditating upon the love and sacrifice of God, we develop the kinds of virtues that distinguish us as Christians.

We differ from many other kinds of explorers in one important way: We know the final outcome of the journey. One day God will come again and establish God's eternal reign on earth as it is in heaven. God will do this because God loves us unconditionally. There is nothing we can do to change that.

Because we know the final destination and because we know that God loves us unconditionally, we should seek to please our maker and our redeemer by glorifying God through lives of self-giving love. We can only hope that when the Master returns, or when we reach the end of our journey on this earth, God will say to us, "Well done, good and faithful servant!" (Matt. 25:21 NIV).

Notes

CHAPTER 1. Exploring Christian Ethics

1. The first known use of the term "Christian ethics" is found in Basil of Caesarea's (330–379) *Principles of Christian Ethics.*

2. The earliest designation for Christians was followers of "the Way" (Acts 9:2). Note how this name for Christians highlights the emphasis on behavior rather than merely intellectual knowledge. The first designation of followers of Christ as "Christians" was in Antioch (Acts 11:26).

3. Minucius Felix, *Octavius.* Quoted in George Wolfgang Forell, *History of Christian Ethics: From the New Testament to Augustine* (Minneapolis: Augsburg, 1979), 51–52.

4. Yahweh is the personal name of the biblical God, as given to Moses on Sinai (Exod. 3:13–15). Most Bibles translate the divine name of Yahweh as "the LORD."

5. The Westminster Larger Catechism, Answer 1, in *The Book of Confessions* (Louisville, KY: Office of the General Assembly, Presbyterian Church (U.S.A.), 1999). A catechism, from the Greek word *katēchein* (to instruct), is a summary of beliefs, usually in the form of questions and answers.

6. Donald G. Luck, *Why Study Theology?* (St. Louis: Chalice Press, 1999), 28.

CHAPTER 2. What Should We *Do?*

1. F. C. Sharp, *Ethics* (Appleton-Century, 1928), 28, as quoted in Louis Pojman, *Ethics: Discovering Right and Wrong* (Belmont, CA: Wadsworth, 1990), 41.

2. Reinhold Niebuhr, *The Nature and Destiny of Man* (New York: Charles Scribner's Sons, 1949), 222.

3. See the treatment of Yoder in Stanley Hauerwas, *Vision and Virtue* (Notre Dame, IN: University of Notre Dame Press, 1974), 202–3.

4. Gilbert Meilander, "Euthanasia and Christian Vision," in *On Moral Medicine: Theological Perspectives in Medical Ethics,* ed. Stephen E. Lammers and Allen Verhey (Grand Rapids: Wm. B. Eerdmans Publishing Co., 1998), 657.

5. Harvey K. McArthur, "Golden Rule," in *The Westminster Dictionary of Christian Ethics,* ed. James F. Childress and John Macquarrie (Philadelphia: Westminster Press, 1986), 251.

6. Some ethicists contend that to be a deontologist one must hold all rules to be absolute. They therefore place "*prima facie* obligationists" in a separate category. I disagree. What distinguishes a deontologist is that he or she believes that there is something inherent in actions that makes them right or wrong regardless of consequences. In my view, this does not necessarily mean

that each and every act of that variety is morally prohibited or obligatory in all cases. The rule or act may carry some moral weight but not absolute weight. The reader should be aware, however, that many ethicists place *prima facie* obligation in a separate category from deontology.

7. W. D. Ross is credited with coining the language of *prima facie* obligations. See W. D. Ross, *The Right and the Good* (Oxford: Clarendon Press, 1930).

8. Tom L. Beauchamp and James F. Childress, *Principles of Biomedical Ethics,* 4th ed. (New York: Oxford University Press, 1994), 34. The following few paragraphs are significantly indebted to the discussion in Beauchamp and Childress, 32–37.

9. Ibid., 34.

10. See Robert Nozick, "Moral Complications and Moral Structures," *Natural Law Forum* 13 (1968): 1–50.

11. Bentham and Mill disagreed, however, over whether happiness and pleasure were equivalent. Mill argued that not all pleasures are equal; some, such as the pleasure of reading or accomplishment of a goal are of a higher value than the mere physical pleasures of eating or sexual activity.

12. Jeremy Bentham, *An Introduction to the Principles of Morals and Legislation* (New York: Hafner Publishing Co., 1948), 2.

13. In response to some of the criticisms raised above, some utilitarians have concluded that it is not *acts* but *rules* that must pass the utilitarian calculation. Thus, we should build the moral life around rules that maximize utility, rules that create the greatest good for the greatest number. For example, rather than asking whether this particular case of lying might be justified by claiming that the good consequences outweigh the harmful ones, the person should ask whether the act of lying is prohibited under a utilitarian rule against lying. A rule utilitarian might prohibit lying because overall the *practice* of lying results in a net harm, even though individual cases of lying might result in more good than harm. Rule utilitarianism is not deontological. It does not hold that there is something inherently wrong with lying. Rather, a rule utilitarian might reason that a general practice of lying results in more harm than good and thus must be prohibited.

14. Joseph Fletcher, *Situation Ethics* (Philadelphia: Westminster Press, 1966), 82.

15. Meilander, "Euthanasia and Christian Vision," 657.

CHAPTER 3. How Should We *Be?*

1. Stanley Hauerwas, *A Community of Character: Toward a Constructive Christian Social Ethic* (Notre Dame, IN: University of Notre Dame Press, 1981), 114.

2. John Calvin, *Institutes of the Christian Religion* 3.3.8; ed. John T. McNeill, trans. Ford Lewis Battles, LCC (Philadelphia: Westminster Press, 1960).

3. Aristotle, *Nichomachean Ethics,* trans. J. A. K. Thompson (London: Penguin Books, 1995), 75.

4. Bruce C. Birch and Larry L. Rasmussen, *Bible and Ethics in the Christian Life,* rev. ed. (Minneapolis: Augsburg, 1989), 122.

5. Ibid., 45.

6. Stanley Hauerwas and Charles Pinches, *Christians among the Virtues: Theological Conversations with Ancient and Modern Ethics* (Notre Dame, IN: University of Notre Dame Press, 1997), xiii.

7. Aristotle, *Nichomachean Ethics,* 76.

8. Ibid., 91–92.

9. Ibid., 79.

10. Philip Melanchthon, *Loci Communes*, in *Melanchthon and Bucer*, ed. Wilhelm Pauck (Philadelphia: Westminster Press, 1969), 35.

11. This view of the emotions as outside of our control is seen in the origin of the words "emotion" and "passion." The word "emotion" comes from the Latin *emovere*, "to be moved." The idea is that we are simply "moved" by our emotions. "Passion" comes from the Greek *passio* which means "to suffer." It is also where we get the word "passive," because it was wrongly believed that we simply "suffer" our emotions and are passive toward them.

12. World Bank, *World Development Report 1993* (New York: Oxford University Press, 1993), 23.

13. Birch and Rasmussen, *Bible and Ethics*, 45.

14. Robin W. Lovin, *Christian Ethics: An Essential Guide* (Nashville: Abingdon Press, 2000), 70.

CHAPTER 4. The Use of Scripture and Other Sources

1. Christopher J. H. Wright, *Walking in the Ways of the Lord: The Ethical Authority of the Old Testament* (Downers Grove, IL: InterVarsity Press, 1995), 14.

2. Edward LeRoy Long, *To Liberate and Redeem: Moral Reflections on the Biblical Narrative* (Cleveland: Pilgrim Press, 1997), 2.

3. Wright, *Walking in the Ways of the Lord*, 15.

4. This section draws heavily upon James M. Gustafson's typology in "The Place of Scripture in Christian Ethics: A Methodological Study," in *Theology and Christian Ethics* (Philadelphia: United Church Press, 1974), 121–45.

5. Harold M. Schulweis, "Judaism: From Either/Or to Both/And," in *Contemporary Jewish Ethics and Morality: A Reader*, ed. Elliot N. Porff and Louis E. Newman (New York: Oxford University Press, 1995), 29.

6. This formulation comes from James M. Gustafson, "The Changing Use of the Bible in Christian Ethics," in *Readings in Moral Theology No. 4: The Use of Scripture in Moral Theology*, ed. Charles E. Curran and Richard A. McCormick (New York: Paulist Press, 1984), 140–44.

7. Bruce C. Birch and Larry L. Rasmussen, *Bible and Ethics in the Christian Life*, rev. ed. (Minneapolis: Augsburg, 1989), 45.

8. Shirley Guthrie, *Christian Doctrine*, rev. ed. (Louisville, KY: Westminster John Knox Press, 1994), 13.

CHAPTER 5. God, Humans, and Creation in Genesis 1–3

1. Karl Barth, *Church Dogmatics*, II/1 (Edinburgh: T. & T. Clark, 1957), 257.

2. In the following few pages, I am very much indebted to Shirley Guthrie's discussion of creation in *Christian Doctrine*, rev. ed. (Louisville, KY: Westminster John Knox Press, 1994), 162–65.

3. Karl Barth, *Church Dogmatics*, III/4 (Edinburgh: T. & T. Clark, 1961), 342.

4. Martin Luther, "A Mighty Fortress Is Our God," in *Lutheran Book of Worship* (Minneapolis: Augsburg, 1997), 228–29.

5. As C. S. Lewis rightly observes, "There are two equal and opposite errors into which our race can fall about the devils. One is to disbelieve in their existence. The other is to believe, and to feel an excessive and unhealthy interest in them." Lewis, preface to *The Screwtape Letters* (New York: Bantam Books, 1982), xiii.

6. Bruce C. Birch, Walter Brueggemann, Terrence E. Fretheim, and Jon L. Petersen, *A*

Theological Introduction to the Old Testament (Nashville: Abingdon Press, 1999), 51.

7. An interesting ethical issue that we will not have time to explore in depth is the depiction of the relationship between male and female in Genesis 1 and in Genesis 2. In Genesis 1, God creates male and female at the same time. They are both made in the image of God, and their union is intended to produce offspring. In Genesis 2, God creates the male first and then the female, and the basis of their relationship is companionship.

8. See 1 Tim. 4:4: "For everything created by God is good, and nothing is to be rejected, provided it is received with thanksgiving."

9. Such reasoning has unfortunately been extended to male-female relationships. Men, so this distorted theory goes, are higher than women because they exemplify reason and rationality while women exemplify the material and the embodied. This kind of dualism is also found in the notion that reason is good and emotions are bad, since emotions are associated with the body.

10. See Andrew Linzey, *Animal Theology* (Urbana, IL: University of Illinois Press, 1995); and Norbert Lohfink, "'Subdue the Earth?' (Genesis 1:28)," in *Theology of the Pentateuch: Themes of the Priestly Narrative and Deuteronomy* (Minneapolis: Fortress Press, 1994), 1–17.

11. J. Philip Wogaman, *Christian Moral Judgment* (Louisville, KY: Westminster/John Knox Press, 1989), 81.

12. One of the most influential writers in all of Christian history, Augustine of Hippo, wrote, "The woman together with her own husband is the image of God . . . but when she is referred to separately in her quality as helpmate, which regards the woman herself alone, then she is not the image of God; but as regards the man alone, he is the image of God as fully and completely as when the woman too is joined with him." Quoted in Lynn Japinga, *Feminism and Christianity* (Nashville: Abingdon Press, 1999), 75.

13. "All real living is meeting," says Buber. Martin Buber, *I and Thou* (New York: Charles Scribner's Sons, 1958), 11.

14. Karl Barth, *Church Dogmatics*, II/1 (Edinburgh: T. & T. Clark, 1957), 275.

15. Nowhere in Scripture is the snake described in Gen. 3 identified as "Satan." However, Satan is described as a snake in Rev. 12:9–15.

16. Guthrie, *Christian Doctrine*, 181–82.

17. Barth, *Church Dogmatics*, III/2 (Edinburgh: T. & T. Clark, 1960), 94.

18. Ibid., 97.

19. Ibid., 231.

CHAPTER 6. The Mosaic Covenant

1. Walter Brueggemann, *The Prophetic Imagination* (Philadelphia: Fortress Press, 1989), 16–17.

2. Bruce C. Birch, *Let Justice Roll Down: The Old Testament, Ethics, and Christian Life* (Louisville, KY: Westminster/John Knox Press, 1991), 169 (my emphasis).

3. Walter Brueggemann, *Theology of the Old Testament* (Minneapolis: Fortress Press, 1997), 184.

4. It is probably the case that Jewish monotheism developed over a considerable period of time, moving from polytheism to henotheism (belief in multiple gods with one standing supreme over the others) to strict monotheism.

5. Amenhotep IV, a fourteenth-century Egyptian pharaoh, instigated a reform of Egyptian worship in which only Aton, the sun disc god, was worshiped.

6. Gerhard von Rad, *Old Testament Theology,* vol. 1 (San Francisco: HarperCollins, 1962), 214.

7. Walter Harrelson, "Decalogue," in *The Westminster Dictionary of Christian Ethics,* ed. James F. Childress and John Macquarrie (Philadelphia: Westminster Press, 1986), 146.

8. Ibid., 147.

9. This does not necessarily mean that capital punishment and warfare are acceptable practices for modern Christians. For a brief but persuasive argument against capital punishment from a Christian perspective, see Glen H. Stassen and David P. Gushee, *Kingdom Ethics: Following Jesus in Contemporary Context* (Downers Grove, IL: InterVarsity Press, 2003), chap. 9. For an argument against the permissibility of warfare, see the works of John Howard Yoder (*He Came Preaching Peace* [Eugene, OR: Wipf & Stock Publishers, 1985]) or Stanley Hauerwas ("Peacemaking: The Virtue of the Church," in *The Hauerwas Reader,* ed. John Berkmond and Michael Cartwright [Durham, NC: Duke University Press, 2001], 318–26). An excellent, succinct argument for pacifism can be found in Richard Hays, *The Moral Vision of the New Testament* (San Francisco: HarperSanFrancisco, 1996), chap. 14.

10. John Calvin, *Institutes of the Christian Religion* 2.8.39; ed. John T. McNeill, trans. Ford Lewis Battles, LCC (Philadelphia: Westminster Press, 1960).

11. Karl Barth, *Church Dogmatics,* III/2 (Edinburgh: T. & T. Clark, 1960), 203.

12. Christopher J. H. Wright, *Walking in the Ways of the Lord: The Ethical Authority of the Old Testament* (Downers Grove, IL: InterVarsity Press, 1995), 155.

13. See Stanley Hauerwas and William H. Willimon, *Resident Aliens: Life in the Christian Colony* (Nashville: Abingdon Press, 1989).

14. Brueggemann, *Theology of the Old Testament,* 185.

15. The version of Sabbath year regulations found in Leviticus does not mention the requirement to give the natural growth to the poor. See Lev. 25:5–7.

16. Richard H. Lowery, *Sabbath and Jubilee* (St. Louis: Chalice Press, 2000), 149.

17. Technically there is a difference between purity and holiness. For a more detailed discussion, see Richard D. Nelson, *Raising Up a Faithful Priest: Community and Priesthood in Biblical Theology* (Louisville, KY: Westminster/John Knox Press, 1993), 17–38.

18. See Jeffrey S. Siker, "Homosexual Christians, the Bible, and Gentile Inclusion: Confessions of a Repenting Heterosexist," in *Homosexuality in the Church: Both Sides of the Debate,* ed. Jeffrey S. Siker (Louisville, KY: Westminster John Knox Press, 1994). For an alternative view on the status of biblical pronouncements on homosexuality, see Richard B. Hays, "Awaiting the Redemption of Our Bodies: The Witness of Scripture Concerning Homosexuality," in the same volume.

CHAPTER 7. Prophets

1. God tells the Israelites, "The land shall not be sold in perpetuity, for the land is mine; with me you are but aliens and tenants" (Lev. 25:23).

2. Frank J. Matera, "Repentance," in *Harper's Bible Dictionary,* ed. Paul J. Achtemeier (San Francisco: Harper & Row, 1985), 861.

3. The Israelites were exiled to Babylon in the sixth century BCE. In 586 the Babylonians destroyed what remained of the nation of Israel and took all the leaders and skilled workers as slaves.

4. Abraham Heschel, *The Prophets,* vol. 1 (New York: Harper Colophon Books, 1962), 9.

5. Bernard Anderson, *Understanding the Old Testament,* 4th ed. (Upper Saddle River, NJ: Prentice-Hall, 1998), 259–60.

6. An *ephah* is a measure of weight, and a *shekel* is a monetary unit. To translate into modern terms, the people are making the "bushel small and the dollar great."

7. Hugo Adam Bedau, "The Case against the Death Penalty." 1997. Capital Punishment Project of the American Civil Liberties Union, www.aclu.org/DeathPenalty.cfm?ID= 9082&c=17.

8. Bruce C. Birch, *Let Justice Roll Down: The Old Testament, Ethics, and Christian Life* (Louisville, KY: Westminster/John Knox Press, 1991), 264.

9. Rabbi Hiyya, *Ketubbot* 68a, cited in C. G. Montifiore and H. Loewe, *A Rabbinic Anthology* (New York: Schocken Books, 1974), 413.

10. Heschel, *Prophets*, 1:9.

11. Walter Brueggemann, *The Prophetic Imagination* (Minneapolis: Fortress Press, 1989), chaps. 2–3.

CHAPTER 8. Discipleship and the Teachings of Jesus

1. The term "gospel" is closely related to the Hebrew word *bashar*, which means "the proclamation of victory in a battle." Likewise, the gospel is the proclamation of God's victory over evil, sin, and death. The word *euangelion* is the source of the modern word "evangelize," meaning "to spread the good news."

2. See also Luke 9:59–60, where Jesus tells a man who wants to follow him, "Let the dead bury their own dead; but as for you, go and proclaim the kingdom of God."

3. This is known as *realized eschatology*.

4. Oscar Cullmann, *Christ and Time*, trans. Floyd V. Filson (Philadelphia: Westminster Press, 1950), 87.

5. Richard B. Hays, *The Moral Vision of the New Testament* (San Francisco: HarperSanFrancisco, 1996), 89.

6. Ibid.

7. In this section, I am indebted to Rudolf Schnackenburg, *The Moral Teaching of the New Testament* (New York: Herder & Herder, 1966).

8. Wolfgang Schrage, *The Ethics of the New Testament*, trans. David E. Green (Philadelphia: Fortress Press, 1988), 29.

9. Ibid., 41–42.

10. Schnackenburg, *Moral Teaching of the New Testament*, 27.

11. Physical death is not evil. It is simply the manifestation of our creatureliness. Here I am using the word "death" in the sense that Paul does, that is, as the separation from God. Death is the natural end of human life and should not and would not be feared if sin did not stand between God and us. Because God must turn his back on sin, human death threatens to separate us eternally from God. But because of God's redeeming love in Christ, we are clothed in his righteousness. Our sins no longer separate us from God, and therefore death is no longer an enemy for those who are "in Christ."

12. John Howard Yoder, *The Politics of Jesus: Vicit Agnus Noster,* 2nd ed. (Grand Rapids: Wm. B. Eerdmans Publishing Co., 2002), 32–33.

13. "On Hermits and Desert Dwellers," in *Ascetic Behavior in Greco-Roman Antiquity*, ed. Vincent L. Wimbush (Minneapolis: Fortress Press, 1990), 70.

14. Clement of Alexandria, "The Rich Man's Salvation," in *From Christ to the World: Introductory Readings in Christian Ethics*, ed. Wayne G. Boulton, Thomas D. Kennedy, and Allen Verhey (Grand Rapids: Wm. B. Eerdmans Publishing Co., 1994), 451.

15. Ronald J. Sider, *Rich Christians in an Age of Hunger: Moving from Affluence to Generosity*, 20th anniversary revision (Dallas: Word Publishing, 1997), 99.

16. Ibid., 27.

17. Ibid., 6.

18. Eugene Borowitz, *Exploring Jewish Ethics: Papers on Covenant Responsibility* (Detroit: Wayne State University Press, 1990), 261. "R. Jacob said: He who has no wife lives without good, or help, or joy, or blessing or atonement. . . . R. Hiyya b. Gammada said that he is not really a complete man, and some say that he diminishes the divine likeness." C. G. Montefiore and H. Loewe, *A Rabbinic Anthology* (New York: Schocken Books, 1979), 507.

19. This phrase comes from Christopher Lasch, *Haven in a Heartless World: The Family Besieged* (New York: Basic Books, 1977).

20. In this section I have taken some liberties by incorporating ideas not only from Luke but from the other Gospels and, more importantly, from other New Testament literature, such as Paul's letters. A more detailed study would lead us to distinguish the ideas of various biblical authors. But as a way of trying to get a handle on how Christians should understand the law, it is necessary to bring in ideas from a number of biblical sources.

21. The idea of Jesus taking upon himself the sins of humanity is much more prevalent in the work of Paul than in the Gospels.

22. Daniel Harrington and James Keenan, *Jesus and Virtue Ethics: Building Bridges between New Testament Studies and Moral Theology* (Chicago: Sheed & Ward, 2002), 66.

23. David P. Scaer, *The Sermon on the Mount* (St. Louis: Concordia Publishing House, 2000), 85.

24. It is no mere coincidence that Jesus' name in Hebrew is Joshua. Just as Joshua led the people into the promised land of Canaan, Jesus leads the people into the promised land of the kingdom of God.

25. See Reinhold Niebuhr, "The Ethic of Jesus" and "The Relevance of an Impossible Ethical Ideal," in *An Interpretation of Christian Ethics* (New York: Harper & Row, 1935). For a cogent and influential critique of Niebuhr, see John Howard Yoder, *The Politics of Jesus* (Grand Rapids: Wm. B. Eerdmans Publishing Co., 1972).

26. Reinhold Niebuhr, *An Interpretation of Christian Ethics*, 30–31.

27. Glen H. Stassen and David P. Gushee, *Kingdom Ethics: Following Jesus in Contemporary Context* (Downers Grove, IL: InterVarsity Press, 2003), 136.

28. Ibid., 143.

CHAPTER 9. Imitation and the Life of Jesus

1. Karl Barth, *Church Dogmatics*, III/2 (Edinburgh: T. & T. Clark, 1960), 3.

2. E. Earle Ellis, *The Gospel of Luke* (Greenwood, SC: Attic Press, 1974), 12.

3. Richard B. Hays, *The Moral Vision of the New Testament* (San Francisco: HarperSanFrancisco, 1996), 202.

4. Paul Ramsey, *Basic Christian Ethics* (New York: Charles Scribner's Sons, 1950), 99–100.

5. See Edward LeRoy Long, *To Liberate and Redeem: Moral Reflections on the Biblical Narrative* (Cleveland: Pilgrim Press, 1997), 157–60.

6. Wolfgang Schrage, *The Ethics of the New Testament,* trans. David E. Green (Philadelphia: Fortress Press, 1988), 91.

7. Søren Kierkegaard, *Works of Love,* trans. Howard and Edna Kong (New York: Harper & Row, 1962), 64–65.

8. John Calvin, *Institutes of the Christian Religion* 3.8.2; ed. John T. McNeill, trans. Ford Lewis Battles, LCC (Philadelphia: Westminster Press, 1960).

9. Dietrich Bonhoeffer, *The Cost of Discipleship* (New York: Simon & Schuster, 1995), 88.

10. Ibid., 89.

11. Robert McAfee Brown, *Unexpected News: Reading the Bible with Third World Eyes* (Philadelphia: Westminster Press, 1984), 96.

CHAPTER 10. The Ethics of Paul

1. This chapter represents a collaboration with my colleague at Ashland University, David E. Aune. Dr. Aune is a Pauline scholar, and his assistance was invaluable.

2. Most translations of Rom. 1:17 have the phrase "righteousness of God," but the NIV correctly renders it "righteousness from God."

3. This case has been made by a number of recent scholars, most notably Richard Hays, in *The Faith of Jesus Christ,* 2nd ed. (Grand Rapids: Wm. B. Eerdmans Publishing Co., 2002).

4. Gregory A. Boyd, *Satan and the Problem of Evil: Constructing a Trinitarian Warfare Theodicy* (Downers Grove, IL: InterVarsity Press, 2001), 80, 82.

5. The term for "sin" (*hamartia*) used here and throughout Paul's letters was sometimes used as an archery term to describe missing the target or going off track.

Index of Scriptural References

Index of Subjects and Authors

Printed in the United States
142474LV00006B/12/A

Made in the USA
Monee, IL
19 November 2020